THE MIRROR OF WAR

The Mirror of War

AMERICAN SOCIETY AND THE SPANISH-AMERICAN WAR

Gerald F. Linderman

ANN ARBOR   THE UNIVERSITY OF MICHIGAN PRESS

For My Mother and Father,
Leonore and Floyd Linderman

Acknowledgments

Debts difficult to pay I can at least acknowledge.

No one explores more skilfully than Robert Wiebe the larger patterns of American history. Much of that set down in the following pages takes as its point of departure the synthesis of late nineteenth-century life that he presents in *The Search for Order, 1877–1920*. Throughout my work, he has encouraged me to touch the limits of my capabilities and has at vital points aided me beyond them. I am grateful for the generosity of his advice, his assistance, and his friendship.

I have benefited, too, from the suggestions and support of Sidney Fine, John Shy, Robert Sklar, Katharine Ehle, George Daniels, Ann McMillan, James Morgan, and Ruth Oldberg. Richard Leopold's close reading of an earlier version saved me from numerous errors of fact. Others have made most pleasant my research visits to various parts of the country—Gervis S. Brady and LaVerne Mercer of the Stark County (Ohio) Historical Center; Watt P. Marchman, Rose Sberna, and Ruth Ballenger of the Rutherford B. Hayes Library; William Ewing of the William L. Clements Library; Winifred Collins and Mrs. Charles Fisher of the Massachusetts Historical Society; Ruth Quimby of the Vermont Historical Society; the staffs of the Library of Congress, the National Archives, and the United States Army Military History Research Collection. Mr. Sanborn Partridge offered me unrestricted access to the Proctor Papers, while Anna McLaughlin of the Proctor Free Library made my work in Vermont a particular pleasure.

I am indebted to the Horace H. Rackham School of Graduate Studies, University of Michigan, for its fellowship and research grants.

Martha Kinney has been a sensitive and inspiriting editor and Yvonne Gillies a helpful and most competent typist. A final, incalculable debt is due my wife Barbara who seems to know, perhaps through her own passion for yoga, all of the best ways to live with someone lost in American history.

Contents

Introduction

A CENTURY AGO most American lives were bounded by locale. A person's conscious concerns seldom moved beyond the narrow, familiar geographical compass of his community. Only a romantic would contend that problems were fewer then, or less troublesome to the individual, but they were of another quality. Particularly in the small towns and their farm hinterlands where three of four Americans lived, life marched to the slower cadence of the seasons; few problems seemed so urgent as our own. Few possessed complex logistical or administrative components. Few required resort to distant agencies for solution. The relative simplicity of problems and the conviction that answers were within one's reach bestowed no assurance of complete control—epidemic disease alone precluded that—but there was in many lives at least a sense of manageability. Most appear to have found within the boundaries of their communities power enough to give satisfactory shape to their lives.

In the 1870s those complexities accompanying the nation's industrial transformation were only beginning to challenge the moralistic influences of gospel and grammar school primer. Americans continued to fit all of life's data within categories of thought far fewer in number than we count today. (Even in

the 1890s a friend's explanation of the distinguishing characteristic of homosexuals would draw from Jacob Riis, the reporter-
reformer who would become middle-class America's guide
to the harshness of life on the Lower East Side, the irate reaction, "Not so. There are no such creatures in this world.")
Fewer conceptual categories allowed that society to assign
within each one explicit, unambiguous moral judgments. The
most compelling aspect of any problem remained its moral
facet; since social evil resulted from the individual's failure to
act as he should, locating the right and the wrong within a
question was always the first and often the only step in for-
mulating the proper response. In ways lost to our century, both
understanding and motivation had clear moral dimensions.

And, as the individual sought the moral truth of a question,
so would he gauge the moral standing of other persons. With
the distance between the small community's richest and poorest still modest and economic status only one of several factors with the power to convey a sense of "fit" within a loosely
graded social structure, a nonmaterial measure of others remained viable. What one person ultimately valued in another
often fell within the category of "character," a term elusive in
its indivisible combinations of proper deportment, elevated
religious sentiment, and moral uprightness. In ways puzzling
today, the import of a man's actions might depend as much on
their ability to reflect these qualities as to achieve material
result.

Given the locale's self-sustaining nature, a second component
—the center—held a lesser importance than it does today.
Townspeople seldom thought it essential or even desirable
that the central government reach into the patterns of their
lives. Washington was a functional irrelevance. It did, nonetheless, still manage to play a cardinal role: it bridged the gap
between locality and totality. It stood as the symbol of unity,
the assurance that the sum of locales equaled a nation united.

Chastened by the society's division in 1861–65, but eschewing any further resort to a federal power that had failed to

effect results during Reconstruction, politicians of the period again returned to that older belief that theirs was a self-regulating and inherently harmonious society. They sent out from the center, with endless repetition and wrapped in that seemingly vacuous rhetoric by which we remember the period, the affirmation that the interests of each served the interests of all, that in their society one *could* calculate the public good from the sum of private goods, that all parts, if left unimpeded by government, would cast themselves into a concordant whole. Still oblivious to industrialization's propensity to create new and not altogether beneficent power, they thus agreed with those at home: there was no need for a standing power in government. A strong national executive was unnecessary, for, with the single exception of the Plains Indian, no component of society required the coercion of federal force. By their design, then, it was to be the glue of common sentiment rather than the pressure of power from the center which promised that the society would remain integral.

While serving as the source of unifying sentiment, the federal government played another role, one both similar to that of other nineteenth-century institutions and consonant with this harmony-of-interest theory. It assisted individuals to attain their personal ends—not, to be sure, every individual, but those within the governing group, those few, generally of higher middle-class strata, interested in holding office at the center. Internally, the system pivoted on personal ties and associations; from these were spun out numberless transactions in jobs, favors, and other species of preferment. Externally, it relied on the apathy which those at home extended to what transpired at the center. It would remain intact as long as they continued to believe either that they had no material stake in Washington's actions; or that despite what seemed to some government's metamorphosis into an endless progression of gluttonous transactions, morality and character did still or would again inform the process; or that, congruent with harmony-of-interest theory, self-serving congressmen somehow continued to serve them as well. As they ceased so to trust, they would insist that locale and center be joined by something more substantial than a symbolism of unity and harmony.

The social consensus which wove itself around this relationship between locale and center was a spacious one and in many ways appropriate to the heterogeneous society of the 1870s and early 1880s, but its disavowel of centralized political power and its reliance on the assumed power of moral judgment left it vulnerable to industrialization's advance. The period manifested an unmistakable movement toward economic aggregation. Industrialism created, with its larger and larger units, widening disparities between rich and poor. New wealth, flaunting itself, became the most important counter in politics. American agriculture, in several of its subsectors already reeling in its dependence on a world market whose fluctuations were neither controllable nor comprehensible, seemed to its followers destined for rapid subordination to burgeoning business. Many Americans, pinched in pride and pocketbook by these processes and no longer able to locate right and wrong in issues of such magnitude and complexity, were less and less inclined to believe that their society rested on a natural harmony of interests.

The crises of the 1890s threatened to sweep away a consensus already eroded by its inability to absorb problems of powerful corporations, labor agitation, and immigrant influx. The nation suffered a depression unprecedented in its duration and severity; industrial strife that touched new levels of violence; an agrarian revolt signaling the collapse of that sector of the economy most still thought pivotal; and a trauma-filled presidential election into which half the population seemed to pour its millennial hopes and the other half its apocalyptic fears. To these crises patent, one must add at least two others, less palpable but in some quarters no less menacing. There appeared the disquieting announcement of the close of the frontier and thus the dissolution of that dynamic which, all assumed, had guided the nation's development by drawing Americans westward for almost three hundred years. And, finally, there emerged a crisis of confidence. Some within the governing group, some who concerned themselves with society's intellectual tone came to fear that character and all other intangible measures of worth were being overwhelmed by values exclusively material; they lamented the decline of behavior, public and private, and the degradation of standards, moral and literary. Just as their apprehensions were breaking the crust of genteel reticence, members of a younger generation shaped by the post-Civil War era revealed their own loss of confidence in many of their fathers' assumptions. It is no surprise that, thirty years after Appomattox, many Americans again worried about the fragility of their society and anxiously asked themselves if the social order were not at another point of peril. As Henry Adams wrote of these years, "The individual crawled as he best could, through the wreck, and found many values of life upset."

Amid these crises, elements essential to the consensus disappeared. Numbers of those previously uninterested in the center's governing group demanded entry or, at a minimum, a series of governmental transactions this time directed to *their* relief. For the first time the unemployed walked on Washington. Farmers in the South and West insisted vociferously that the center act to recoup their interests. Immigrants, though still organized only in city machines that exploited as often as they expressed their interests, seemed to those in office equally menacing. Local apathy vis-à-vis Washington dissolved.

The apparent climax came in the presidential election of 1896. The prosperous insisted on the fixed quality of their society and rejected any suggestion that the consensus—*the* proper and abiding basis of society—should not remain valid for their lifetimes. To such people, angered and frightened by their sense of numberless, unqualified others crowding into the political process, the only issue of 1896 was that of social order.

The clergy called William Jennings Bryan a blasphemer. Doctors diagnosed him a psychopath. Editors and educators attested that agrarian democracy was lawlessness in feeble disguise. For an antidote to anarchism these established forces returned almost instinctively to the symbols of unity. Intensifying the appeal to patriotism on the assumption that dividing allegiances might still be bound by devotion to nation, McKinley commandeered the flag.

Those on the other side, principally agrarians, denounced the power of business wealth and vowed to sweep away that governing group which had acquiesced in its aggrandizement.

McKinley's victory at the polls had about it the appearance of tidy resolution: the governing group remained in place. Economic prosperity's return six months later and the rapid wilting of Populist organizations added to the semblance of conclusiveness. Election day, however, proved less than complete catharsis. The issue of social order, in aligning the governing group with emergent business against the forces of disrupted locale, had temporarily obscured business' role in undermining that consensus so vital to the governing group's interests. What re-emerged to agitate many minds was that which Bryan termed "the fight between the money power and the people." Once the specter of social collapse had been at least partially exorcised, the Great Commoner's issue would again present itself, this time in a context much less menacing to respectables.

The verdict of 1896 was thus appealed and, in its probusiness aspect, symbolically overturned in the preliminaries to the Spanish-American War.

Crucial here are two formulations widely accepted by Americans in 1898: the popular dedication to the Spanish-American War as a humanitarian and antimaterialist crusade, and the popular denunciation of the American businessman-financier as an internal enemy initially capable of eliciting almost as much hostility as the external foe, the Spaniard.

It is within the context of the first formulation that Redfield

Proctor's address before the Senate on March 17, 1898, became the crucial event. The Vermonter, in ways to be discussed in chapter two, drew from his countrymen a moral impulse of overpowering strength. Senator George F. Hoar of Massachusetts spoke for many when he said that Americans thenceforth could feel free to anticipate "the most honorable single war in all history." On the other political flank, even American Socialists applauded this war of altruism. As William McKinley discovered in attempting to resist the movement to war, there was no significant dissent from this view of American motives.

By extension, sympathy for the Cuban became the test of human kindness, and those who remained so unmoved by the island's plight that they opposed war became morally suspect. It was the wealthy businessman who became this sentiment's special target.

There is a nub of truth in the contention that large-scale business stood aloof from the rush to war. Some businessmen, notably those in the largest commercial centers of the eastern seaboard, believed economic recovery much too tenuous to risk war. Amid the historians' efforts to determine *which* businessmen, by location and industry, did or did not oppose the war's coming, one should not, however, lose sight of the force ultimately conclusive, the *conviction* of so many Americans, justified or not, that business did indeed block a war for humanity.

The larger significance of this widespread animosity toward business rests in its ability to reconstitute social unity by reuniting in 1898 segments of society bitterly opposed in 1896. The governing group adopted, without attribution, much of the vocabulary of William Jennings Bryan. Henry Cabot Lodge, who had speculated that a Democratic victory "would mean almost revolution," now joined in decrying "the money power." Similar Bryanite echoes ring through the words of Theodore Roosevelt; earlier a proponent of pruning Populism by shooting its leaders, in 1898 he denounced "the craven fear and brutal selfishness of the mere money-makers," those who were "anxious to court any infamy" for peace. And beyond the governing group, Peter Finley Dunne's syndicated creation, Mr. Dooley, caught a corresponding popular mood both angry and sardonic when he told Hennessey,

> Ye cud niver be a rale pathrite.
> Ye have no stock ticker in ye'er house.

The Spanish-American War was thus conceived both as the triumph of moral judgment and as a repudiation of those whom Americans sensed had most severely impaired the governing consensus of twenty-five years. The forces creating war were less the first proclamations of twentieth-century capitalism than twilight expressions of a disappearing nineteenth-century social structure.

The book's six essays probe the social consensus, particularly its reliance on simple, limited categories of thought and its trust in elemental, unambiguous moral judgment. They explore equally the faltering of consensus, particularly its inability to incorporate new problems that seem to demand that power be marshaled at the center and extended to the domestic economy and to foreign affairs. Even when most potent, however, the consensus was not one of lock-step; it offered to the various parts of the nation a broad latitude, a generous heterogeneity further increased by its gradual erosion. The following studies, predicated like the consensus itself on the looseness and diversity of nineteenth-century life, attempt to probe an American society caught by war at a time of special tension.

CHAPTER I *William McKinley*
and the Decision for War

AN AMERICAN HISTORIAN of the telephone has recorded that
"for temperamental reasons" neither Benjamin Harrison nor
Grover Cleveland took pleasure in that infant instrument.
William McKinley to the contrary was "the one President who
really revelled in the comforts of telephony." He employed
daily the single White House telephone unused in previous
administrations and ordered a second installed. He valued
the telephone, he said, because "[it] is bringing us all closer
together." [1]

McKinley judged events and propositions as he judged inventions. Throughout his political career he attached the
highest value to those that promised to reduce American dis-
unities, for his early experiences had riveted in him a sense
of the perils of division. The Civil War overtook him on the
threshold of manhood. Four years of combat did not eradicate
the values of his youth; they did mark him with an enduring
apprehension that those values could survive only if the society that supported them were held together. As a series of
subsequent personal blows reinforced this consciousness of
vulnerability, he took as his special task the diminution of dis-
sensions in his private life and the life of the nation.

Experience joined temperament in commissioning McKinley

9

to protect and nurture America's reestablished but very fragile unity, for what he called "American values" were gems in a frayed sack. The stones themselves were clear and lustrous and of unquestioned worth as the source of future social prosperity and tranquility. If, however, the sack were rent again, the contents would scatter and be lost. McKinley's determination to knit closer and stronger the social fabric enclosing the values he cherished provides a thematic unity to the style and substance of his public life.

So focused, McKinley's political career was remarkably successful. By 1898, as the country's twenty-fifth chief executive, he presided over a society emerging from a period of economic depression, social strife, and sectional animosity. Just as he might have been tempted to congratulate himself on the return of social repose, however, there reappeared the problem of America's response to the renewal of the Cuban revolt against Spain. What had been for Grover Cleveland in 1895 a prickly but minor irritant had become in three years' time an emotion-freighted issue threatening to involve the United States in full-scale war with a European power. Largely from that earlier sense of war as the destroyer of social unity, McKinley opposed the popular demand for war against Spain. The period of his resistance—February, March, and April of 1898—constituted the supreme crisis of his life.

A secure Ohio boyhood imparted to William McKinley a cluster of optimistic assumptions about God, man, and the United States. His midcentury Methodism remained soft—reassuring, sympathetic, conciliatory. God was a daily reality, a benevolent and very personal deity who guided the lives of his people. McKinley's belief in theological determinism would, if abstractions ruled, have destroyed man's sphere of effective action; in practice McKinley was confident of his ability to discern God's intent and to act so as to remove obstacles from God's path.[2] Ultimate power, however, rested in the hands of a God solicitous of the prosperous future of citizen and nation.

For McKinley, the end of American life required no intellectual speculation. It was a given. That it could be defined in terms no more specific than "progress" and "prosperity" and "improvement" was a source of no discomfort. The United States was a nation in the ascendant, and few people paid serious attention to the pessimistic pronouncements of a handful of intellectuals on the fringes of American life. Who could feel that the apocalyptic visions of Brooks Adams or the laments of William Dean Howells touched reality? How could America be "coming out all wrong in the end?" [3] For McKinley, as for the vast majority of his contemporaries, the road led upward. As he put it to an Atlanta audience: "At peace with all the world and with one another, what can stand in the pathway of our progress and prosperity?" [4]

It would be an error, however, to think McKinely's confidence impenetrable. "At peace with all the world and with one another" represents an important qualification, for McKinley believed that movement into that beneficent future was possible only if Americans remained a united people. Indeed, his introduction to the fragility of American unity and his tendency to conciliation came early in life. The Civil War was McKinley's bridge to manhood. Feeling no exaltation, no soaring spirit at its outset, he watched the first volunteer contingent depart. Later, after discussing the matter with a cousin, he decided "in cold blood" that it was his duty to enlist. [5] A private at eighteen, in four years he rose through the ranks to become a brevet major. He attended prayer meetings whenever possible, received a single furlough, participated in more than a dozen battles and suffered neither wound nor serious illness. [6]

McKinley was cited for courageous action at least three times, and the pattern of his heroism is suggestive. At Antietam, as a commissary sergeant of the Twenty-Third Ohio Volunteer Infantry, he drove his mules through heavy musketry to deliver hot food and coffee to the men on the firing line. It was an unusual solicitude that won the commendation of his colonel, Rutherford B. Hayes.[7] Later in the retreat from Kernstown, Virginia, McKinley, then a staff officer, again rode through heavy fire to deliver an order permitting an exposed regiment to retire. In the same campaign he led a volunteer force to save Union artillery pieces abandoned by their crews.[8] One can seldom separate elements of chance and will in war, but McKinley in each of these instances acted the conservator whose responses were directed to the succor of his companions or charges rather than the destruction of the enemy. He was never reported to have killed a Confederate soldier, nor did he ever speak of such an action. Had he done so, he would have worn the event as a burden rather than a badge.

Late in the war while at Winchester, Virginia, McKinley noticed the special concern of a Union surgeon for Confederate prisoners. Investigating, he found that this man and others whose friendships crossed sectional lines were Masons aiding Southern confreres. On the basis of that discovery he joined the Winchester lodge and remained a Mason throughout his life.[9]

McKinley reached his maturity as the nation was being torn apart. He emerged from the Civil War with body intact and with a sense that a society no longer able to take its unity for granted would require, and might reward, the arts of the conciliator.

Few presidents have surpassed the social distance William McKinley traveled between impecunious, semirural origins and the White House. Prior to his enlistment he taught school and clerked in a post office after his father's business failure ended his attempt to complete college. On his return to civilian life he studied law and passed the bar examination before beginning his climb: Canton, Ohio, attorney and Y.M.C.A. president; political speaker and secretary of the Republican county committee; Stark County prosecuting attorney; delegate and later committee chairman at state party conventions; congressman; governor of Ohio; president. This thirty-year progress, impressive but deceptive if from a list of McKinley's steps to the top one should infer that he early charted a route to the White House, was not without its severe political and personal reverses.

In 1871 McKinley failed in his bid for re-election as prosecuting attorney. Fifteen years later he was ousted from his seat in the House of Representatives by a party vote on disputed election charges. In 1890 he was defeated in a regular congressional election. Despite such reverses, McKinley refused to believe that anyone wished him ill. He was confident that suasion and the conciliation of opposing forces would eventually set matters right and until 1898 experience gave him no cause to doubt the efficacy of such tactics. They enabled him to run unscathed the gauntlet of savage Ohio political cliques. Although in the end he joined with Mark Hanna, he always managed to avoid final disruptive breaks with the factions led by Joseph B. Foraker, Asa S. Bushnell, and George B. Cox. On his way up, his abstention from acrimony aided him in converting several failures into bases of future success. The lost House election of 1890 was made to seem an object lesson in the injustice of legislative gerrymandering. McKinley refused to say a word in extenuation of his defeat, but his friends made it clear that he was victim rather than loser. His political return in the gubernatorial election of the following year drew national attention, and his victory appeared to many Americans a matter of elementary justice.

In retrospect the celebrated Walker affair acquires the same cast of disaster averted, failure converted. The collapse of Robert L. Walker's tin business in 1893 revealed that McKinley, in gratitude for an old school loan, had endorsed many of Walker's notes. Believing that he was simply renewing the original commitment of $17,000, McKinley had signed without examination documents obligating him to redeem more than $130,000. When the storm broke, McKinley reassured the man

who had bilked him, then old and ill, and proposed to retire
from politics to meet his debts. Hard pressed themselves by a
serious economic depression, Americans might have rejoiced
in the announced departure of an irresponsible public official;
instead, many of scant means attempted to contribute to Mc-
Kinley's relief. At a time when the acquisition of large fortunes
seemed to depend less and less on a man's character, when
congressmen continued to engage in business and law during
their terms of office and the Senate was becoming the "rich
man's club," McKinley had obviously made few dollars. He
had, moreover, signed away innocently dollars that he did not
possess. In the end a consortium of wealthy friends led by
Hanna, William R. Day, Myron T. Herrick, and H. H. Kohlsaat
contributed the necessary amount, and McKinley retained his
governorship.[10]

In the presidential campaign three years later McKinley
presented himself as "the advance agent of prosperity." The
Democratic opposition, and especially the newspapers of William Randolph Hearst, countered with charges that McKinley
was the prisoner of business interests.[11] The election result
suggests that the numerous victims of the depression of 1893
may have remembered the fact of McKinley's victimization
before the manner of his redemption.

McKinley's response to crushing personal problems was
similarly propitiatory and the results for McKinley the politician equally advantageous. In 1871 McKinley married Ida
Saxton, the daughter of a Canton family prominent in Stark
County publishing and banking. Their first daughter lived
three-and-one-half years, their second only five months. By
1876 Ida McKinley had become the captive of a chronic in-
validism and was thereafter subject to periodic depression and
epileptic seizures. She became shrewish, but McKinley nursed
her through each crisis with elaborate attention and deep af-
fection. His concern for his wife was unceasing. As Thomas
Beer put it, McKinley became "a soft-spoken, watchful nurse
in his own house and a worried guest if he was in company

without his charge. . . . [He] ascended into the headlines of newspapers with this burden, and it was genuine, wasting his time, hurting his health, and wearying his friends so that they canonized him before he was forty years old." [12]

As McKinley had refused to speak in extenuation of his political and financial failures, so he deflected inquiries about Mrs. McKinley's health. He shared neither his disappointments nor his fears, but Americans of the 1890s knew of his relationship with his wife and thought it a character qualification for occupancy of the White House.[13]

When governor of Ohio, McKinley waved to Ida each morning from a nearby intersection on his way to the capitol, and from his office window he saluted her with handkerchief each afternoon at the same hour no matter what the work at hand.[14] In such patterns McKinley revealed a rough identity in his responses to public and private problems. Because of Ida McKinley's illness it was absolutely essential to avoid emotional eruption. The present was assumed to be the ideal and any change a change for the worse. There could be no long-term planning; the task was to move gracefully and quietly from day to day. Order and regularity were indispensable, but they could not be imposed. Harmony and well-being would grow only from conciliation and the repeated gesture of reassurance.

Shortly after he entered the House of Representatives in 1878 McKinley chose to become a specialist in tariff matters. He did so principally because his friend and counselor, President Hayes, suggested the tariff as the way to political preferment.[15] As a good congressman, he was also interested in the protection of the infant steel and tinplate industries of Stark County, Ohio. Beyond these considerations McKinley saw the tariff in a way unusual for his day. He was unhappy that the process of framing tariff schedules was invariably divisive; it required descent into the legislative pit, haggling and wrestling and trading limited favors for limited but locally powerful interests. Although pleased enough to carry home his own prizes, he insisted that there be a way to gauge the social effect of those myriad "deals" called a tariff schedule, to judge "the highest good to the greatest number." [16]

McKinley's early speeches relied on the traditional conception of the tariff as a wall, but again with significant extensions. The immediate danger, he held, was that foreign business capitalizing on its lower labor costs might destroy new American industry. High tariffs would protect the country's economy against capture by foreign monopolies and at the same time spur internal industrial growth and high wages. Agriculture too would be served through an expanding home market. Far from a design to serve "the interests" here at home, McKinley's tariff theory looked to isolate the nation from external threat and thus enable the natural harmonies of American employer, worker, and farmer to express themselves. Only in the last year of his life did McKinley's faith in the automatic compatibility of farm, factory, and front office begin to waver. Until then, foreign not domestic monopoly was the danger.

At the end of McKinley's twelve years in the House of Representatives, his colleagues acknowledged his expertise. Tariff-making remained a welter of head-on collisions among numberless interest groups. McKinley's optimistic theory received no more than a polite lip-service. Yet he alone could claim to identify the effects of individual items within the whole tariff system. His insistence that such an effort should be made appealed both to those who cast their eyes back to periods of greater social tranquility and to those who looked ahead to an America of large-scale industry and nationwide markets.

McKinley's presidency was not one of vigorous executive action. He accepted the common belief that national political power resided in the Congress, not the White House.[17] Precedent reinforced temperament: McKinley tried to confine himself to endorsing whatever combinations were made by others. When he could not ignore a problem—his first inclination—he invariably attempted to compromise within the terms of the problem itself. That is, he preferred to conciliate the elements whose disagreement constituted the problem. If such tactics failed, he would often accept tactical defeat rather than risk the bitter residue of an imposed settlement.

In the spring of 1897 he called a special session of the Congress to raise tariff rates established under the Cleveland administration. The Senate immediately embarked on an unusually wild free-for-all that mocked the president's hopes for a systematic tariff and sent the rates far beyond what he thought healthy for the nation. He signed the bill without demurral. McKinley favored the annexation of Hawaii, but he had no word of reproach for a Senate that refused to give his treaty serious attention until the Spanish-American War. The administration's allies brought to a vote the Olney-Pauncefote Anglo-American Arbitration Treaty—and failed to muster the necessary two-thirds majority. Hanna's brain child, a merchant marine subsidy bill, received little White House support and was also defeated. The single successful executive initiative was the Gold Standard Act of 1900, but it simply ratified prior administration practice and set a seal on what most Americans deemed the judgment of 1896. Generally, McKinley believed the consequences of inaction less troublesome than those of division.

It is with some surprise then that one encounters numerous statements establishing McKinley's high standing with legislative branch and public. Senator Shelby Cullom maintained that there had never been a president with more influence over Congress; [18] the Democrat John Crisp told McKinley the people felt that "you and they are the same kind. You are to them what no other President since Lincoln has been." [19] How did a man of such apparent passivity retain such holds on congressmen and voters? The answer rests partially in the lineaments of a remarkable personal style and partially in the sense of himself that he succeeded in conveying to the American people.

Within the limits he set for himself, William McKinley was a consummate politician. Harrison and Cleveland had been dour chief executives; they resisted the intrusions of press and public and defended the White House as if it were a besieged fortress. McKinley was the Accessible President. His secretary, John Addison Porter, admitted without hesitation congressmen who claimed the privilege of presenting newly married couples from home districts. Senator Stephen B. Elkins of West Virginia boasted that he introduced a thousand men to the president.[20] Samuel Gompers later wrote that no other president had offered him easier access.[21] Even sightseers could ordinarily chat with McKinley.[22]

In fact McKinley enjoyed his visitors and delighted in the public reception. Perhaps he found in the shaking of many hands confirmation of that identity, asserted by Crisp, between people and president. Somehow the gesture never staled, never lost its attraction for McKinley as a ritual of reassurance. "I feel better after that contact," he said.[23] When he discovered that the fastidious Porter planned to exclude all but the invited from the first White House diplomatic reception of 1898, McKinley refused to permit the barring of gate-crashers.[24]

Moving from issue to issue, McKinley put to his office visitors and reception guests the question, "What do people up your way think of it?"[25] He sought public response to a problem, not specific information about a problem's constituent parts. He read widely in the newspapers of the day but to divine sentiment rather than to accumulate data. His intellectual and analytical powers were distinctly limited, and he continued to resist the role of president as problem-solver. Refreshed by thousands of handshakes, he was drained of his energies by visitors and officials who came to him with specific problems: "I have to meet and resist all that force not once or twice each day but all day without interruption."[26]

When events did not compel him to arbitrate but permitted him to preside, William McKinley was very much at home in the world of politics. He had a fine memory for names and faces, and despite his heavy dignity he relished public speaking. The contrast between his ordered and sedate frontporch campaign and William Jennings Bryan's sweep through the country in 1896 is deceptive, for McKinley built much of his national reputation on the stump. In the previous campaign, between September 25 and November 2, 1894, he delivered three hundred and seventy-one speeches, ranging through three hundred towns in sixteen states.[27] Estimates of his speaking style differ, but Robert La Follette for one thought it superb.[28]

McKinley managed men as he managed problems: he stressed that which united and obscured that which divided. Whatever Bryan might say, there was for McKinley no "enemy's country" on either side of the Alleghenies. Every opponent was a potential ally. Every opponent had interests that might be buffed and rounded and shaped to fit within larger combinations of interest, and the larger those combinations the more secure the national unity. Such a conception applied with finesse enabled McKinley to control some difficult temperaments. Shelby Cullom objected to many of the president's appointments in his native Illinois; he remonstrated regularly and was as regularly soothed with soft words.[29] New Hampshire's Senator William E. Chandler, according to his biographer, was an "excitable, erratic, enthusiastic and radical" man whom McKinley alone could manage.[30] Men found moving the few glimpses that the outwardly reserved and dignified McKinley permitted into a deeper stratum of feeling. Senator George F. Hoar of Massachusetts, the leading Republican opponent of McKinley's colonial policy, recorded that at the climax of a heated discussion McKinley cried out in a vocabulary of emotion now depreciated, "I shall always love you, whatever you do." And Hoar reciprocated the president's feelings: McKinley was his "beloved friend." [31]

McKinley's particular strength, approaching genius, was the conciliating and healing gesture converting or at least neutralizing opposition.[32] Archbishop John Ireland, who supported McKinley's candidacy in 1896 and 1900, was aggrieved at the absence of what he considered a fair return. He was not made a member of the United States delegation to the Hague Peace

Conference nor had McKinley praised him to the pope. In a
few moments of conversation the president nonetheless persuaded the archbishop that he had always had the cleric's
interests at heart. McKinley then sent him off to Paris, completely mollified, to present a statue of Lafayette.[33] Even the
acerbic Henry Adams, certainly no friend of the president,
conceded that McKinley was a "marvelous manager of men." [34]

Not surprisingly, McKinley lacked a sense of institutional
relationships. The executive branch was to him not a collection
of offices and bureaus, each standing in certain formal arrangement with the others and all parts of an ongoing bureaucratic process. It more resembled an intricate web of personal
relationships in which men, in exchange for their advice and
support, traded jobs, favors, and preferment.[35] McKinley
equated the executive power with the length of the presidential reach, and he took extraordinary care in picking the men
who would fall within its compass. Those intimates within
would provide whatever was needed to conduct a satisfactory
presidency. Quite logically then, McKinley made no effort to
familiarize himself with the agencies of the executive or to
tap their resources of information and support. When he required information beyond his reach, he employed a series of
emissaries. He was most comfortable working with men like
Assistant Secretary (later Secretary) of State William R. Day,
products of long and intimate friendships.

The McKinley style of executive leadership rested on his
ability to spin wide that web of personal influence and to ma-
nipulate resources to tie men within it to his own interests.
Civil Service reform threatened to limit his access to men and
to deprive him of such traditional fasteners as patronage jobs.
He ignored Cleveland's executive order requiring competitive
examinations for Foreign Service aspirants.[36] Prior to the 1900
presidential election he removed nine thousand places from
protected categories.[37] Though these steps violated the pledge
of the Republican platform and brought anguished appeals

from reformers, McKinley thought them essential. He was dependent on the "habit of conference" [38] and he required the political wherewithal to keep within reach those men whom he knew and trusted.

This politics of personal persuasion requires some elaboration of Shelby Cullom's assertion that there had never been a president with more influence over the Congress. To this statement the Illinois senator appended a second to the effect that there had not been the slightest friction between the president and the congressional party leaders.[39] Both are misleading if taken to imply significant presidential influence on congressional movement. McKinley did assuage individual congressmen with great success, but larger congressional-executive harmonies were in large measure dependent on presidential deference. After each election, at Hanna's urging, McKinley balanced factions and pacified cliques, but once patronage appointments had created a rough equilibrium, McKinley considered his object achieved. There was no further patronage manipulation to specific legislative ends. There was nothing to compare with Cleveland's determined effort to compel repeal of the Sherman Silver Purchase Act. The Congress understandably considered McKinley one of its own: he shared its prescription for congressional-executive harmony.

Respectful of congressional power, William McKinley feared presidential power. Theodore Roosevelt was already impressed with its possibilities; McKinley was always aware of its responsibilities. Grover Cleveland noted this at a private preinaugural dinner he offered the McKinleys: "Of all the interviews I have ever held during the whole of my career, none ever impressed me as being so full of settled sadness and sincerity." [40] Several years later Henry L. Stoddard realized that in contemplating the shape of the peace McKinley was very uncomfortable with his unqualified power to exact terms of Spain. The president, concluded Stoddard, had "no flair to be absolute." [41]

If the Congress valued McKinley for what he did—or perhaps for what he did not do—the public esteemed him for what he was, the "Christian Statesman."

He attended church regularly. He prayed frequently on matters official and personal. He read the Bible nightly to Ida McKinley. He was a teetotaler. He eschewed sexual matters to such a degree that his most conspicuous recorded interest was his request for a photograph of the wife of the man he intended to appoint secretary of the treasury. Looking at it, McKinley said of Mrs. Lyman Gage that she would certainly "ornament the social side of the President's family." [42] The McKinleys lived in the White House exactly as they lived in Canton, Ohio: dinner at 6:30, perhaps a game of euchre, perhaps the president reading newspapers while his wife knitted. He forgave his assassin and died with a prayer. His hypocrisies were few and gentle: he enjoyed cigars but, fearing that he would set a bad example for the young men of the country, he would not be photographed with one. [43]

Today one looks for contrivance in a man who makes his sentiments obvious and pitches them at an exalted level. In retrospect McKinley appears so much the model "Christian Statesman" that the very consistency of his behavior verges on parody of a stock figure. Americans of the 1890s, however, judging him at a distance, found him in earnest. More surprising, there was no disenchantment among those closest to the president. [44] Men as disparate as Charles Dawes and Samuel Gompers admired McKinley. Even his political opponents granted that there was no defect in McKinley's virtues. Their only recourse was to paint his virtues too perfect, a source of weakness and vacillation. Unable to deny him uprightness, they denied him power. In this rendering, at its most savage in Homer Davenport's cartoons for the New York *Journal,* McKinley became an overdressed Buddha, the smiling, impotent, unidimensional "virtuous man" manipulated by the strings of others. This image drew far less response from

McKinley's contemporaries than from later historians of the period.

This divergence of opinion is at least partially attributable to the loss after World War I of that earlier sense of "character" as an almost tangible substance. When Americans of the 1890s spoke of McKinley, they spoke of his character, and one can almost hear in their tones the capitalization of the "c." Its constituent parts were even more obscure than those of "progress," but in rough terms it may be used as that quality of uprightness and honorable dealing that a man such as McKinley was confident he possessed and was certain others recognized in him. McKinley's early Canton law rival and later friend, William R. Day, supported such assumptions: "In the trial of a case Major McKinley gained the confidence of the jury by the fairness and courtesy of his conduct, and into all his arguments was thrown the silent but potent influence of a character beyond reproach." [45]

McKinley had no doubts about the canons of proper behavior. He appears throughout to have lived comfortably with his parents' values, secular and religious. Whatever the components of character, McKinley thought them timeless and of equal applicability in every generation. Never questioning the adequacy of the old values, he did not recognize new situations of increasing ethical complexity [46] incident to the industrial transformation of American life. Few of the uncertainties that troubled Theodore Roosevelt touched McKinley. In his serenity he did not understand the New Yorker's insistence that character could grow flabby with neglect; nor did he share Roosevelt's penchant for framing action so as to test and prod and, where found wanting, improve character.

McKinley seemed to know intuitively that his bearing was central to his task. From that office which he honored not for its potential as an agency of action but for its exemplary qualities, an office symbolically to be set above the political process by its ability to inspire lives of virtue, he offered the country

the picture of a benevolent presiding officer affirming and re-
affirming what he never ceased to assume bound all Americans:
belief in God; love of country; confidence in progress through
individual effort. His personal and official lives stood surety for
his disinterestedness. His demeanor conveyed the continuity
of American values, the continuing validity of character and
self-help during a period of vast change and transformation.
No matter how formidable divisions appear, he seemed to say,
they are but artificial and transient. McKinley was the promise
of the seamlessness of American life.

Public and congressional pressure to compel intervention in
behalf of the Cuban rebels mounted in the spring of 1896.
Undulating with the course of the rebellion and the availability of domestic diversion,[47] it reached its apogee two years
later following the destruction of the *Maine* on February 15,
1898. During the first months of his term McKinley avoided the
subject of Cuba whenever possible; he shook off the impor-
tunities of White House visitors.[48] When he did choose to act,
he responded first to those human elements of the problem
with which he was most comfortable. He secured a congressional appropriation of $50,000 for the relief of American citi-
zens in Cuba, most of whom were of Cuban birth. He later
organized a drive for private contributions to feed a large part
of the Cuban population. Here he applied the same techniques
that he had employed when, as governor of Ohio, he had
undertaken the relief of the destitute miners in the Hocking
and Sunday Creek Valleys: the use of a personal emissary to
verify need; minimal resort to government channels and resources; the appeal to the goodwill of the people; the contri-
bution made by McKinley personally but anonymously.[49] In
April 1898 the president reported to Congress that the $200,000
received had saved many Cuban lives. White House correspondence records indicate the importance McKinley attached to
this project.[50] He was never happier or more energetic than

when he could act less as an elected official than as the individual best situated to mobilize the neighbors to meet elemental human needs.

By late summer 1897, however, events compelled McKinley to face the more complex aspects of the Cuban situation. Captain-General Valeriano Weyler's draconian measures—notably his attempts to divide the island into compartments separated by impenetrable military barriers and to "reconcentrate" country people in urban centers under tight Spanish control—produced distress but no decision. Weyler several times persuaded Madrid that total success required no more than an additional increment of force, and the Conservative ministry of Canovas del Castillo was emboldened to insist on rebel submission as a prerequisite to any negotiation. The rebels, however, would not capitulate, and the Spanish could not conquer. Washington detected the outlines of a protracted stalemate. Meanwhile, as Cubans starved in cities whose administrative systems were hopelessly inadequate to the needs of the forced migration, sugar fields, mills, and ranches (some of them American owned) were destroyed by rebel torches.

In August 1897, with McKinley's new minister, General Stewart L. Woodford, enroute to Madrid with instructions to bring heavier pressure on the Spaniards, Canovas—Spain's prime minister since March 1895—was assassinated. Delaying his arrival until the Liberals under Praxedes Sagasta had established a new government, Woodford chose to speak softly and was rewarded when on November 25 the queen regent proclaimed a new policy. Her government had decided to repudiate Weyler's methods and to grant Cuba autonomy under the Spanish crown.

McKinley welcomed this apparent reversal. In his annual message to Congress in December he urged that the American press and public give Spain "a reasonable chance" to make good her promises. The Sagasta government, however, disastrously overestimating its own power, had merely mollified Washington with pleasing policies it could not implement.

After some hesitation Weyler agreed to abide by Sagasta's order recalling him to Spain, but on January 12, 1898, Spanish *colons* abetted by regular Army personnel rioted through Havana streets in protest against the queen's reform program and against suspected United States pressure. Shocked, American officials realized Madrid's powerlessness: no matter how imposing the structure of Cuban autonomy displayed on ministry desktops, it would never be realized in Havana.

With Sagasta and the queen regent appealing for more time and McKinley contemplating the implications of a diplomatic victory suddenly turned sour, the New York *Journal* on February 9 printed an intercepted private letter in which Spain's minister to Washington denounced the president as "weak and a bidder for the admiration of the crowd." Enrique Dupuy de Lome resigned. One week later the Spanish government issued an official apology, its tone haughty and condescending. It drew little attention, for by that time the battleship *Maine* was already resting on the bottom of Havana harbor and Americans needed no additional incitement to anger against Spain.

So impatient with Spain was American opinion in mid-February of 1898 that if war were to be averted the official investigating commission appointed by McKinley would have to prove the Spanish government *innocent* of any responsibility for the loss of the *Maine* and two hundred and sixty American lives. This proved impossible. After a delay of six weeks McKinley forwarded to Congress a final report alleging the *Maine* a victim of an external explosion, a verdict establishing in many American minds the guilt of Spaniards, if not Spain. Two days earlier, on March 26, the president had authorized Woodford to demand that Sagasta's government grant Cuba "full self-government, with reasonable indemnity," a phrase whose meaning a subsequent dispatch admitted now moved beyond autonomy to "Cuban independence." On March 27 there followed an American ultimatum: Washington demanded an immediate armistice, an end to reconcentration, and the opening of negotiations between Spanish authorities and Cuban insurgents. "If possible" the president was to act as "final arbiter" on any points remaining unresolved on October 1.[51] The Spanish, debating endlessly intricate points of honor, agreed five days later to suspend reconcentration but rejected arbitration and renewed their insistence that the rebels ask for a suspension of hostilities. McKinley saw no escape. He began to draft his war message to the Congress.

With the deterioration of relations between Washington and Madrid the pressures on the president became intense. The first four months of the new year marked the deepest crisis of McKinley's life. He required drugs in order to sleep.[52] He aged visibly. He paced a path through the White House grounds.[53] In mid-February the secretary of the Navy thought him "more oppressed and careworn" than ever before.[54] In April when his Chicago friend H. H. Kohlsaat called at the president's invitation, McKinley "broke down and cried like a boy of thirteen." [55]

The source of his anguish—and ultimately of his confusion and paralysis—lay in incompatible concepts of war, the presidency, and public opinion. As congressman, governor, and president, McKinley set an unusually high value on public opinion.[56] Chauncey Depew said of him that his "faith in the public intelligence and conscience was supreme. He believed that people knew more than any man. He never tried to lead but studied so constantly public opinion that he became almost infallible in its interpretation." [57]

McKinley attached great importance to public responses that reached him along those fragile and shifting lines of personal contact he spun from the White House.[58] He assembled other indications from responses to questions during those long public receptions and from his reading of White House mail and newspapers, as many as a dozen a day. By these methods he believed that he tapped the thinking of a significant number of Americans and that such thinking was his best guide to action.

In early 1898 the yellow press capitalized on a train of events, created reinforcing "events," and with the help of the Associated Press spoke the voice of war in many of the nation's cities. William Randolph Hearst was successful in articulating the themes by which Americans came to interpret what was happening in Cuba. They were variants on the major refrain of Spanish inhumanity and were illustrated effectively by persons whose plights Hearst chronicled in endless detail. His message—the Spanish are ravaging this or that innocent and appealing individual; the Spanish must be stopped— stirred Americans. If some other, less elementary definition were to be given the Cuban problem—the absence of any threat to the country's national interest, for example, or the inevitability of a satisfactory peaceful settlement or the inhumanity of war—another voice would be necessary.

Here McKinley was cruelly caught. He at first hoped that public opinion was not bellicose; his decision to stop reading newspapers [59] was another attempt to ignore a troublesome problem. He was unsuccessful, partially because indications of the popular temper continued to reach him through other sources, partially because he too found irresistible the terms in which Hearst cast the Cuban question. As always, the alleviation of small-scale, unambiguous human predicaments appealed to his temperament.

When he could no longer ignore the public demand for war —crowds hissed his name in the music halls and burned his effigy [60]—McKinley had to choose to embrace, to reject, or to attempt to alter the mandate of public opinion. Although he believed it his presidential duty to obey public opinion,[61] he found it impossible to accept the first alternative: he could not happily, nor even willingly, lead the country to war. The passage of years did not alter the perception of war that McKinley had gained as a boy. The horror of the killing never dimmed. In later years he would praise the concern of com-

rade for comrade that he had shared in his regiment, but of
the unit's raison d'être, of the cannon and the musket, he said
nothing. Unlike Oliver Wendell Holmes, Jr., he had not entered the Civil War in an excess of zeal. Nor was he later
gripped by the disillusionment and fatigue that fill the Massachusetts officer's letters of 1864–65.[62]

Postwar rituals—the G.A.R. encampments, the Fourth of
July and "bloody shirt" oratory, the flags and reviews—had by
1890 transformed the conviction of many Union veterans that
war was hell. Holmes himself began to wear a military mus-
tache and to observe battle anniversaries.[63] He had not forgotten the destruction and cruelty, but he had discovered a
higher rationale. "War, when you are at it, is horrible and dull,"
he told the Harvard graduating class of 1895. "It is only when
time has passed that you see that its message was divine. . . .
We need it in this time of individualistic negations. . . . We
need it everywhere and at all times. . . . Out of heroism grows
faith in the worth of heroism." [64]

By all this McKinley was untouched. To Holmes and many
other Americans war had become for the individual an exercise in personal virtue and for communities of men the final
arbiter of competing moral values. There is no record that
Theodore Roosevelt or anyone else of the Holmes camp put
these propositions to the president, but McKinley could not
have agreed that anyone should *require* a violent setting in
which to demonstrate the highest personal qualities. He would
have found it stranger still that those moral values in which he
had such confidence should be subject to challenge and
change. His view of war remained simple, the direct descen-
dant of the sights, sounds, and smells of the battlefield. Soon
after the destruction of the *Maine,* the last Civil War soldier
to live in the White House told Leonard Wood, "I have been
through one war; I have seen the dead piled up, and I do not
want to see another." [65]

McKinley could no more reject than espouse the public's
call for war. To do so would have meant renouncing a life-

time's dedication to public opinion. He was not unconscious of possible aberrations in public sentiment. He had conducted several campaigns on planks he thought unassailable, and he had lost. Vindication, however, had never lagged far behind. With public opinion proving itself self-correcting in short order, McKinley could continue to believe that the "people knew more than any man." Nevertheless, in April 1898 not even the old and perhaps almost forgotten suspicion that public opinion might be temporarily mistaken offered McKinley solace. It was one thing to recoup an election defeat, but how did a president recoup the losses of a war he profoundly believed unjustifiable?

It is doubtful that McKinley considered seriously the third alternative, giving new voice to the presidency by speaking out against the drift to war. Though he told Minister Woodford that the Spanish Ministry of Foreign Affairs might be given "unqualified permission to publish every word, written or spoken," addressed by Washington to Madrid,[66] he eschewed such candor at home. He did not mention Cuba in a public address prior to the outbreak of the war. He said nothing when the *Maine* sank. In the six weeks between the vessel's destruction and the publication of the official report, the *Journal's* editorials and diagrams of alleged Spanish infernal machines flatly asserted official Spanish treachery. McKinley said nothing to inhibit the leap of the public mind from the inquiry's finding of "external explosion" to outright Spanish culpability.[67]

Had he chosen to speak, McKinley might have found a rough precedent in the presidential campaign of 1896. Then too hysteria was loose in the land, at least by Republican definition.[68] In the campaign's early months the free-silver craze appeared irresistible and to compound McKinley's difficulty, public sentiment seemed to sweep in the wrong direction on the wrong issue. He wanted to stand on the tariff, not the currency issue. In the end, however, Mark Hanna's "campaign of education" flooded the nation with hundreds of speakers and millions of pieces of literature.[69] Hanna recognized the techniques capable of speaking to the country at large, raised the necessary funds and carried the election.

There is no evidence that McKinley considered in 1898 the tactics of 1896. The party might use private funds to win an election, but the American presidency was not yet an agency whose mission could justifiably encompass a broad manipulation of public opinion. An office of peace information employing Hanna's speakers, literature, and press handouts was in McKinley's conception beyond the limits of presidential propriety.[70]

More surprising was his failure to set out his position through other channels more familiar and orthodox. He might have dispatched personal emissaries—or gone himself—to the nation's largest cities. He might have made allies of those newsmen who, as Long wrote, "cluster like bees" around the White House.[71] McKinley enjoyed their company and provided a press desk in the executive mansion, but it was the ineffectual Porter who talked to newsmen each evening during the months of crisis.[72] Even without a bold decision to enlarge the sphere of presidential activity, some instruments of communication were available. There were many Americans waiting for some word of direction from the White House. They received none.[73]

William McKinley could not bring himself to act in response to public opinion demanding war. Nor could he free himself of a lifelong allegiance in order to resist its claims. Nor could he move beyond a limited conception of his office prohibiting any serious attempt to alter the substance of public opinion's demands upon him. He could not choose. In a period of acute national crisis the executive was paralyzed.

Another presidential secretary, George Cortelyou, said that 90 percent of the mail addressed to the White House in the last months of peace endorsed McKinley's course of action. Yet the incoming letters reveal a wide divergence in public assumptions about the president's policy. This is nowhere more

apparent than in the public response to McKinley's message of
April 11 yielding the entire Cuban problem to congressional
action. Abram Hewitt applauded the president and saw in the
message a guarantee of peace. The Women's Christian Temperance Union responded similarly: "Peace hath her victories.
. . ." Oscar S. Straus was also laudatory but as he saw it, the
presidential message was neither war nor peace; it was "powerful in its reserve for such further action as may be necessary."
Veterans groups and informal military companies sent their
approval of McKinley's policy; they assumed it included war
and offered themselves for active duty against Spain. No matter how contradictory these interpretations of McKinley's position, the White House returned to each correspondent "the
President's sincere appreciation of your cordial words of approval of the policy of the administration." [74]

The congressional leadership was considerably more sensitive to the president's confusion. Until the arrival of McKinley's
war message, the Senate's "Big Six" [75]—Nelson W. Aldrich,
William B. Allison, Hanna, Hoar, Orville H. Platt, and John C.
Spooner—together with Speaker Thomas B. Reed in the
House, managed to block at one stage or another short of the
president's desk every resolution conferring belligerent rights
or otherwise recognizing the Cuban rebels. Yet, as the crisis
approached, even they felt uncertain of McKinley's stand.
Their puzzlement, their sense of contact lost, runs through a
letter from Hanna to McKinley on April 3: "I have been talking with some of our friends this morning, particularly Senators Platt of Conn[ecticut] and Spooner. They think . . . it
is *very* important that some *one man* (Senator) should be so
far taken into confidence and consulted before your Message
went to Congress that your friends in the Senate . . . should
be *prepared* to meet the situation and intelligently support
your policy. . . ." [76] The President did not act on Hanna's
advice. [77]

So fearful of rupturing traditional relationships with Congress and the public, yet so loathe to lead the country into war,

McKinley stood immobile. His defenders would later argue that he had not wished to avoid war entirely, but simply to postpone it in the interests of military preparation. The country *was* almost totally unprepared, so the argument runs, and the war itself was undeniably short and glorious; thus any delay must have been as purposeful as it was beneficial. Those who could not admit that McKinley might have been compelled against his will to begin a triumphant war rallied to the theme set out by Senator Charles W. Fairbanks of Indiana: the president had with one hand "delayed the oncoming storm" and with the other pushed preparations.[78]

There were undoubtedly administration officials making hurried provisions for war. Theodore Roosevelt's frenzied efforts to set in motion the Navy's war-plan were facilitated by Secretary Long's decision to leave all "technical matters" to those bureau chiefs who were Roosevelt's intimates, and by Long's convenient need for a day of rest on February 24, 1898.[79] The dispatch of Dewey's famous orders should serve to suggest not how much Roosevelt and the naval command did but how much was left undone. Even then they were partially overruled. Ordered Long the next day: "Revoke your order for moving guns til you can consult the President. Do not take any such step affecting the policy of the administration without consulting him or me. . . ."[80]

Two weeks later McKinley asked and received a $50,000,000 appropriation "for the national defense," but he compelled Secretary of War Russell A. Alger, the cabinet's warhawk, to limit the Army's share to the repair of coastal defenses.[81] Active preparations for combat were delayed until the president had surrendered the Cuban problem to Congress. As late as April 13, Alger begged the president to "get troops ready" in order "to show the country you are getting ready for war."[82] Obviously, Alger knew that McKinley had not been preparing for war. The president's physical deterioration and that sense of acute suffering he conveyed to visitors speak of a man with a dilemma, not a tactic.

A series of encounters in late March and early April persuaded McKinley that he had no alternative but to yield to the congressional and popular will. Henry Cabot Lodge was the author of a shrewd private appeal to the president on March 21:

> The unanimity with which you are supported at this moment has never I think been equalled at any crisis in our history. . . . It is an awful trust which is thus placed in you Mr. President at this moment. . . . It is equally true that this unanimity of support, so freely & patriotically given, would disintegrate in a day if there were to be hesitation or weakness shown in dealing with the Maine incident or the Cuban question at large, & instead of silent union of all we should have warring factions & bitter debates.[83]

Shortly thereafter a commmittee representing between forty and fifty members of the Republican caucus called on the president and told him that the party faced disastrous defeat unless McKinley acquiesced in war.[84] Vice-President Garret A. Hobart, whom McKinley liked and respected, took his chief for an afternoon carriage ride and delivered an ultimatum of his own: "Mr. President, I can no longer hold back action by the Senate; they will act without you if you do not act at once." [85] These threats of new disunity in the country, Congress, and party were the sort to weigh heaviest on McKinley the conciliator.

Despite the push of such pressures and the pull of such popular sophistries, McKinley even in the end did not choose war. As his vague and inconclusive message to the Congress demonstrates, he simply slipped over the line between peace and war in moving as slowly as possible to accommodate demands he could no longer resist.[86] Implicit in his capitulation was the hope to establish concord in Cuba; far more immediate and insistent was the need to preserve concord at home.

Once he had signed Congress' war resolution, some of the president's resiliency returned. His management of the war was forceful and energetic.[87] He accepted the political fruits of the war and did not doubt the value of winning freedom for the Cubans. But he never claimed the Spanish-American War as his own. He never employed the argument of his friends that only the requirements of military preparedness had restrained him from an earlier move against Spain.

McKinley's later public addresses suggest the pursuit of some psychic indemnity for the fact and cost of the war. He once spoke of the "magnificent army . . . mustered in less than sixty days" and of the military victories won,[88] but his chief stress was reserved for the themes of North-South reunification and an enhanced national identity flowing from the war. In Decatur, Illinois: "There was no division in any part of the country. North and South and East and West alike cheerfully responded. . . ."[89] In Atlanta: "From camp and campaign there comes the magic healing which has closed ancient wounds and effaced their scars."[90] There had been compensations, McKinley said often. Sectionalism had been made to disappear. Immigrant and minority religious and racial groups had proven their loyalty. Europe could no longer deny America's power.

In private conversation, however, he was less certain of the value of the war, less confident of his role in its origins. He pictured himself as victim rather than principal actor. Without doubting that he had done everything within his power to avert war, he nonetheless acknowledged that he had sat in the leader's chair when the nation rose to wage war, a fact no indemnity could balance.

In the autumn of 1900, less than a year before his assassination in Buffalo, McKinley told his former private secretary that the "declaration of war against Spain was an act which has been and will always be the greatest grief of my life. I never wanted to go to war with Spain. Had I been let [alone] I could have prevented [it]. All I wanted was more time."[91]

William McKinley's career converged on the repair of social damage suffered in war. The last of the Civil War's soldiers to sit in the White House could preserve that work only at the price of another war.

CHAPTER II   *Redfield Proctor:*
Character, Conversion, and
the Commitment to War

IN THE COURSE of the Senate session of March 17, 1898, Redfield Proctor easily gained his colleagues' consent to interrupt a leaden debate on the quarantine powers of the Marine-Hospital Service. The senator from Vermont—tall and grey-bearded, with a Lincolnian economy of body and a bearing that conveyed calm and a dignity rimming austerity—rose and offered brief observations on his recent visit to Cuba. The struggle there, he reported, had polarized the populace; Cubans fought Spaniards, with the insurgents controlling the countryside and government forces supreme in town and city. Each side possessed power sufficient to resist compromise but neither was strong enough to force its will on the other. Many were dead; the Spanish reconcentration policy was indeed expensive of life.[1]

By general agreement of contemporary opinion and subsequent historical judgment, Redfield Proctor's half-hour speech so excited the proponents of war and converted the proponents of peace that it supplied the nation's final propulsion to war against Spain. The Reverend Washington Gladden wrote that Proctor's address "swept away the ethical restraints and let the elemental passions loose." It "formulated in the popular mind a proclamation of war," declared the editor Henry Watterson. No speech "in any legislative assembly in the world in fifty years," said former President Benjamin Harrison, ". . . so powerfully affected the public sentiment"; Proctor's "quiet recital . . . aroused the nation." [2]

If the impact of Proctor's speech is clear, the sources of its extraordinary influence remain clouded. Its surface appears to offer nothing exceptional. Proctor advanced no new facts, no new perspective on events in Cuba. He urged no specific course of action. He spoke without passion. Nor do the data of his life reveal any unusual force of personality or impressive weight of accomplishment in themselves capable of riveting the nation's attention. Although he enjoyed the public reputation of a man of character, dignity, and solid reliability, it was one that could be matched by tens of his colleagues. Still, some combination of the man and his words struck a deep emotional resonance in American society and rapidly demolished the last important resistance to war.

Educated at Dartmouth and Albany Law School, Redfield Proctor practiced law in Boston until the outbreak of the Civil War. A volunteer, he rose to the rank of colonel in his Vermont regiment. After Appomattox he returned to the bar only long enough to discover that army life had "made sitting in a chair irksome." [3] He thereupon immersed himself in business and in 1870 organized the Sutherland Falls Marble Company. Though serving in the late 1860s and 1870s as a congressman and as Vermont's lieutenant-governor, he continued to invest his principal energies in business. While governor (1878–80), he absorbed his chief competition and created the Vermont Marble Company. In 1883, aided by special state legislation, he led the organization of the Producers' Marble Company, a five-member sales partnership designed to support marble prices by eliminating competitive bidding. Though this agency lasted only four years, Proctor was able to position himself to profit by its demise; he purchased the three firms that remained solvent. By 1891 the Vermont Marble Company was a prestigious and profitable concern with branches in at least six large cities. Its original 60 employees grew to 3,500. By 1903 it was Vermont's largest industry and the world's largest marble company.[4]

Redfield Proctor submitted formal resignations as company president and director incident to his tenure as Benjamin Harrison's secretary of war (1889–91) and as a senator (1891–1908), but he remained the firm's controlling force. He continued personally to endorse its notes.[5] To those who sought to sell, Proctor replied that he was no longer active in business; to those whom he thought might buy, he continued to promote his product. (He wrote to a Washington newspaper planning to erect a new building that he "should be pleased if you saw your way clear to put up a front of Vermont marble.") [6] Such efforts returned their rewards. The company's poorest year in twenty-nine, 1896, still yielded a $100,000 profit.[7] At the time of his death Proctor was reported the wealthiest man in the Congress, with at least $1,000,000 invested in Washington real estate alone.[8] Such pursuit of private profit was hardly unusual in the Senate of the 1890s, but some sensed in Redfield Proctor a singular fervor for money-making. It was this that gave the point to the jibe with which Thomas Reed skewered the senator's speech. "Proctor's position," chided the isolated, antiwar Speaker of the House, "might have been expected. A war will make a large market for gravestones." [9]

Private correspondence confirms Proctor's absorption in narrow-gauge economic and political concerns. Seldom did a discussion of public policy capture a paragraph from letters stuffed with marble bids, dividends, interest rates, share prices, and property purchases or with pensions, patronage posts, and political favors. He rarely granted interviews; he never wrote for publication; he offered few public addresses. A member of the Committee on Military Affairs and the chairman of the

Committee on Agriculture and Forestry, he remained a step
from the Senate's innermost circle and devoted himself to
profits, patronage, and elections.

❖ ❖ ❖

Redfield Proctor's business background is material to the
first of three sources of that concussion which his Senate appearance delivered to the public consciousness. Businessmen,
among the first to feel its impact, found in Proctor's words a
series of vital reassurances offered by one of their own. They
saw in Proctor the dispassionate assessor who had visited Cuba
with ledger book in hand.

Indeed, with his first words Proctor assumed the stance of
an objective observer. He disputed numerous reports that the
White House had suggested or sponsored his Cuban journey.
His services were not for hire. He mentioned a letter of introduction, signed by Assistant Secretary of State Day, that he
had carried to Fitzhugh Lee, the American consul general in
Havana, but he insisted that William McKinley had done
nothing save to remark that he had no objection to the journey.

And, Proctor averred, he had been no more committed to
prior positions than to other persons. On the Cuban issue, his
mind had been a perfect *tabula rasa*. He held no opinion regarding the destruction of the *Maine*. ("Let us calmly wait
for the report.") He had had no contact with members of the
Cuban Junta. He went to Cuba on grounds strictly personal
and eminently reasonable: he wished to learn the truth.

Thinking himself the objective observer, Proctor sought out
in Cuba equally disinterested informants. "My inquiries were
entirely outside of sensational sources"—American consuls and
medical officers; local *alcades;* municipal relief committees;
"leading merchants and bankers, physicians, and lawyers."
"Most of my informants were business men who had taken no
sides and rarely expressed themselves." Nor had Proctor solicited rebel opinion. Though he reported that at least one Cuban
field officer had approached him with information, Proctor de-

cided that "Having called on . . . [Spanish Governor-General] Blanco, I could not with propriety seek communication with insurgents."

The note of self-depreciation that sounds through the speech contrasts with the fervid, assured tones in which others were discussing Cuba. Proctor went far beyond the rejection of a White House role. From his opening remarks

> Mr. President, more importance seems to be attached by others to my recent visit to Cuba than I have given it . . .

to his closing words

> . . . it is not my purpose at this time, nor do I consider it my province, to suggest any plan. I merely speak of the symptoms as I saw them, but do not undertake to prescribe. Such remedial steps as may be required may safely be left to an American President and the American people

Proctor disclaimed *any* role.

Businessmen who found a guarantee of objectivity in Proctor's moderate tones, his denial of self-interest, his refusal to draw conclusions, and his reputation as a man of character and substance were impressed by the favorable reading which the senator then proceeded to give the Cuban balance sheet. Let me, one whom you can trust, here offer you the facts of the matter, he seems to say.

While Cuba's present produces an economic deficit—"when will the need for this . . . [American financial help] end? Not until peace comes . . ."—its presumably post-Spanish future promises excellent investment prospects. It is a land of "surpassing richness." "I have never seen one to compare with it." (Proctor later explored investment in cheap Cuban lands and eventually took an option on a mineral-water resort, while his friend and companion, Colonel M. M. Parker, conveyed to reporters the travelers' assurance that Cuba's climate would induce settlement by American citizens.) [10]

Contrary to others' suggestions, Cuban racial strains will pose no problem. Cuban whites "are of pure Spanish blood and, like the Spaniards, dark in complexion, but oftener light or blond, as far as I noticed." Though one-third of the Cuban army was black, the population's proportion of colored to white "has been steadily diminishing for more than fifty years" and at that moment stood no higher than one in four. Moreover, the dominant Cuban temperament is "less excitable" and "quieter" than that of the Spaniard. Here Proctor recounted how his Cuban contacts had spoken out against the bullfight, "a brutal institution, introduced and mainly patronized by the Spaniards." The fear that such Cubans, once freed, would prove a revolutionary force was, Proctor insisted, "not so well-founded." "[T]he conditions for good self-government are far more favorable."

Finally, a war against Spain was unlikely to prove expensive to the United States. Her Majesty's soldiers, though "quiet and obedient," were "not at all equal to our men."

Proctor thus offered prospects of an easy military decision opening lucrative investment opportunities among a capable people whose racial and temperamental characteristics were compatible with those of Americans.

Only two days later the *Wall Street Journal* reported that Proctor's speech had "converted a great many people in Wall Street, who have heretofore taken the ground that the United States had no business to interfere in a revolution on Spanish soil." The *American Banker* announced in favor of an intervention it had firmly opposed. Within ten days, the *Literary Digest* detected, the nation's most conservative newspapers had similarly reversed themselves.[11]

Redfield Proctor's disinterestedness may have appealed to businessmen intent on questions of investment opportunity, social stability, and the compatibility of racial types, but it alone was unlikely to "let the elemental passions loose." As the New York *World* pointed out, it was important to such persons that the senator spoke not as a jingo, a Westerner, a poor man, a Southerner, or a newspaperman, but as one of the respectables.[12] As businessmen were responding to the words of a successful colleague, however, a much larger number of Americans thought that they heard another, quite different speech. That initial stance of objectivity that led in one direction to a cool calculation of self-interest pointed in another, toward an image of much greater emotional intensity, the individual experiencing conversion.

For those who remained rooted in nineteenth-century America, an assemblage of facts seldom offered the key to decision on a pressing issue. A problem was not an empty frame to be filled with relevant data, piece by piece, until one had before him a completed image certain to reveal the proper response. Such an approach was impracticable. Information was rarely complete and its circulation almost always erratic and sporadic.[13] The individual, for whom issues were in any case basically simple and essentially moral, thus relied on his own experience or on that of a trusted witness. What he desired were those facts that would expose to him the moral essence of the issue—only those facts necessary to uncover that inner moral sensibility, that understanding that he assumed penetrated beyond reason, that ultimate revelation of Moral Truth. By this route might a nineteenth-century American find Christ or discover the villainy of drink. By this route did Tom Johnson, who in the early 1900s would win for Cleveland a reputation as the nation's best-governed city, encounter "the incident which was to change my whole outlook on the universe." Happening to read Henry George's *Social Problems* while traveling by train to Indianapolis, he experienced revelation: "He felt like Joshua marching into a new land, and seeing new things." [14] His contemporaries had no difficulty understanding the powerful, converting impulse that could reverse the thrust of a traction magnate's life and propel him into reform politics.

Many felt that Redfield Proctor, too—studying the Cuban

situation at first-hand—reached beneath the facts to seize the core of their moral meaning. His Senate speech was thus simultaneously a businessman's report and a moral testimony.

Here again Proctor began by disclaiming any prior faith. "I went to Cuba with a strong conviction that the picture had been overdrawn; that a few cases of starvation and suffering had inspired and stimulated the press correspondents, and that they had given free play to a strong, natural, and highly cultivated imagination. Before starting I received through the mail a leaflet published by the Christian Herald, with cuts of some of the sick and starving reconcentrados, and took it with me, thinking these must be rare specimens, got up to make the worst possible showing." And then, the truth: "I saw plenty as bad or worse; many that should not be photographed and shown."

Outside of Havana, he reported, "it is desolation and distress, misery and starvation." Towns garrisoned and fortified by the Spaniards were "virtually prison yards." Hospitals were indescribable. As for the four hundred thousand Cubans subjected to Weyler's reconcentration policy:

> Torn from their homes, with foul earth, foul air, foul water, and foul food or none, what wonder that one-half have died and that one-quarter of the living are so diseased that they can not be saved? . . . Little children are still walking about with arms and chest terribly emaciated, eyes swollen, and abdomen bloated to three times the natural size. The physicians say these cases are hopeless. . . . [Cubans] have been found dead about the markets in the morning, where they had crawled, hoping to get some stray bits of food . . .

In such phrases did Redfield Proctor convey to his countrymen the results of his findings and simultaneously profess his insight. His declaration that

> [most important] is the spectacle of a million and a half
> of people, the entire native population of Cuba, struggling
> for freedom and deliverance from the worst misgovern-
> ment of which I ever had knowledge

offered a moral truth that Americans recognized and accepted.
And as deplorable as the situation thus described might be,
hinted Proctor, there existed an even more wretched reality
beyond his powers of expression. The "sight . . . makes an appeal stronger than words." "It is not within the narrow limits
of my vocabulary to portray it." "What I saw I can not tell so
that others can see it. It must be seen to be realized."

There is then throughout Proctor's address a variety of
speech-within-a-speech that elicited response from his contemporaries. Beneath the surface detachment urging calm,
denying involvement, eschewing conclusions, they felt a moral
fervor offered as Proctor's direct response to experience. Never,
for all its attempts, would Hearst's New York *Journal* match
Proctor in witnessing to the profound horrors that Americans
then decided were being inflicted on Cubans. There was in
the practices of the Spaniard an evil to be obliterated, a sin-
fulness of which Americans too had to be absolved.

Those who measured Proctor's impact from this second
source ascribed to his remarks the force of an emotional con-
vulsion. Mark Hanna, tracing to Proctor the people's war fever,
saw in the Vermonter's phrases "so many fire-brands thrown
broadcast over the country." A report from Washington noted
that the administration was being bombarded by letters from
"the religious element . . . thoroughly aroused." "The blood
of innocents is on our doorsteps," proclaimed the Chicago
Post, "and it must be wiped away." [15]

A final source of impact is of a different quality. It derives
not from what Proctor said but from what others said of him—
that he traveled and spoke as the emissary of William McKinley.

From the moment that they learned of Proctor's plan to visit

Cuba, journalists—by then desperate for *any* indication of McKinley's feelings about Cuba, confident that a president of the United States must be taking *some* measures to translate his perceptions of a critical problem into policy—were convinced that Proctor was playing an important official role. Indeed, a strong prima facie case existed. The senator, a frequent White House guest and the beneficiary of numerous "little talks" with the president, was a close friend of William McKinley.[16] An early supporter of the Ohioan's presidential aspirations, Proctor brought Vermont to McKinley's support at a time most politicians still counted all of New England safe for the candidacy of Thomas Reed. Proctor moved on to play a role in framing the famous gold plank that emerged from the Republicans' St. Louis convention. Following McKinley's election, he was offered but declined a cabinet seat.[17] He was apparently able to control the dispensation of administration patronage in Vermont, New Hampshire, and, partially, in Maine. Colonel Parker, his protégé, received a presidential appointment as marshal of the District of Columbia.

The Vermonter enjoyed wielding his influence. He dined the vice-president; dispatched letters of political wisdom to Mark Hanna; and occasionally ordered Russell Alger to do his bidding. ("Now there are two or three things I want you to do, because they are right and in the interest of good administration, and it doesn't hurt the case any that they are special favors to me. The wisdom and propriety of them is [sic] easily seen. I wish [that] you might notify me before I go away that they are all attended to.") [18]

It was not surprising, then, that Redfield Proctor would consult with the president prior to his departure for Cuba; that he would negotiate for an Army officer to accompany him as escort and interpreter; or that Consul General Lee, once in receipt of Day's letter describing Proctor as "one of the closest friends of the President," would squire his visitor with the greatest solicitude.[19] Such official assistance lent plausibility to the picture of Proctor as presidential operative.

Proctor himself fueled this view with an unwillingness or

inability to offer a convincing alternative explanation for the Cuban visit. To some reporters he said that any journey to Cuba would come only as a casual extension of a Florida fishing holiday with Colonel Parker. To others he claimed that he might go to Cuba for his health, though the island's reputation in 1898 was not precisely that of a spa. To others he hinted an investigation of a real-estate investment. He would come no closer to his suspected political concern than to confess that the island's conflict lured him: "To tell the truth, we are just going over there to see what's going on, to be where the excitement is. Doesn't everybody want to get there? Don't you?" [20]

Other relationships, had knowledge of them broken beyond tight official circles, would have heightened suspicion of Proctor's official role. The Vermonter was in the midst of protracted commercial negotiations with Russell Alger. In October, 1897, the senator had proposed that the secretary of war purchase a portion of Proctor's interest in a Canadian timber-water-power project. Shortly thereafter Proctor, Alger, and Sir William Horne, president of the Canadian Pacific Railway, inspected the site at Grand Falls, New Brunswick. There followed detailed bargaining in "daily interviews" with Alger, who apparently thought some of Proctor's plans grandiose. Nevertheless, by January 6, 1898, the principals had agreed upon an initial transaction, Alger's purchase of a two-thirds interest in the Grand Falls Waterpower and Boom Company. In February they prepared to make "a portion" of the shares available to Horne and Vice-President Hobart, and as the result of a final distribution in mid-April, Horne and his Canadian associates held one-half of the shares, while Proctor, Alger, and Hobart each retained one-sixth.[21]

Not much better known at the time than this investment partnership was Redfield Proctor's intercession on behalf of that Vermont sailor, George Dewey.

One day in the autumn of 1897 Dewey . . . informed me that he would like to be assigned to the command of the Asiatic squadron. . . . The day before . . . however, Mr.

Roosevelt informed him that the outlook was not encouraging, and asked him if he could get Congressional assistance. Dewey said he was acquainted with me, and Roosevelt replied: "He is the man who can help."

. . . I told the President that the Dewey family and the Proctors had been intimate for many years. . . . "Moreover," I said, "George Dewey is a consistently, honestly, and intelligently pugnacious man. He is a fine officer, with a splendid record, and will not weaken 5,000 miles away from home and out of reach by telegraph, but will rely upon his own sound judgment." I made the case pretty strong, but none too strong, as history has shown.

The President took a card from a drawer . . . and wrote to Long, saying: "Please assign Commodore Dewey to the command of the Asiatic squadron." . . . Dewey received his assignment the next day.[22]

Proctor later wrote that he had "never done my country a greater service than the part I had in Dewey's going to Hong-Kong." [23]

There was thus considerable substance to the view of Proctor as a person in intimate and influential association with prominent members of the administration. Newspapers, knowing parts of the whole, immediately extended the logic of the situation. Headlines such as those of the Cincinnati *Inquirer,* February 20:

SENATOR PROCTOR
Sent by McKinley, It Is Said, on an
Important Mission

and the New York *Journal,* February 23:

LEE COMING TO KEY WEST
TO MEET MCKINLEY'S EMISSARY AND IMPART
STARTLING SECRET NEWS;

reports such as those of the Montpelier (Vermont) *Record,* February 21, that "general opinion" believed that Proctor "has been sent direct from the administration"; even Proctor's denials published by such newspapers as the New York *Times* and the Boston *Advertiser* [24]—all served to fix attention on the senator. So persistent was the faith in Proctor as presidential agent that not even his Senate disclaimer could quash it. At the time of his death ten years later reputable newspapers (among them the Springfield *Republican,* the Washington *Star,* and the Philadelphia *Telegraph*) [25] continued to assert that McKinley had asked Proctor to undertake the Cuban mission.

Clearly, the conviction that Proctor's words were those of the president augmented the impact of the Senate speech. To isolate the force delivered from a single source, or to measure combinations of force from three sources is of course impossible, but the impression remains that this element was the least important in mobilizing Americans. Its influence may largely have been felt before the fact; reports of Proctor's official connection likely served to focus attention on his travels and by heightening curiosity open Americans to his Senate appearance. Nevertheless, even after March 17 many continued to look through the speech to the White House. Senator Shelby Cullom, quoted in the New York *Evening Journal,* believed the speech "meant that the President has decided to move forward with rapidity." A cabinet member was reported to find in Proctor's words McKinley's decision finally to permit the truth to circulate. The New York *Press* saw in the erasures and pastings on Proctor's manuscript evidence of administration editing, while the Boston *Herald* concluded that Proctor had summarized the facts contained in consular reports previously withheld by the administration.[26]

❖ ❖ ❖

Popular perceptions of Proctor as commercial assessor, convert, and spokesman were potent but not altogether accurate.

In all three instances the disjunction between Proctor's impact and the realities of his life is striking.

His credentials as dispassionate observer or as the skeptic on the threshold of illumination are vulnerable to challenge. His profession of neutrality impressed many—"this calm, judicial exhibit," the Philadelphia *Evening Telegraph* called his speech [27]—but Proctor had in fact decided *prior* to his departure for Cuba that McKinley was remiss in failing to act against Spain. Theodore Roosevelt's insistence that Proctor was from the first pro-intervention [28] finds substantiation in the senator's letters. On February 14 he wrote in confidence to an America friend living in Cuba:

> I very much regret that we have not done more to aid the Cuban cause, but . . . it seemed to rest mainly with the administration, and the pressure of business interests has prevented possible action so far. The city interests have made strenuous protests against action that they have claimed would bring on commercial disaster, etc. just as there seemed to be a chance for returning prosperity. I do not take any stock in this view of the case, but have been helpless to do very much.[29]

As with other Americans, judgment on this issue came to Redfield Proctor without long reflection, and that anti-Spanish verdict he carried with him *to* Cuba.

If Proctor lacked the objectivity his words proclaimed, there is less cause to doubt that he experienced the feelings that others identified as signals of the convert's emotional intensity. One cannot read the Senate speech without sensing that, beneath the requisite genteel forms, he had been stirred by what he saw in Cuba. More striking, however, is the fleeting quality of that emotion and its ardent identification with the Cuban people.

Though before the Senate he had opposed annexation and

pronounced favorably on Cuban self-government, he soon moved in easy stages to the view that the United States must "manage" the Cuban people. This transition derived largely from what Proctor believed the exigencies of the Philippines situation. By November, 1898, he had concluded that the "fortunes of war" had thrust the islands upon the United States and that, though the nation had not sought such responsibility, it must now accept it "for the betterment of the people of those islands and in the interest of humanity." So persuaded, he was instrumental in moving the Vermont legislature to endorse McKinley's policy of colonial acquisitions.[30]

Though his views of Cubans did not reverse as precipitately as those of most Americans—the islanders remained in his eyes "kindly and hospitable, easily influenced for good or ill, but very appreciative of kindness and good will from others"—Proctor began to worry about a Cuban unruliness that had found no mention in his speech. "Firmness" became his principal advice to American military commanders. Gone, too, was that sense of broad similarities tying Americans and the peoples of the Caribbean: "Of course they are very different from . . . [Americans] and far inferior. . . ." By 1902 so altered was the Cuban in Proctor's estimation that the senator was willing to admit a silent support for annexation.

Of course conditions have changed, and I might perhaps consistently favor it now if it was an open question, but we have promised . . . [the Cubans] independence. . . . To advocate . . . [annexation] here would be not only unfair to them but would tend to obstruct instead of forwarding annexation.

In short, it was too late to annex without engendering significant Cuban opposition.[31] Proctor offered friends another reason for leaving unpublicized his altered views.

I had better let well enough alone . . . Some might take
it that I was recanting, which I do not wish to do, and
it is always a little difficult to explain without its having
that effect.[32]

Peculiarly, given the impact of his words on the nation, Redfield Proctor made the progress of the war itself no cause of
his own. It became a bore, an impediment to a European
visit he wished to make. "[T]hough I hate . . . very much [to
abandon those travel plans] . . . I fear it would not look just
right [,] would it [,] to leave the country at this time." He
did make a second visit to Cuba in early 1899, but his reactions were muted. The single concern to which he devoted
energy was his proposal that a Cuban regiment be recruited to
fight for the United States against Filipino insurrectionists, an
idea greeted by Cuban and administration derision.[33]

The conversion impulse that Americans felt in Redfield
Proctor's words held no more than the appearance of trans-
formative power. In his life, as in the lives of his countrymen,
the emotions of March, 1898, in which were rooted the American idealization of the Cuban and the dedication to Cuba's
salvation, proved transient.

No better reflector of reality is the conviction that Proctor
stood as William McKinley's surrogate. In the end, the public's
picture of Proctor's complicity in an administration effort is
compelling and, almost certainly, totally false. Despite appearances, Proctor was neither an official emissary nor even a
presidential observer. One detects in his private letters no
hint of another man's commission. There is instead the struggling idea of a visit to Cuba, appearing quite late, growing
and shrinking as it competes with Proctor's other, principally
commercial interests. His planning was casual and erratic. As
late as January 3, 1898, he told an associate that he was preparing a spring journey to Europe. On January 10 there appeared the first reference to "a trip South during the month
[of February]." On February 8 he told the Army officer whom

he hoped would accompany him: "My plans in regard to Cuba are very indefinite so far. I think I can get away within a fortnight to go to Florida. Rather think of going down to Miami, and doubt if I decide to go to Cuba until I have stopped a few days in Florida. . . . I think the chances are not even that I shall go at all." One week later he wrote, "I think it exceedingly doubtful about my going to Cuba. Am going to Florida, and possibly may cross. . . ." Tentative almost to the hour of his departure on February 17, he wrote to his Chicago attorney just two days earlier: "I expect to start Thursday on a trip to Florida. Possibly may go to Cuba, unless the lawsuit is likely to come on." Nothing in his letters suggests more than a modest personal curiosity about events in Cuba, a curiosity that by a very narrow margin he resolves to satisfy.[34]

The postlude, like the preliminaries, supports a view of Redfield Proctor's Cuban visit as a purely private endeavor. The thrust of the speech establishes his distance from McKinley. At that juncture when the president desperately wished delay, Americans read Proctor's words as counsel for immediate intervention. The damage—a public reaction that destroyed whatever remained of McKinley's power to ignore the demand for intervention—was inadvertent, since the senator knew no more than anyone else of the president's paralytic inner turmoil. He seems to have remained unaware for at least a month that McKinley might have thought his speech a disservice. He wrote to the president in early May praising Dewey's victory at Manila Bay in terms of a jovial informality that few essayed with William McKinley: "We may run . . . [Dewey] against you for President. He would make a good one." There is no record that McKinley reciprocated. In early September it required a special appeal to Alger to win Proctor inclusion in the presidential party welcoming the troops' return at Montauk Point. He encountered increasing resistance to his patronage recommendations. In November he wrote of "some peculiar things in the appointments and promotions." In December he complained to his colleague, Senator George F. Edmunds: "I have tried faithfully for young Lawrence, but all to no avail. . . . I confess that I am out of patience and feel hurt in the matter, because I think the President might have fixed it, and you doubtless know that he might have done so, but I said everything to him. . . . I confess I don't see any opening for further effort." Six days later hurt had moved to anger. "I talked very earnestly to . . . [McKinley], and, to tell the truth, I was quite mad though I held it in. . . ." Restraint, too, was unavailing for in early February, 1899, Proctor wrote to Alger that the president "has no use for my services or opinions on any matter." [35]

Several weeks before his death in March, 1908, Redfield Proctor took a rare step: he granted a newspaper interview. Predictably, the circumstances were unusual. Henry Cabot Lodge, in a talk with James B. Morrow of the Washington *Post,* had claimed that the gold plank of 1896 had been the good work of Reed's managers, not McKinley's. Proctor, who had declined several requests to meet with Morrow, reversed himself and apparently came to like the journalist, for they spoke several times. Once Proctor's anger at Lodge had evaporated, he proved willing to talk of other matters, notably the great adventure of 1898. The resultant account was published after Proctor's sudden death; though apparently failing to dent the popular view, it is substantiated in all but its final assertion by the senator's private correspondence.

Did you go to Cuba . . . at President McKinley's request?

It was rumored at the time . . . that I had gone there in a secretly official capacity, but the report was untrue. The Maine had been blown up and I knew that something was very likely to follow. Boys love adventure and don't outgrow it as they become men. . . .

I told President McKinley that I was going, and he seemed to be glad of it. Anyway, he wasn't displeased. I didn't ask permission to go, understand, but I thought he ought to know. He was President and I was his friend. I went as a private citizen, paid my own bills, and represented nobody but myself. . . .

When I left the boat and came ashore in Florida [on my return] newspaper reporters pressed me to talk, but I wasn't ready, and declined. Several Washington correspondents boarded my train in Virginia, but I didn't say anything to them. I conversed privately with friends in the Senate, and they urged me to make my story public. So one day I remained at home and wrote out a simple narrative of my trip in pencil. I intended to give it to the newspapers for simultaneous publication in all parts of the country. But I meant to show it to Mr. Day [the Assistant Secretary of State who also urges him to speak out]. . . .

From the State Departmet I went to the White House. Mr. McKinley and I retired to his library, where he read the statement with a great deal of care. When he had finished reading, he remarked: "You have not said that the normal condition of the Cubans is entirely unlike the normal condition of the Americans."

"No . . . but I shall do so."

Then he asked if I intended to present the statement to the Senate that day.

"I don't think I shall." . . . "It is simply a draft in pencil, and I had thought of having it typewritten."

Going to the Senate I met Mr. Frye, of Maine, in the cloakroom. "You must speak now." . . . "The people should know at once what you have seen."

"I'll have it typewritten," . . . "and read it to-morrow."

"But to-morrow is Friday," . . . "and the Senate will adjourn early, and not meet again til Monday."

Whereupon he hastily entered the chamber of the Senate. Mr. Mallory, of Florida, was making a speech on a quarantine bill, the passage of which was in charge of Mr. Vest, of Missouri. Frye went to Vest and asked if he would consent to have the bill put aside for a short time. Then he walked over to Mr. Mallory and whispered, and Mallory said he would yield the floor to me.

In five minutes Frye was back in the cloakroom. He actually pushed me into the Senate chamber. Following right behind me, he asked that I might have unanimous consent to read a statement bearing on my recent trip to Cuba. The consent was given, Mallory sat down, and I took the floor. . . . When I had concluded I was handed a scrap of an envelope from William E. Chandler, of New Hampshire, who was presiding. "God bless you," he wrote, "I love you for that speech."

But it wasn't a speech. No matter what it may have been the Associated Press telegraphed it in full, and it was printed all over the world. . . .

What did President McKinley say? . . .

Of course, he was doing everything possible to maintain peace between the United States and Spain. All kinds of stories got about concerning my action, and it was even said that I had broken a promise given to the President. I saw McKinley several days later after I had submitted my narrative to the Senate—it is my impression that Mr. Lodge, of Massachusetts, was present—and took occasion to refer to the rumors.

"You know," . . . "that I did not promise to withhold the statement."

"That is true," . . . "but I thought you would wait. I wanted Senator Hoar to read what you had written."

"I have a very high opinion of Hoar," . . . "but I am not in the habit of consulting him as to what I shall say."

"Had I known what you meant to do," Senator Hanna remarked to me later, "I should have got down on my knees and tried to stop you."

"And I should have been tempted to go on," I answered, "just to see Mark Hanna on his knees."

And your relations with the President. . . ?

They remained unchanged . . . until the day of his death.[36]

Redfield Proctor was never able to decide what precise role he had played in the coming of the Spanish-American War. Since he had not acted as a presidential agent, he had only to weigh his own performance within the rush of events, but here his readings vacillated. He never faltered in his belief that the war had been a noble cause, and he occasionally revealed a desire to claim it (though never the cause of the Cubans) as his own. When Russell Alger wrote, "Your war is closed. Are you satisfied [?]" Proctor responded, "You know it is not my war, nor anybody else's, but the people's; but call it mine if you will. Yes, I am satisfied. The result is grand. . . ." He recognized that his speech had "tremendously stirred" the country, but he regularly insisted that he had been granted too much credit for influencing the march to war. The nation, he believed, had been engaged in the process of making up its mind; his speech arrived at the propitious moment and to his surprise happened to "take wonderfully," but the war would have come without his words. He sensed, quite accurately, that the historical impact of his speech had rapidly transcended his intent, his experience, his words, and all other perimeters of his life.[37]

Redfield Proctor's address before the Senate was nonetheless a crucial event: Americans embraced it for its ability to establish the highest possible rationale for a war against Spain.

No one could argue convincingly that American security or national interest or economic well-being was being jeopardized by the situation in Cuba. Even the sinking of the *Maine* remained an elusive basis for intervention. The authors of the

act were unidentified. Surmise, though violent in its denunciation of the Spaniard, was not entirely persuasive.

Redfield Proctor rendered totally unambiguous the morality
of the situation. In place of a dubious vengeance, he offered
war founded on an undiluted humanitarianism. In place of a
specifically American interest, he invited the nation's willingness to act unselfishly as an agency of civilization. Its cause
was to be that of good employed against evil; its concern was
to be international rather than national; its representation was
to be that, not of ourselves, but of all right-thinking peoples.

Contemporary commentators recognized Proctor's speech
rather than the sinking of the *Maine* as the sharpest spur to
war. Senator Hoar insisted that Proctor, not the tragedy of
Havana harbor, galvanized the Congress. Lyman Abbott
thought March 17 the "real occasion of the war." Wrote the
New York *Commercial Advertiser:*

> This is a far more serious matter than determination of
> responsibility for loss of the *Maine*. That is a mere cause
> of international law. This involves the destiny of a whole
> people and our duty to civilization.

Similarly, the Sacramento *Bee:*

> The blowing up of the *Maine* may be proved to have been
> accidental, but the American nation, great in heart and
> ever ready to champion the cause of the oppressed, must
> not, without sacrifice to its honor, much longer remain
> deaf to the cries of the starving Cubans which are ring-
> ing in its ears!

The Pittsburgh *Times,* the Boston *Journal,* the Chicago *Record,*
and the Washington *Star,* among others, were convinced that
Proctor's address, more than any other event, was responsible
for the war.[38]

Looking back three months later, *Scribner's Magazine*

judged that Proctor had distilled the complexities of the Cuban situation to one question and one answer:

> [W]hat was this country's duty in the sight of God?
> [War,] For humanity's sake.[39]

It was, many concluded, "America's highest and best justification for going to war." [40]

The private reality of Redfield Proctor's life coincided much less than William McKinley's with the public reputation as a man of character. He dissembled frequently. Gruff and abrupt, frequently mean-minded and almost always impenetrable to humor, he was an authoritarian in family relationships and the author of extramarital adventures extensive enough to alienate his wife permanently. He left the world of marble briefly, almost inadvertently. Entering another, larger world, he spoke for thirty minutes and retired again to the cloakrooms of Washington politics. In that brief span, a man of little idealism struck responses that in ways specific to his society mobilized the nation's highest idealism. The impact of Redfield Proctor's speech, though relying on appearances that ornamented reality, propelled the nation to war.

CHAPTER III *The War and the*
Small-town Community

WILLIAM MCKINLEY knew that the regular Army, a lean
professional force of fewer than thirty thousand men, was inadequate to defeat an enemy that deployed six times its numbers in Cuba alone. He recognized too that whatever the
Army's capacities, the popular clamor for participation would
compel a broad expansion of American land forces; the war
would be a people's war in its execution as in its origins. In
a situation offering little room for maneuver, the president
attempted to compromise political and military requirements.
By inviting the mobilization of the citizen-soldiers of the National Guard he moved to accommodate popular pressure
while upholding the necessity for some minimal military proficiency among thousands of insistent volunteers.

Regular Army units, themselves doubled in size and barely
able to maintain cohesion, won the battles, but the hometown
National Guard company became the prism through which
many Americans viewed and interpreted the Spanish-American
War. In peace the company played an important role in the
life of its town. In war soldiers and townsmen alike saw the
company, wherever located, as an extension of their community. This perception supported greater social informality and
wider spheres of individual action than professional soldiers

60

thought consistent with the demands of a national military effort. Throughout the war the Army attempted to stamp volunteers with a greater respect for hierarchy and discipline. This effort, impeded by the regular Army's own structural weakness and political vulnerability, was vigorously opposed by guardsmen who unhesitatingly invoked hometown ties to resist the imposition of bureaucratic order.

No one believed that the regular Army alone could fight the Spaniards in Cuba. Memories of Grant's great army persisted and G.A.R. veterans reminisced about the march of two hundred thousand, sixty abreast, down Pennsylvania Avenue at the war's end, but the land force of 1898 bore almost no resemblance to the Union Army of 1865. Charged with policing the Indians, the postwar Army had functioned as a frontier constabulary. That role, modestly supplemented by the infrequent dispatch of small units to curb labor disorders in eastern and midwestern cities, required no more than 27,472 officers and men: so Congress had decided in the Army bills of 1874–76.[1] Over the next twenty years that force developed sinew—the Indian wars required and produced effective, small-scale organization and tight discipline among the long-term enlistees in the ranks—but the regular Army added fewer than one thousand men to its rolls and remained minute by European standards. Dispersed throughout the West in company units, it did not once function or even exercise as a national Army.[2]

In early 1898 Secretary of War Russell A. Alger could deploy 28,183 officers and men distributed among seventy-seven garrisons. The enemy, it was estimated, counted 180,000 regulars in Cuba.[3]

With the passage of the war resolutions, the McKinley administration could no longer delay a decision on Army expansion. The obvious first step was the use of the regular Army as cadre for an enlarged national Army: the congressional act of April 26 more than doubled the regular Army. Perhaps one million young Americans were simultaneously volunteering to fight Spain.[4] The addition of a mere 30,000 to the regular Army could not begin to relieve the pressures generated in every section of the country by those who first offered and then demanded participation. Indeed, there were 30,000 pertinacious applicants for general and general staff officer positions alone.[5] The president's problems might have been severe. To open the Army to such numbers would overwhelm the regulars, destroying the only effective units available to the government. To ignore the clamor of volunteers would jeopardize national unity and court political disaster in the fall elections. Fortunately, there were available to McKinley in National Guard organizations bodies of ardent volunteers who possessed at least a nominal military proficiency.

There was in fact nothing national about the National Guards. They were "forty-five little state armies,"[6] with no uniformity of organization, equipment, or expertise. There were no links between state organizations. Only tentative, still fragile ties connected each state National Guard and the national government. In 1880 the War Department, suddenly alarmed that state militias offered nothing approximating a trained reserve on which the regular Army might draw in time of emergency, began to detail regular officers to inspect state summer encampments. Small detachments of regular troops occasionally went along, but to inspire and exhort rather than instruct. The regulars accomplished little. Training remained perfunctory. National Guard firearms, different from those of the regulars and requiring ammunition no longer manufactured in this country, were not replaced. In 1885 the secretary of war conceded that militias were, and would remain, hopelessly outmoded and disparate.[7]

In the late 1880s a few professional soldiers, impressed by programs in Europe to rationalize and reorganize national armies, began to urge a coherent American military system linking local and federal organizations. Congress, however, opposed the extension of War Department controls over state organizations with the same diligence that it so strictly limited regular Army appropriations, whether for expansion or modernization. Its only concession to the professionals' case was to increase federal aid to the National Guards. In 1887 it doubled the $200,000 that it had divided among state militias since 1808,[8] though the sum devolving on each of the forty-five organizations remained a pittance. In the absence of any threat to the country's safety, standardization of state units or their integration into a national system was far beyond the resources Congess was willing to grant the War Department. All such schemes remained chimerical.

Whatever their military capabilities in 1898, the National Guards offered to a harried president existing organizations staffed with men who thought themselves soldiers. Their expansion and deployment would channel volunteer fervor, leave regular Army units to cope with no more than a two-fold expansion, and assuage powerful state political organizations gratified to see militias recognized and strengthened, though no less determined to control their use. In the end there was no choice but to call on the guardsmen.

The method of their mobilization caused some hesitation. The president himself had doubts about the constitutionality of ordering Guard units beyond America's borders, so the War Department devised an artifice to bring state units intact into the national Army. Governors would mobilize their Guards *en bloc*. At assembly camps throughout the country regular officers would then call on each guardsman individually to enlist for the duration of the war. Once pledged to federal service, the guardsman would immediately rejoin his fellows in reelecting his former officers, thus reconstituting the old state unit within the national Army.

The Spanish-American War "was as hard to get into as later world wars were hard to keep out of."[9] It was, a postbellum Army War College study would conclude, "the most popular foreign war in which the United States has ever been engaged. . . ." [10] Thousands of young men were, like the light-hearted Tennessean and later secretary of state, Cordell Hull, "wildly eager to leave at once." [11] The regular Army might reject 77,000 of 102,000 applicants—75 percent—and the volunteer forces refuse 25 percent in pre-muster physicals and an equal proportion after induction, but the commanding general would still complain that the Army had admitted 100,000 more than were needed or could be equipped.[12] This popular enthusiasm had forced McKinley to a war from which he shrank; it continued to distract the administration insofar as military units had to be chosen from and within the various states with the same delicacy that the most succulent political plums were apportioned. As Governor John R. Tanner of Illinois set out the problem: "If no one wanted to go, and the government had to draught, any one Congressional district would object to allowing more than its proportionate share. On the other hand, where everybody wants to go . . . the equities suggest that each . . . district have its proportionate share in the glory." [13] Perplexing as were these problems, volunteer enthusiasm did spare Washington at least one of Abraham Lincoln's difficulties. It enabled the government to exact terms of enlistment more stringent than those of 1861. There would be no three-month or hundred-day men among the 233,000 guardsmen who moved by this circuitous route into the national Army.

Though regular Army units were to be decisive in the land victories of the Cuban campaign, the small-town National Guard company was in the view of many Americans the essential and preeminent unit of the Spanish-American War. Americans thought it appropriate, indeed necessary, that a foreign war should be fought by the hometown military unit acting as an extension of their community.

If it is true, as the Kansas editor William Allen White wrote, that "Johnny of the American Army, the Johnny who responded to the President's call for troops is a country boy—

a boy of the country town," [14] it is also true that in 1898 the place held by the small town in the consciousness and daily life of its citizens was diminishing. American small towns were losing their self-sufficient and self-contained qualities. The older sense of belonging in totality within the local community was rapidly slipping away as 1900 approached. The railroads, regional and national advertising, standardized products and the mail order houses had already established in men's minds many points of reference and identification beyond the town limits.[15] Large-scale movements toward corporate concentration which small towns were powerless to influence—but also their own desires for superior services and more and cheaper goods—prodded townspeople into a larger world and made them increasingly dependent on decisions made there.

Though weakening, the power of locale remained in 1898 a measurable force in American life. Most Americans continued to believe that there were important distinctions between the values, virtues, and styles of life prevailing in their own and other corners of the United States. Locale still served them as a primary focus of emotional attachment and allegiance. An Ohioan serving in the Fifth Mississippi Volunteer Infantry in 1898 wrote the father of a dead soldier, "I know it is some comfort to you to know that an Ohio boy was with your son when he died. After he learned I was from Ohio he called me 'brother'." [16] Brigadier General William C. Oates, a former Confederate soldier, spent much of his time and all of his influence in 1898–99 attempting to obtain Alabama staff officers and Alabama regiments for his command. He wanted Alabamians for what he deemed their unique qualities, and he was angry when Alger ignored all of his petitions.[17]

To the more cosmopolitan, this identification with locale was a residual provincialism, an American failing. They rejoiced at evidence of new national standards and congruencies. Augustus Peabody Gardner, the son-in-law of Senator Henry Cabot Lodge of Massachusetts, was pleased and proud "to see [in the Army] thousands on thousands of lads with clean-cut faces and clean habits all looking exactly alike whether from North, South, East or West." [18] Jennie Hobart, the wife of McKinley's vice-president, reported of cabinet members that "hailing . . . from all sections of the country, each one wore the clothes fashionable in his community." Watching for opportunities to "gently correct" the statesmen of the executive branch, she was delighted when she succeeded in establishing sartorial uniformity.[19] Both defender and detractor testified that localism retained some force.

The National Guard company was a local institution with a prominent niche in the social and political life of its community. For the old, the hometown unit was a source of pride and security and commemoration; for the young, it signified excitement and adventure and social aspiration.[20] Carl Sandburg, twenty years old in 1898 and a member of Company C, Sixth Illinois National Guard Regiment, called his unit a "living part" of the town of Galesburg.[21] His company, like others throughout the country, paraded on holidays, mustered for important visitors, sponsored an "annual ball and reception," and conducted in its own armory a weekly drill that had all the marks of a public entertainment. With companies from surrounding towns it traveled to a summer encampment. There each guardsman might fire five or ten cartridges in target practice, provided that the legislature had not eliminated the ammunition appropriation as a matter of economy and that the men had not eliminated weapons firing as a matter of preference. There were few hours given to serious training, almost none to long marches. Civilian caterers provided the food; regimental armorers looked after the rifles. The same hometown relations and friends who gathered for drill nights often came along to summer camp, sometimes in chartered excursion trains. The five-day schedule of these "regimental maneuvers" ordinarily included a little close-order drill, a sham fight, and the governor's review. Summer camp was truly a "jolly lark." [22]

The only company activity that moved beyond the ceremonial, social, or political was the riot duty to which a state administration would occasionally summon a hometown unit. The governor of Illinois called out Galesburg's Company C against striking laborers in East St. Louis in 1886 and against striking miners in Pekin and Spring Valley in 1894.[23] Sherwood Anderson's hometown unit—Company I, Sixteenth Ohio National Guard Regiment, of Clyde, Ohio—moved into Tiffin on riot patrol in November 1895 and later helped to control disorders in Cincinnati and a strike near Wheeling.[24] Though obviously less than a "jolly lark," such duty was seldom onerous. The appearance of Guard units was usually sufficient to restore order. Violent confrontations were rare.

With so little necessity for rigorous military performance, the company mirrored with minimal distortion the social patterns of its community. Although upholding in principle democratic and cooperative ideals, the town seldom realized them in its social setting. There existed instead an influential scale of deference, though one whose increments were so subtle that the modern eye would perhaps miss them and whose gradations remained inseparable even to that exemplar of small-town life, William Allen White.[25] Based on shifting combinations of wealth, occupation, education, and term of residence,[26] it operated principally to diminish the expectations of those at the bottom: neither Carl Sandburg nor Sherwood Anderson thought himself entitled to earn as much money as the town's banker or to become the captain of the town's company. Though this system did impart to townspeople an almost intuitive sense of social superiors and inferiors, few seem to have thought it oppressive. It seldom jeopardized the town's ambience of intimacy. (Wrote Carl Sandburg of his company, "I knew most of the privates. [I] had worked for Corporal Cully Rose at the Auditorium and had gone to school with the Q[uincy railroad] boiler-maker, Con Byloff, who was first lieutenant.") [27] It was, moreover, deemed "the town's way," and thus a mark of the community's independence from external control. Most important, individuals generally found the resultant social patterns sufficiently limber to permit a latitude of action they thought satisfactory.

Thus, all anticipated that those respectables who had lobbied legislative authority at the state capital and had done the preliminary work of organizing the town's military unit would be those whom the enlisted men would select as their officers in the required company elections—a fair return, it was understood, for the positions they occupied and the uses to which they had put the attached status. Retention of command, however, by a major or captain who had assumed his rank by virtue of a station accorded deference depended on the maintenance of social relationships consonant with the fluidity of community patterns, often as interpreted by the company's privates. They *spoke* of the shoulderstrap not as the emblem of their deference but as the sign of a neighbor's greater interest in military affairs or his willingness to work a bit harder or even his endowment with a certain leadership ability. They remained suspicious that the wearer, if unwatched, would develop dangerous tastes for the prerogatives of office. They required that he give frequent signs that he thought himself not much better than those he ranked. They expected that officers and men would address one another by first name.

Action the men considered unduly arbitrary might produce a move for new elections or a flurry of resignations. With the strength of the local company a mark of the town's standing in competition with its neighbors, such disaffection could be a serious matter. Town officials thus tended to support the men's assumption that authority inhered principally not in community status nor in the rank of officer but, democratically, in commonly recognized qualities of the incumbent. With the men retaining the right to reconsider their choice of officers on social grounds and with the community sometimes standing in their support, the officer's sphere of command was a narrow one. The call to war did not alter these essential relationships within National Guard companies.

The pattern of interaction between regular and volunteer soldiers during the Spanish-American War was one of muted conflict: the regulars attempted to impose hierarchical controls on hometown units; the volunteers, determined to uphold the informal relationships of the Galesburgs and Clydes, resisted. In the end, organizational weakness within the regular Army, the brevity of the war, and the multiplicity and resilience of the National Guard company's links with home enabled the volunteers to forestall major change.

Professional soldiers equated discipline and technical proficiency in a way alien to volunteer thought. Guardsmen were confident of their ability to do everything that a war would require of them, and they saw no necessary connection between what they did and how they did it. Regular Army leaders, insisting that control and performance were inseparable, recognized from the first that the chain of command would lack the power to constrain volunteers until informal social relationships between officers and men were suppressed. It was apparent with the first attempts, however, that the Army leadership would be unable to force observance of military manual relationships. In part, the Army's own structural weaknesses were responsible.

The secretary of war and the commanding general of the Army entered the war with independent powers in overlapping jurisdictions, a legacy of the 1820s assuring friction at the highest level of command.[28] The ten bureau heads were accorded permanent tenure—"elderly incompetents," Theodore Roosevelt called those who held the desks in 1898.[29] Almost to the day the war began the Army seems to have contemplated no contingencies beyond Indian fighting. It had no high command, no war plans, no experience in large-unit operations, no formal liaison with the Navy, no mechanism for resolving interservice controversies short of the president's desk. Then, with the coming of war but without a blueprint for expansion, the old Army assumed control of volunteers numbering eight times its own personnel while itself doubling in size and assuming a new role. To know how to provision cavalry squadrons setting out to chase Indians was obviously to know only a small part of how to outfit a 300,000-man Army, including an overseas expeditionary force. With no one giving thought to structural change, a constabulary could not be transformed overnight into a national Army. Without realizing that reform was a requisite to expansion, the War Department attempted exactly that metamorphosis.

The Army suffered from other problems beyond structural weakness and rapid enlargement. After the Civil War few Americans took an interest in the Army. No one insisted that it share its skirmishes against the Indians. Public attention was fitful, and minute appropriations signaled congressional indifference. This disinterest, however, had two faces: balancing the limitations imposed by the most stringent economies was the Army's ability to develop cohesiveness undisturbed by large-scale political intervention.[30] In 1898 the outbreak of war reversed this situation: with massive appropriations came political intrusion. Everyone seemed to demand a share of the fight.[31]

Civilian motives varied, of course, but many of them ran counter to the Army's aim of subduing the enemy as quickly as possible. McKinley himself stressed the theme of sectional reunification and appointed to high commands former Confederates such as Joseph Wheeler and Fitzhugh Lee. These men understood the extramilitary role that the president intended for them and exploited the power it conferred to ignore orders originating higher in the Army's chain of command. With his impetuous push inland from the beaches of Daiquiri in opposition to the orders of his commanding general, "Fighting Joe" Wheeler gave notice that he would be very difficult to control.[32] Others followed his lead.

Similarly, the organization of three federal volunteer cavalry regiments—superfluous supplements to the regular Army and National Guard units—worked to dilute professionalism. Here too appointees like Theodore Roosevelt ("Well, General,

I really don't know whether we would obey an order to fall back.") [33] capitalized on their political immunity. A third element undermining Army cohesiveness was the lure of promotion beyond the sluggish pace of the peacetime Army that led one-fifth of the regular Army officers to accept volunteer appointments.[34] Thus, with its own integrity threatened by the departure of a part of its officer corps, the arrival of political immunes, and the swelling of its ranks, the regular Army was able to enforce few standards of organization, procedure, or performance. It could decree but it could not enforce in the new national Army the discipline of the constabulary. Moreover, unlike the Civil War, the Spanish-American War did not go badly enough or last long enough to compel organizational unity and discipline as matters of military necessity.

Even without problems of its own, the regular Army would have found it difficult to assimilate National Guard units because of the diversity and vitality of the latters' links with their communities. Each Galesburg, each Clyde assumed that the hometown company was *its* military unit, an extension first of itself rather than the nation. The community thereby accepted the largest measure of responsibility for the unit's welfare, and that meant hard work to establish and maintain ties to its soldiers.

Communication was the foremost problem. How were people at home to remain in contact with a company that had marched away? The difficulty of obtaining information increased of course with the distance between town and unit, but the community was seldom without detailed news of the condition of its soldiers. While the company remained in an assembly camp within the United States, streams of curious and voluble visitors shuttled back and forth on excursion trains. Sick soldiers convalesced at home and could be counted on for the latest news. More reliable than either of these links, however, was the correspondent.

Large-city newspapers assigned a correspondent to accompany each of the state's regiments wherever it might go. In a

common pattern the Chicago *Daily News* had reporters with
each of Illinois' three regiments, and their dispatches were
distributed to small-town newspapers within the regiment's
home territory.[35] Smaller papers strained their resources to
send a regular correspondent with the local company, a practice that delighted the townspeople but disgusted professional
war correspondents. Richard Harding Davis publicly prophe-
sied the demise of quality reportage as the result of the small-
town amateur's invasion of his fraternity.[36]

When there was insufficient money to send a reporter, the
local newspaper ordinarily commissioned a soldier to send
back regular letters for its columns. Though Carl Sandburg
apparently aspired to the job, Private George Martin, a min-
er's son and the former captain of the Knox College football
team, served as the correspondent of the Galesburg *Evening
Mail*. In five months he sent home for publication more than
thirty letters filled with innumerable details of daily routine;
of the poor food served and promised rations undelivered; of
activities in and out of camp; of sickness and morale.[37] Such
reports were personal and candid. Galesburg read in another
of its newspapers, the *Republican-Register,* the letters of the
company commander reporting the progressive deterioration
into insanity of a Company C private identified by name.[38]
That was a collective concern just as much as the accounts of
adventure and mischief or the daily denunciations of those
held responsible for the troops' misfortunes.

Such dispatches continued to appear regularly in most newspapers after the secretary of war formally prohibited military
personnel from writing for publication. Many units simply ignored Alger's order. Where it did receive notice, it was circumvented. Correspondents addressed their letters to hometown friends who in turn offered them to the newspapers as
of "possible interest" to the community. Privates, noncommis-
sioned officers, chaplains, occasionally lieutenants and captains
—and, according to the journalist Ray Stannard Baker, naval
officers acting as correspondents aboard war vessels [39]—con-

stituted an informal communications network more extensive than has been appreciated.

Regular sources of information, often revealing the troops' immediate needs, guided those at home who were committed to the support of the company. The first steps of organization actually preceded the boys' departure: the farewell reception, the speeches, the parade to the railroad station, the presentation of company colors. The town ladies soon discovered that some of the soldiers had left needy families behind and that the trains that carried away their sons would soon pass through again with other hungry and thirsty boys. These concerns required new organizations. A Women's Auxiliary War League, a Citizens' War Committee, or an Army-Navy League appeared in every town. As news reached them from their companies, these groups expanded their activities. Many established commissary operations. They made or bought articles company members said were needed. A popular, though probably unsolicited, effort at the beginning of the war was the knitting of red or white bellybands, abdominal protectors of stitched flannel believed to ward off tropical fevers. The boys threw them away; the food, pieces of clothing, pocket cases of pins, needles, buttons, and thread they kept.[40]

The arrival of news was often the prelude to other varieties of community action, for on very few counts did the community conceive its role as a passive one. The town dispatched special delegations to check reports of soldier sickness or suffering. It occasionally sent local doctors and even hospital trains to camps in the southeastern United States.[41] Hometown leaders were equally dedicated to another kind of guardianship: they watched for news of promotions and were quick to bombard their congressmen with indignant delegations and complaining letters if an officer vacancy was filled by someone from another company or regiment.

Clearly, hometown companies affected the way small-town citizens thought about the war. Though the quantum leaps in communications were still in the future and all Americans except those on the eastern shoreline must have realized that there was virtually no chance that they would experience war directly, people had less difficulty than one might imagine in engendering a feeling of the immediacy of war. The existence of Company C testified that it was Galesburg, Illinois, and only secondarily the federal government, that was waging war. Galesburg and other small towns assumed—without justification, as it turned out—that theirs would be a decisive influence on the war's outcome. Confident of their power to affect what happened to their companies, they had little sense of consigning their young men to the care of the federal government, and thus assumed that Washington would interpose only infrequently and unimportantly between them and their military companies.

Those at home seldom pressed the War Department to release news of their sons, for the simple reason that they did not view the United States government as an important source of information. Controlling their own lines, townspeople felt with justification that they had fuller information about their boys than had the secretary of war. And for news of the broader movements of the war they could rely on the wire services feeding the local newspaper. Local people celebrated of course the great victories of Manila and Santiago, but they did so without impinging on the centrality of the relationship between town and company. Many of the manifestations of that relationship seem today merely quaint. At the same time that the nationally minded Theodore Roosevelt was soliciting Rough Rider testimonials in a forlorn attempt to win the Congressional medal of honor for his actions on Kettle Hill,[42] the women of the Clyde Ladies Society began to collect funds to provide each of the members of Company I a medal (cost: fifty cents) struck on behalf of the town.[43] To the ladies, the gesture did not lack substance. Service to the community should be rewarded by the community.

In 1917–18 and 1941–45 Americans would again follow the large movements of war in their newspapers and would trace in personal letters the exploits of their sons. In twentieth-century wars, however, the federal government would control newspaper content, and letters like those of 1898 conveying full details of daily routine, diet, illness, and adventure, would be censored as damaging to morale and security. Tied in such ways to their soldiers, many of America's small towns experienced the Spanish-American War more intimately than would be possible for civilians in subsequent wars.

◈ ◈ ◈

No doubt many young men welcomed war as an escape from monotonous jobs—or as an invitation to adventure of a sort rarely available to them. Happy to enlist, they nonetheless conceived their escape as strictly temporary. Anticipating nothing more exceptional than a return home at the war's end, officers and men were content to accept their role as representatives of their communities. On the occasion of his unit's departure for the Caribbean, Carl Sandburg's company commander acknowledged Galesburg's mandate by addressing a farewell letter to the entire town.[44] Letters home bear similar evidence that the soldiers recognized themselves as guardians of the town's honor. They too would work to retain links between town and unit and to resist any intrusive element threatening to make the company less representative of its community.

When shortly after the passage of the war resolutions the House of Representatives debated an Army bill that endangered the election of company officers by increasing the governors' appointive powers, the Galesburg *Republican-Register* reported that the "boys [of the National Guard comapny] were worked up and vowed they would not go into service with other than their own officers." [45] In this instance the House bill became law, but so strong was small-town opposition that politically sensitive governors invited local "recommendations" for officer positions, thereby preserving the substance of the elections system.

In cases where there were no such concessions to community

control, the men sometimes acted on their threats to stay at home. The members of Galesburg's Artillery Battery B remained civilians rather than merge with another town's battery, a condition stipulated by the War Department for Battery B's activation. "In this [amalgamation]," explained the *Evening Mail,* "they would lose their organization, identification and officers, and they did not choose to accept the offer." [46]

Those who did accept did not cease to concern themselves with the composition of the unit. When, following the departure from home of most National Guard organizations, the War Department directed that companies be increased from sixty-eight to one hundred and eight, sergeants returned to home towns to recruit the additional men. Such soldiers, to whom the manpower depots of World War I would have seemed alien inventions, assumed that replacements should come from home. "The boys are hoping," wrote Sergeant A. I. Robinson, the correspondent in Sherwood Anderson's company, "that the . . . new men will all be from Clyde." [47]

The soldiers were less exercised than their townsmen over the promotion of outsiders, but it remained a point of dissatisfaction. Robinson wrote home in mid-May of 1898 that "members of the company were very much chagrined" at the appointment of a "Toledo man" as captain of Company I, "but like good soldiers they made the best of it." Later he was less resigned. The men suspected "political chicanery" when a Clyde man was passed over in favor of a candidate from rival Fremont; that constituted "an outrage." [48] Unit sentiment as reflected in his letters throughout the war strongly supported promotion from the company ranks. There is in his criticisms of the Toledo men who would "hog" promotions something beyond small-group solidarity and normal desire for personal preferment. His opposition, and the protests of those at home, signal the deeper conviction that other officers were less capable and trustworthy *because* they were not from Clyde.

Men from home made easier the maintenance of informal

social relationships, perhaps the soldiers' principal concern beyond their safe return to civilian life. Out of this concern grew their resistance to the pretensions of their own officers and the incursions of regular officers intent on establishing professional discipline and impersonality. A complicating factor in this struggle was a measure of ambivalence in volunteer attitudes toward the regulars. Hometown soldiers admired the capabilities of the professionals. "As good as the regulars" was an encomium that volunteer units would happily accept, so long as professional leadership was not imposed on their own ranks. Volunteers could not entirely ignore the returns of professionalism, even when they calculated its price too high to pay. In one of his letters to the Galesburg *Evening Mail,* Private Martin assured townspeople that the order and discipline in Company C would be "much the same" as in the regulars, but, he added with no sense of contradiction, "of course, the officers will hardly be as strict." [49] Carl Sandburg wrote with less ambiguity of the same volunteers: "They elected their own officers and you could hear fellows [say], 'No West Pointers in *this* regiment.'" [50] The Seventh New York, perhaps the best National Guard regiment in the country, refused induction into federal service because its members feared they would be compelled to serve under West Point graduates.[51]

The source of such widespread aversion to the regular officer was the volunteer's conviction that professional discipline would cheat him of the critical personal experience that the war was expected to supply.[52] Close ties of company and town and their united resistance to external authority in no sense implied a high degree of subordination of the volunteer to his hometown unit. The "boy of the country town" still thought of warmaking as personal expression and scarcely at all as concerted group action. Face to face with the enemy, the individual was the integer of meaning. It was he testing himself. It was his battle performance—and only peripherally his unit's —that counted. Many volunteers considered their membership in a company a matter of administrative convenience, the result of their need for a vehicle that would carry them to war. Once there, each would be judged, by himself and others, as an individual combatant.

It was this individual expresison in warfare that the volunteers believed regular officers determined to prevent: West Point martinets would compel the volunteer to subordinate himself to an organization. So believing, volunteers throughout the war resisted those attempts at discipline and regimentation that threatened their image as personal combatants. It was thus not only the familiarity and security of the hometown unit, the presence of childhood friends, that brought volunteers to the company's defense against the threat of outside control. In equal measure it was the freedom offered in such units to fight in a style that volunteers thought would supply the personal meaning of war.

Volunteers further resisted the imposition of impersonal authority because they saw no basis for a careful distinction between officer and enlisted man. They were unpersuaded that anything inherent in the category "officer" established superior soldiership. Relevant military experience earned the volunteers' respect, but almost all their officers were as innocent of it as they were. Neither regular nor volunteer had faced a European enemy or fought over a tropical terrain. Moreover, the implements of land warfare, unlike those huge, complex and risky machines employed since the 1880s in the United States Navy, required no specialized training. Volunteers were confident that their proficiency with the weapons available to fight Spaniards in Cuba equaled—many thought surpassed— that of the regulars. In the eyes of the men, their officers had no claim to authority or even respect—neither superior experience, expertise, nor anything else by which they had *earned* the right to issue peremptory orders and enjoy privileges denied the men.

The writings of Sherwood Anderson make clear the volunteer's assumption that hometown social patterns should prevail and his determination to resist their suspension. "I was a soldier," he wrote a quarter century later, "and had picked the right war. We of the local military companies were taken into the national service just as we were. Our local companies had been built up on a democratic basis. I had got what I wanted. . . ."[53] To keep what he wanted required some effort. The professionals, fearing that intimacy would translate into partiality in combat, insisted on the social separation of officers and men. But Anderson had grown up with his lieutenants, had lived side by side with them on terms of intimacy and informality and expected to resume such a life in Clyde as soon as the war was over. At first the situation in each company must have resembled that described by a citizen of neighboring Fremont who visited his town's company at Camp Bushnell in Columbus. "There are no regular Army officers in camp . . . and officers and men of the Guard mingle on a plane of beautiful equality. Privates invade the tents of their officers at will, and yell at them half the length of the street. The recruits talk and smoke cigars in ranks, and officers frequently associate in the pastimes of the men."[54] The Army's adjutant-general would later cite as one of the most serious defects in the American military effort the "utter disregard for the most elementary principles of military life in large camps."[55]

In mid-May 1898 volunteer companies received orders prohibiting officers and men messing together.[56] Anderson was at first bemused. "Ed and Dug [company officers] are all right. They have to live off by themselves and act as though they were something special, kind of grand and wise and gaudy. It's kind of a bluff, I guess, that has to be kept up. . . ."[57] He took delight in his inability to separate the company commander from the janitor he had known at home. In his mind the first lieutenant would remain a celery-raiser and the second lieutenant a knife-sharpener.[58] Throughout the war Anderson doubted the Army's ability to invest those men with additional powers that he would be inclined to recognize.

Some intrusions of formality were simply laughed away. Returning from an evening in town without benefit of pass,

Anderson mocked the challenging sentry. "Ah, cut it Will, you big boob. Don't make such a racket." With that, he proceeded into camp.[59]

The limitations of jeering became obvious, however, as volunteers found restrictions imposed by the regular Army increasingly onerous. The men then made clear to their own officers that they would appeal questions of personal relationships, not to higher military authority but to the home town. In one form the process involved threats of a vigilante justice that volunteers expected the community to condone. Wrote Anderson: "An officer might conceivably 'get away' with some sort of injustice for the moment—but a year from now, when we were all at home again [?] . . . Did the fool want to take the chance of four or five huskies giving him a beating some night in the alleyway?" [60]

More overt and genteel appeals to community values were equally effective. Newspapers did not hesitate to print letters, from their own correspondents or unnamed persons, denouncing the "airs" put on by an always-named officer. One potent petition to the people at home was that of Wiz Brown, a private in Sandburg's unit. The company commander, Captain Thomas Leslie McGirr (whom Sandburg described as "a second-rank Galesburg lawyer") [61] believed that Brown had threatened him and resolved to retaliate by giving the private a dishonorable discharge. When he learned of the matter, Brown apparently gave no consideration to an appeal through the chain of command. Even if the idea had occurred to him, a reversal of McGirr's decision would not have accomplished his purpose, for Brown was much less disturbed by the nature of his discharge than by the effrontery of McGirr's conduct. Instead he instigated an article that appeared in the Galesburg *Evening Mail* on the day before the company's return. It reported that all except three of the unit's members had signed a petition, requesting that McGirr be denied the honors of homecoming, leading the parade, and making the principal speech. Specifically, the signers charged the captain with improprieties in the maintenance of the company accounts and with treating some of the men with favoritism, others with undue severity. The newspaper seems to have accepted Brown's letter as prima facie evidence of McGirr's guilt; it summoned no more in his defense than the observation of one of the captain's friends that "he is not well." Nothing more was heard of the charges against McGirr. He did speak, very briefly, at the banquet given the returned heroes by the Army and Navy League at the Universalist Church. Whatever the justice of the matter, Captain McGirr, and all those other volunteer officers so precariously balanced between town, company, and Army, must have been acutely aware of the narrow range of the command prerogative.[62]

Those in command positions could not miss the fact that the men judged them on their willingness to maintain pliant social relationships. In an angry diary Private Charles Johnson Post reserved a special rage for the chaplain who pressed charges against shipboard food thieves and later ousted enlisted men from a Y.M.C.A. tent reserved for officers.[63] To acknowledge the official division between officers and men was mischievous, to enforce it intolerable. Conversely, a Captain Rafferty won Post's praise when he joined the men each night at the fire for reminiscence and discussion of religion and politics.[64] Enlisted men whose letters filled hometown newspapers could find no higher compliment for an officer than the assertion that military life had in no way altered his demeanor. Colonel D. Jack Foster of Sandburg's regiment was one who retained popularity because he continued to act like a civilian. There was about him "no assumed military dignity nor overbearing manners." [65]

To volunteers the handshake was the litmus of the egalitarian ideal. A Rough Rider cowboy introduced himself to Leonard Wood, his regimental commander: "Say, Colonel, I want to shake hands with you and tell you that I like you a damn sight better than I expected to. . . ." [66] Another began his harangue of the Rough Riders' second in command, Theodore

Roosevelt, with "Well, Colonel, I want to shake hands and say we're with you. . . ." [67] There was tentative flattery and further testing in these remarks. An officer willing to shake hands was an officer whose men assured one another that they could expect "man-to-man" treatment. On the other hand, volunteers despised the salute [68] and castigated as a tyrant the officer who insisted upon it. So caustic were the men on this count that even regular officers ceased to require military courtesy. A career officer of the Tenth United States Cavalry, Captain John Bigelow, Jr., wrote with self-mocking resignation at the end of the war, "Few of the enlisted men whom I pass on the streets of Huntsville [Alabama] salute: I do not know why, unless it is that they are not in the habit of saluting their officers." [69]

If Bigelow typifies regular officers frustrated by their inability to enforce the professional ideal, William Jennings Bryan might stand for that minority of volunteer officers who escaped the tension between egalitarian and professional ideals by remaining unconscious of the latter's existence. A colonel in a Nebraska regiment accurately described as a "neighborhood organization," [70] the Great Commoner perceived no distinctions between officers and men. [71] Not the drillfield but the campfire—and the opportunities it offered to discuss with the men "how to live and how to die" [72]—fixed the pivot on which his Army life turned. Nothing professionals said of military efficiency or discipline chipped his vision of the Army as co-operative movement. For Bryan and others who thought as he did there was no interior conflict. Larger numbers of volunteer officers, however, found themselves jostled between personal desires to make their units "as good as the regulars" and the volunteers' disapproval of officer "airs." Again the experience of the unhappy McGirr is instructive. On a hot march from Guanica to Ponce during the Puerto Rican campaign the tired, dust-covered boys of Galesburg's Company C saw a chance to spare their backs by transferring blanket rolls to a hired ox cart. McGirr hesitated; he "did not think it a military thing to do." Confused, a bit embarrassed, a bit angry at his inability to feel in full control of the situation, he finally gave his consent.[73] His was the dilemma of the hometown company officer.

The efforts of Theodore Roosevelt and Leonard Wood to reshape an older friendship to meet the requirements of a new hierarchical relationship reflected all the tensions inherent in a dual approach to war. Eager for a commission, Roosevelt cited as one of his qualifications for a lieutenant colonelcy his very perfunctory service in a New York National Guard unit.[74] Wood, Roosevelt's fellow outdoorsman and nominal superior, had by contrast more than a decade's experience in the old Army as regimental surgeon and Indian fighter. In the year prior to the war Roosevelt, while serving as assistant secretary of the Navy, had built friendships with Wood and a group of young naval officers. Influenced by such associations, Roosevelt became a convert to the standards of the regulars. When war came, he announced his determination to be "professional" in all aspects of soldiering. To his surprise he could not shed the preconceptions planted in his National Guard days. Pleased when a contingent of Rough Riders properly executed a difficult drill, he showed his appreciation by buying each man a schooner of beer. Wood, with other officers present, rebuked his friend for unprofessional conduct. Stung at first but soon repentant, Roosevelt returned to tell Wood, "I wish to say, sir, that I agree with what you said. I consider myself the damndest ass within ten miles of this camp." [75]

Contrition did not insulate the future president from his basic ambivalence on the proper manner of producing American soldiers. He said of his Rough Riders that "what was necessary was to teach them to act together, and to obey orders." To this professional formula Roosevelt the guardsman added: "The men were singularly quick to respond to any appeal to their intelligence and patriotism." [76]

Biographer Hermann Hagedorn saw here the essential difference between professional and volunteer. Wood, he said, came to the Rough Riders expecting to command and be obeyed; Roosevelt felt it essential "to win over the minds" of his men.[77] It must be added that if Roosevelt's problem was the inability to reconcile his persuasion-inspiration tactic with a power theoretically self-sufficient, Wood's was the frustration of dedication to an ideal beyond realization. Passing sprawling soldiers, he heard his corporal rebuke one of the lounging volunteers: "Didn't yo' hear me shout *ATTENTION?*" Came the reply: "Sure, I did. I thought yo' jest wanted me to look alive to somethin' interestin'." [78]

Friedrich Wilhelm von Steuben had observed of American soldiers one hundred and twenty years earlier that "one must first explain—and then give the order." [79] His remark was no less applicable to the volunteers of 1898, although professional soldiers were by then less likely than von Steuben to regard the trait as a part of the genius of the American people.[80] Unable to enforce orders, the Leonard Woods of the Army were loathe to explain them. Like his friend Theodore, he pondered whether the officer's duty was to instill in his men automatic response to command, or to offer a personal example of intelligence and patriotism inspiring others to follow where he led.

The Spanish-American War proved partially correct the regulars' contention that social informality would produce volunteer indiscipline and officer indecision. While still near their communities, volunteers so comported themselves that Alger advised his commanders to transport troops from their home states as soon as possible, an obvious effort to escape what an investigating commission chaired by Grenville M. Dodge would later term "the disturbing influences of home locality." [81] Distance, however, proved no panacea. In training camps the men simply disregarded elementary sanitary precautions; repeated orders and daily inspections were unavailing.[82] Fist fights between individual officers and men were frequent. In the war zone, ranks often crumbled when there was the prospect of a view or a show, whether bombardment or dance troupe.[83] Tired marchers regularly ignored orders and pitched into the

William McKinley
as he appeared in 1900.
Courtesy of the Library of Congress.

Ida and William McKinley, 1900.
Courtesy of the Library of Congress.

McKinley as he appeared during the Civil War.
Courtesy of the Western Reserve Historical Society Library.

Mark Hanna, McKinley's friend and political supporter.
Courtesy of the Library of Congress.

M'KINLEY---Please, sir, can I have the core?
MARK HANNA---There aint goin' to be no core.

In Homer Davenport's cartoon a servile McKinley pleads
with a swollen Hanna dressed in dollar-sign suit.
Courtesy of the Library of Congress.

Henry Cabot Lodge, Senate intellectual
and confidant of Theodore Roosevelt.
Courtesy of the Library of Congress.

Russell A. Alger, a secretary of war
impatient with the president's unwillingness
to hasten military preparations.
Courtesy of the Library of Congress.

Speaker of the House Thomas B. Reed, a man
as cynical of war as of most other human undertakings.
Courtesy of the Library of Congress.

John D. Long, imperturbable Massachusetts politician
and secretary of the navy whose lack of militancy irritated
those intent on war.
Courtesy of the Library of Congress.

Senator Redfield Proctor whose speech of March 17, 1898, converted many to intervention in Cuba. *Courtesy of the Library of Congress.*

Infantrymen relaxing at Tampa, Florida camp, 1898.
U.S. Signal Corps photograph courtesy of the National Archives.

Sherwood Anderson in an army training camp, 1898.
Courtesy of Thaddeus Hurd and Glen Giffen, Clyde, Ohio.

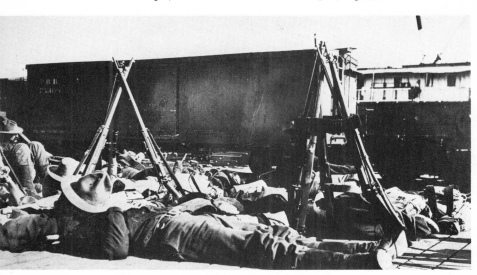

Troops at Port Tampa awaiting the departure of the Cuban expeditionary force.
U.S. Signal Corps photograph courtesy of the National Archives.

The sailing of the troopship *Concho*.
U.S. Signal Corps photograph courtesy of the National Archives.

The landing of the V Corps at Daiquiri in southeastern Cuba.
U.S. Signal Corps photograph courtesy of the National Archives.

William Glackens's combat sketch of the ford of the San Juan River,
called the "Bloody Bend" and the site of severe American casualties.
Courtesy of the Library of Congress.

Glackens's rendering of the disorganized charge against Spanish fortifications
on the San Juan ridges. *Courtesy of the Library of Congress.*

Theodore Roosevelt in Rough Rider uniform, 1898.
Courtesy of the Library of Congress.

Roosevelt and the Rough Riders on San Juan Hill.
Courtesy of the Library of Congress.

American soldiers, the effects of fever and poor food
already apparent, cheer the news of Santiago's surrender.
U.S. Signal Corps photograph courtesy of the National Archives.

"Fighting Joe" Wheeler, one of several former Confederate commanders who accepted army commissions in 1898. *U.S. Signal Corps photograph courtesy of the National Archives.*

Major General William A. Shafter, the commander of the Cuban expeditionary force. *U.S. Signal Corps photograph courtesy of the National Archives.*

Valeriano Weyler, Spanish governor-general of Cuba, called "The Butcher" by the American popular press. *Courtesy of the Library of Congress.*

Cubans as pictured in American periodicals. Light-complexioned
rebels swearing loyalty to the insurrectionary cause.
Reprinted from Harper's Pictorial History of the War with Spain.

A rendering of combat suggesting the Cubans' imagined
capacity to wage a traditional war.
Reprinted from Harper's Pictorial History of the War with Spain.

A Cuban commander, Calixto Garcia (with brow
dented by bullet wound) and his headquarters staff.
U.S. Signal Corps photograph courtesy of the National Archives.

William Randolph Hearst, publisher of the New York *Journal*.
Courtesy of the Library of Congress.

Cuban soldiers as they were at first encounter with Americans.
U.S. Signal Corps photograph courtesy of the National Archives.

Joseph Pulitzer, publisher of the New York *World*.
Courtesy of the Library of Congress.

Stephen Crane, the most famous of the Spanish-American War correspondents. *Courtesy of the Library of Congress.*

Richard Harding Davis, the *beau-ideal* of correspondents. *Courtesy of the Library of Congress.*

jungle scarce supplies of ammunition. Officers hesitated to invoke military justice. Shafter reported that in the Fifth Corps "not an officer was brought to trial by court-martial, and, as far as I know, no enlisted man." [84] In extreme cases where discipline fell below the minimal standard necessary to maintain the semblance of a military unit, the Army could at best request the resignations of officers it held accountable.

Ultimately, however, despite such evidence, the professionals' indictment proved unpersuasive, for in the crucial moments the volunteers' battle discipline—resting not on officer authority but on a particular personal motivation—was adequate to the test of combat.[85] To most Americans, that alone was the performance that counted.

Better than any other writer, Stephen Crane captured the tension that played between volunteer and professional concepts of war. In Crane's short story, *Virtue in War*, Private Lige approaches the tent of Major Gates, a former regular commanding a volunteer unit:

"Well, Maje," said the newcomer, genially, "how goes it?"

The major's head flashed up, but he spoke without heat. "Come to attention and salute."

The private looked at him in resentful amazement, and then inquired: "Ye ain't mad, are ye? Ain't nothin' to get huffy about, is there?"

"I—Come to attention and salute."

"Well," drawled the private, as he stared, "seein' as ye are so darn particular, I don't care if I do—if it'll make yer meals set on yer stummick any better."

Drawing a long breath and grinning ironically, he lazily pulled his heels together and saluted with a flourish.

"There," he said, with a return to his earlier genial manner. "How's that suit ye, Maje?"

There was a silence which to an impartial observer would have seemed pregnant with dynamite and bloody death. Then the major cleared his throat and coldly said: "And now, what is your business?"

"Who—me?" asked the private. "Oh, I just sorter dropped in." With a deeper meaning he added: "Sorter dropped in in a friendly way, thinkin' ye was mebbe a different kind of feller from what ye be."

The inference was clearly marked.

It was now Gates's turn to stare, and stare he unfeignedly did. "Go back to your quarters," he said at length.

The volunteer became very angry.

"Oh, ye needn't be so up-in-th'-air, need ye? Don't know's I'm dead anxious to inflict my company on yer since I've had a good look at ye. There may be men in this here battalion what's had just as much edjewcation as you have, and I'm damned if they ain't got better *manners*. Good mornin'," he said, with dignity; and passing out of the tent, he flung the flap back in place with an air of slamming it as if it had been a door. He made his way back to his company street. . . . He was furious.[86]

Lige complains to his friends that Gates "won't have no truck with jest common—*men,* like you be." He and the major are both wounded in an attack on a Spanish blockhouse. Again, Lige attempts to persuade Gates to acknowledge his individuality. As if his pardon were important to Gates, Lige tells the major he is no longer angry. Again Gates responds from the manual, ordering Lige to "Go to the rear!" Lige refuses, though the major rather desperately threatens him with drawn revolver. The volunteer stays, but he can do nothing, neither win Gates' recognition of his personal worth nor save the major's life. In the end Lige perceives a "certain hopeless gulf" separating him from the other man.[87]

❖ ❖ ❖

In contemplating the quandary of 1898's professional officers, whether Leonard Wood or Crane's Major Gates, one must take

care not to rely on too strict a dichotomy between the desire
for automatic response and the necessity of inspirational leadership rooted in character. In fact, the issue was not so sharply
etched in 1898. Not even the most dedicated professionals yet
conceived of the Army as a machine, or soldiers as cogwheels
that could be made to rotate independently of individual will.
Men continued to believe in varying degrees that the success
of an army flowed from the personal qualities of its members:
professionals insisted that obedience to command was the most
important, not the sole, quality required. No one, least of all
those generals like Oates who insisted in surrounding themselves with men from home, thought of a national army of
interchangeable parts. No one, least of all those who in 1898
believed that directing others in peacetime pursuits constituted grounds for refusing direction in war, foresaw that another war would dissolve those large areas of continuity between civilian and military life, leaving all equally vulnerable
to a power of command enhanced psychologically and insti-
tutionally.

Change thus came with no rush to the American Army of
1900–1917. With many officers still professing to value a certain latitude in individual behavior, with an American public
persistent in its belief that the experience of 1898 had validated
the nation's reliance on a volunteer system, and with the exemplar of individualized warfare sitting in the White House,
the interwar debate on military reform quite understandably
focused on inefficiency rather than on indiscipline. (Although
professionals asserted to one another that the volunteers would
have fared poorly in combat without the heavy stiffening of
the regulars,[88] incompetence, especially in the care of the sick,
had in truth cost far more lives than had lack of discipline in
battle.) The objective of Army reformers was thus a "more
intimate relation" between the general government and National Guard units,[89] one assuming that the militiaman taught
how to act professionally would thereby *wish* to act professionally. Sufficient exposure to the values of the regulars would
of itself purge informality, without resort to coercion. As the

Dodge Comission concluded, "Until the individual soldier appreciates the necessity of complying fully with the regulations and confines himself to the regular food—and this the soldier never does until *experience* teaches him the necessity— he will drink polluted water, eat noxious food . . . and will not take care of himself, and *no discipline or watching will prevent it.*" [90]

Varieties of proposals were offered to shape the experience of guardsmen toward professional standards. Secretary of War Elihu Root opened to members of the National Guard the Army's new specialized schools. [91] The Dick Act of 1903 provided that the Guard was to be organized, equipped, and trained in uniformity with the regular Army. The latter, moreover, received authority to detail to the states professional instructors and to establish minimum standards for weekly drill and summer camp. From other sources came suggestions for combined maneuvers, joint encampments, and experimental mobilizations. If ideas were profuse, however, movement was rare. Old exhortations could not do work for which new mechanisms were required. In 1908 the election of officers continued in the Guard units of several states. [92] In 1916 the mobilization of the National Guard during the Mexican border crisis revealed so few organizational advances beyond 1898 that Leonard Wood's claim of the previous year that the volunteer system had proven a failure seemed borne out. [93]

To be sure, the pace of change was already accelerating with the approach of war in Europe. Americans, granted almost three years to contemplate from afar the horrors of trench warfare, were untouched in 1917 by the massive enthusiasm of 1898. Guard rosters were as a rule undersubscribed; even the introduction of conscripts sometimes failed to forestall the consolidation of units. Guardsmen for the first time took a double oath, to the national as well as the state government. Within a year of America's entry into war, most divisions thoroughly blended regulars, guardsmen, and draftees. [94]

In 1917–18 the homogeneous hometown unit—and with it

any intermediate level of loyalty and identification between soldier and the national Army—was rapidly disappearing. A stronger military institutional structure,[95] a growing national-mindedness and the exigencies of a war of immensely greater scope and severity were combining to produce units of greater geographical mix and officers whose professional qualifications rather than community affiliations would become the requisites of military leadership.

In the spring of 1898 Sherwood Anderson had quit his job in a Chicago cold-storage warehouse and had returned to Clyde to rejoin Company I, a gesture for which even the hoboes on the train on which he stole a ride had paid him honor.[96] In 1917 fewer Americans felt so strongly a direct relationship between war and hometown. No longer did many feel it important to approach a national conflict through one's local community.

The same Sherwood Anderson who ridiculed the command pretensions of "Ed and Dug" did seem to enter a strikingly different conceptual cosmos when in 1917 he wrote a book presenting man as "ineffectual until, absorbed into a faceless mass led by a charismatic leader, he contributed his will and body to an invincible social entity." [97] Though rich in hyperbole when applied to the American soldier of 1917–18, such a statement does help to mark the diminution of individualized expression in war. It gives shape to a tendency advanced by the introduction during World War I of psychological placement and standardized testing.[98] And it finds rough counterparts in the professionals' reconceptualization of war. Reflecting on the experience of 1917–18, General Henry Jervey told brother officers in 1920:

A man could not be considered as merely a man. He was something more. He was part of [a] machine made up of many different parts, each a man it is true, but having to play a highly specialized part. Consequently it became necessary to economize the specialized abilities of these

various spare parts and assign them where their specialized abilities would do the most good. In other words,
round pegs had to be selected to fill round holes. This
required a careful classification of the men before assignment . . .[99]

Invincible social entity. A machine of many parts. Pegs and
holes. No longer would men discuss war in the imagery of
character, citizenship, energy, and physical prowess.

If by 1920 no issue survived, twenty-two years earlier two
conceptions of warmaking still remained in an unstable suspension.

The Spanish-American War did not bridge the gulf between
volunteer and professional. The enemy was too weak and the
war too short to force efficiency; the weapons were not so
destructive as to force discipline. The nation for the last
time thought appropriate, and could afford, volunteer informality.

CHAPTER IV

The War of Personal Encounter

. . . *the book for the army is a war song, not a hospital sketch.*

OLIVER WENDELL HOLMES, JR.[1]

IN THE MIND of Theodore Roosevelt there evolved a theoretic conception of combat shared in part by other volunteers preparing to go to war against Spain. His ideas offer the opportunity to measure, against American expectations, the actual experience of a war in which men were determined to "[fight] the issue out with bullet, butt and bayonet in a deadly personal encounter."[2]

Theodore Roosevelt hoped and worked for war. He spoke of it as a geopolitical necessity: the United States had reached that stage of its development where it must expel from the hemisphere all remaining European powers, beginning with Spain.[3] On another level of thought, one that tapped Roosevelt's deeper emotions, he found a more potent persuasion. The nation, he said, needed a war [4]—not to relieve a Spanish threat to American security or prosperity, not to rescue suffering Cubans, not even to avenge the sinking of the *Maine*. A war was essential to provide experiences that would test and temper Theodore Roosevelt and other American participants and by some mystic transfer rejuvenate their society.

Brooding over the state of American society, Roosevelt began his critique with the assumption of loss. Americans of his
generation had let slip some important constituent of character, some spiritual element that sustained those of McKinley's age. American society was a warrior gone to fat. Losing
"the fighting edge," Americans had surrendered to "mere animal sloth and ease" or "material gain" and had thus set in
train "a gradual failure of vitality." [5] With more fervor than
logic, Roosevelt charged that his countrymen were too energetic in their material pursuits, too lethargic otherwise.

Conscious of the rapid social change that eluded the president, Roosevelt could not share McKinley's certainties and so
ridiculed them. Had Roosevelt been able to persuade McKinley that America was ill, however, the two would have had
no difficulty agreeing on the cure. There was nothing unortho-
dox in the younger man's conceptualization of the problem in
terms of deteriorating individual standards rather than the
industrial transformation of their society. Convinced that a
composite of individual values set a society's tone and course,
ignoring institutional relationships [6] but sensing a growing
social malaise, Roosevelt prescribed a reinvigoration of individual character.

What was required was to identify and duplicate the experience that had imparted vigor and spirituality to the older
generation, for then changes in American life would prove re-
versible. There was hope in the belief that a young man, denied a vital experience, was being reduced to impotence by the
the decline of his character, not by the tyranny of his machines.

The missing element, Roosevelt concluded, was an experience comparable to the Civil War. Thirty years after Robert
E. Lee's capitulation, there had appeared what Norman
Thomas would later call the "social and collective memory of
. . . [war] which softens reality." [7] By 1898 many Americans
had lost the sense of the Civil War as tragedy and waste. Older
Republicans assured themselves that the Civil War had acted
as a political guide for their generation. But what was to lead

the new generation, those carrying memories of their fathers'
Civil War tales, of G.A.R. contingents leading countless pa-
rades but, as Walter Hines Page complained, coming "to manhood . . . [with] no part in any great adventure"? [8] Wrote
Carl Sandburg on his way to the Spanish-American War:
"Over all of us in 1898 was the shadow of the Civil War and
the men who fought it to the end." [9] From that shadow the
fear of war and its costs had departed, leaving behind a challenge and a reproach to the young men of the 1890s.

It is not surprising that Theodore Roosevelt fixed on war as
the essential social restorative. As an adolescent during the
Civil War he had marched in Zouave shirt, prayed to God
that the Southern troops might be ground to powder, and pes-
tered family friends for battlefield mementos.[10] He found excitement in the stories of two uncles whose service in the Confederate Navy he quickly forgave.[11] He was less generous with
his father; it rankled that the elder Theodore Roosevelt had
not enlisted.[12] As a Harvard undergraduate, the son began
work on his *Naval History of the War of 1812*. He was already
an avid hunter of whom a college friend said, "He wants to be
killing something all the time." [13] He admired and emulated
military men. On his appointment to second-in-command of
the Rough Riders, he "swelled with pride at being addressed
as 'colonel.'" [14] Throughout his life he measured problems by
the increments of force necessary to overcome them, and he
regularly employed a vocabulary of power. Such phrases as
"It is better to hit than to parry" and "I always hate words
unless they mean blows" were characteristic.[15]

A corollary of Theodore Roosevelt's respect for war was
his deprecation of peace.[16] He asserted that righteousness
should come before peace and then proceeded to attach to
peace values that made it unrighteous. Peace would not provide that which made a people great. "I believe most earnestly
and sincerely in peace, but as things are yet in this world the
nation that cannot fight, the people that have lost the fighting
edge, that have lost the virile virtues, occupy a position as dan-

gerous as it is ignoble." [17] The companions of peace were those reprehensible tendencies to the "soft life" and materialism; its agents were the "peace-at-any-price universal arbitration types" and the "peace faction." [18] Unrelieved peace, Roosevelt feared, would prove fatal to society.

For those of his friends still unpersuaded that war was both necessary and beneficent, still insistent that the primacy of peace was more than a philosophical abstraction easily yielded to "realism," Roosevelt had an ingenious answer. The Spanish treatment of Cubans, he argued, constituted murder. American abstention from war prolonged murderous behavior, thus condoning a false peace. War on the other hand would halt murder and inaugurate true peace. No matter, then, whether one valued or discounted peace, Roosevelt's prescription was war.

Locating on the individual level the source of the problem war would cure, Theodore Roosevelt conceived of war as a pitting of himself against evil others in an unimpeachable cause. He did not submit to war. He was spared that later sense of yielding oneself to a powerful military organization capable of enforcing strict discipline, of surrendering to war as a phenomenon inevitably overwhelming the individual. He sought war as a vehicle of self-expression. With so many of those young Americans eager to fight against Spain, Roosevelt envisioned the war as a single set-piece scene: the American soldier would charge, would meet the Spaniard [19] hand-to-hand and, by invoking personal and racial qualities and converting them to physical force, would kill the enemy. The process would not be automatic. Some Americans would be found wanting and would fall. Those, however, who succeeded in bringing to bear the best American virtues would enlarge the supply of those virtues within society. So conceived, the war would bring a positive return to each successful participant and, by extension from the individual, would restore America's "virile virtues," her martial spirit. A sufficient number of personal transformations would create a social transformation, a society reinvigorated.

To this reading of war's meaning the personal experience—especially the personal encounter with the enemy, "the thrill of grappling with him and hating him," as the poet Ernest Crosby put it [20]—was central. Organizational relationships were tolerated proportionate to their perceived ability to produce that vital experience. In joining a military unit Theodore Roosevelt did not aspire to *become* a soldier. As we have seen, few Americans yet equated ability to serve as an Army officer with technical qualifications. Despite his flirtation with professionalism, Roosevelt relied heavily on the attributes of character: certain qualities, again left unspecified, identified the best citizens and in the tradition of the citizen Army the latter were easily transformed into the best soldiers.[21] It required little more than putting on a uniform. Thus, Roosevelt valued his Rough Riders as "soldiers ready made." [22] He was proud of the cowboys' ability to ride and shoot, but that was not their chief commendation. Roosevelt accepted with equal enthusiasm the applications of Ivy Leaguers and other eastern "swells" who matched the Westerners in ruggedness, individualism, confidence, and the like.[23] Character preceded technical proficiency.

The unit itself was conceived not as a piece among pieces that, once fitted properly, would produce a united military effort. Rather it was a convenient vehicle to carry the American soldier to his confrontation with the enemy. It might require a level of organization distasteful to the men, but because a vehicle was essential, those in the ranks recognized the inevitability of some temporary infringement of their freedoms. Roosevelt bound the Ivy League clubmen to obey cowboy officers to whom they would have paid no attention in civilian life.[24] This subordination was extremely fragile, based as it was on what Roosevelt labeled the necessity to observe "the rules of the game."

The celebrated war correspondent Richard Harding Davis found offensive the sight of Lieutenant Colonel Roosevelt dining in a hotel with two sergeants, probably eastern friends.

"It was a bad break," Davis concluded; "Roosevelt gave the regiment a bad name by that one act that it does not deserve." [25] Focusing as usual on punctilio, the correspondent missed the point. Roosevelt still reserved to himself the prerogative of judging where rank defined relationships. Military etiquette was not yet the necessary and outward sign of hierarchical relationships securing military discipline. The essential discipline, Roosevelt insisted by his actions, could only be generated internally. The proprieties might have their place, but *he* would decide where the "rules of the game" applied.

Training, with its stress on long marches rather than unit drill or combined exercises, fit the same preconception of the individual's role in war. The objective was not proficiency in the use of weapons,[26] not large-scale unit maneuverability or disciplined response to command but the hardening of bodies. It was assumed that each man moving to meet the enemy would struggle with himself to mobilize the highest ideals of which he was capable, to conquer the quaking and shirking enemy within. Training was a method to prevent the intrusion of irrelevant physical factors into that essentially moral encounter first with oneself and then with the Spaniard.

Theodore Roosevelt spoke of the possibility of that personal disgrace so feared by American soldiers of 1898. The Rough Rider officers, he said, "all earnestly wished for a chance to distinguish themselves, and fully appreciated that they ran the risk not merely of death, but of what was infinitely worse —namely, failure at the crisis to perform duty well. . . ." [27] Training aimed not at the survival of the soldier but at the delivery of the individual, physically unimpaired, to the crisis. It sought to minimize the danger of dishonor outside the true zone of testing. In conceptual terms it differed little from the pledge of total abstinence taken by departing units, including the boys of McKinley's home county.[28]

❖ ❖ ❖

A few Americans of various sections, parties, and classes shared in varying degrees Roosevelt's sense of social malaise;

his conviction that the deterioration of individual standards was responsible; his characterization of war and peace;
and his desire to exploit war's transforming power. America
was too prosperous, thought the novelist Owen Wister, and
needed misfortune to return her to fundamental standards.
William Allen White welcomed a war whose sorrow would
chasten a nation deserving of punishment. Senator William
Allen, a Nebraska Populist, hoped that war would consume
American society's "dry rot," and the Kansas poet Eugene Ware
embraced war as the instrument to overcome American ava-
rice. Ambrose Bierce welcomed "war, famine, pestilence, anything that will stop people from cheating. . . ." The bellicose
were not the only ones to agree with Roosevelt. William James,
who attacked Roosevelt for treating peace "as a condition of
blubberlike and swollen ignobility, fit only for huckstering
weaklings, dwelling in gray twilight and heedless of the higher
life," nonetheless agreed with Roosevelt that American character was in danger of disintegration and that the vitality re-
leased by war might "hammer us into decency." His brother
Henry read military books, memoirs, and Napoleonic lore
and contrasted himself, a "poor worm of peace," with the
"brilliant man of action." [29]

Clearly, most of the elements of Roosevelt's critique were
circulating in American intellectual circles. The prominence
of several critics should not, however, obscure the fact that
their sallies, delivered against a backdrop of McKinleyite opti-
mism, were muted and narrowly confined. Roosevelt, though
committed to a comprehensive indictment of American society,
never became public critic. Indeed when the writer William
Dean Howells permitted circulation of his worry that America
was coming out all wrong, Roosevelt was angry. He denounced
as decadent literati those like Howells and Hamlin Garland
who refused to celebrate that same American character that
Roosevelt feared, and so informed his friends in private letters,
was failing.[30] He found statements like Howells' unbearable,
for they issued from spirits apparently resigned to the corrosion of America and clearly exacerbated the problem by parad-

ing it in public. To Roosevelt it made a great difference where
one offered his criticisms and whether one accepted or fought
to reverse destructive social trends. The objective was a restorative war, not a public discussion of character's decline.

Few American enlistees agreed with—or even knew of—
Roosevelt's critique of their society or his insistence that war
was essential to the nation's future. He might divert himself
with war aims defined in national terms, might look forward to
a country rejuvenated by its soldiers' successes, but the men
shared only his terminal point: the centrality of the individual performance against the enemy. The public cry to war
focused on the relief of suffering Cubans and the punishment
of Spain. For most of the country's young men the humanitarian impulse marched arm-in-arm with the expectation of the
encounter with the Spaniard. The intellectual route between
them was a simple one. What more reasonable way to deliver
Cubans than to strike at the nation oppressing them? What
simpler way to chastise Spain than to kill the Spaniard?

In an exercise in prophecy repeated at the outset of many
wars, Americans foresaw a short conflict and, this time, were
correct. They treated the war as if it were a necessary com-
modity in very short supply: there would not be enough for
everyone and unless one got there quickly, it would be gone.
The volunteers' conviction that the essence of the war could
be found only in a combat experience posed a serious problem
for those in command. The belief, soon substantiated, that
there would be very limited access to the war zone and even
less to the battlefield [31] weakened further that fragile cooperation among the American forces.

"This is going to be a short war," Roosevelt declared. "I am
going into it and get all there is out of it." [32] In such a setting
comrade sometimes became competitor. His jog from one War
Department bureau to another, smiling broadly but tensely insistent that the chiefs immediately authorize his requisitions

for the outfitting of the Rough Riders, was inspired by the presence of a rival cavalry commander. This man, unnamed in Roosevelt's *Autobiography*, was either Melvin Grigsby or Jay L. Torrey, commanding officers of the second and third volunteer cavalry regiments.[33] Both raced Roosevelt to war; neither had his combination of energy, influence, and good fortune. "Grigsby's Cowboys" got no closer to Cuba than Camp Thomas, Georgia. "Torrey's Rocky Mountain Riders" foundered in Florida.

The same assumptions of the centrality of combat and its limited accessibility account for the desperate machinations employed by those assembled at Tampa to win space in the invasion fleet. When the Fifth Corps commander General William R. Shafter found men and supplies hopelessly jammed along a single-track railroad running through sandy wastes, with neither staff nor time to develop administrative procedures capable of supporting a 15,000-man expeditionary force, and with Washington issuing almost hourly peremptory orders for his departure,[34] he could only abandon the pretense of military organization: he announced the hour of the expedition's sailing and warned that those not aboard would be left behind.[35] In the rush for the boats, Roosevelt blocked the gangway of a vessel assigned to other units, employing varieties of deceit, bluff, and intimidation until his own Rough Riders came up the wharf. He was determined not to be numbered among the 10,000 for whom no space could be found.[36]

It was not only "that runaway rainbow chase for glory"[37] that impelled many to act as Roosevelt did. Equally influential was the narrowness of the terms commonly used to define significant participation in the war. No soldier consented to his unit's assignment to support activities. What formal support forces existed—companies of teamsters, for example—were civilians under contract to the Army. The soldier based his participation on the assumption he was, and should only be, a fighter.

These, then, were the assumptions that gave impulse to

American participants in the war, premises whose logic led
them to seek a San Juan Hill or its equivalent. Without gross
simplification one might therefore reduce the principal ex-
periential thrust of the war to the image of a barrier-strewn,
often intersected road leading to the hill and the encounter it
seemed to promise. Since so many sought to make the journey and so few completed it, the figure of the road might also
mark those numerous crossings at which most volunteers left
the straight-away or, more accurately, were shunted from it.
Those who did ultimately arrive at their destination were, as
we shall see, surprised to discover much that their preconceptions did not encompass.

To be sure, there were those who quit the race to combat
almost before it began. Some older guardsmen, discovering
themselves no longer interested in anything beyond what a
War Department study would later castigate as "the club fea-
tures of militia organizations," declined to serve and departed
in peace.[38] More exacting were the experiences of that small
number of young guardsmen who found camp life hard or
responsibilities at home compelling and refused to transfer to
federal service. Those in Galesburg's Company C choosing
to return home were "jeered unmercifully . . . and were ordered to remove their uniforms and get out of camp." [39] Taunts
of "traitor" and "Spaniard" and "Go home to momma" fell on
the heads of those lacking "sand." Seven of Clyde's Company I
were stretched around trees and their buttocks beaten while
officers looked on.[40] Company H of Fremont, Ohio, clipped all
the hair of its single defector, then rode him from camp on a
rail.[41] To fail the test of war was a personal failure; to refuse
to submit to that test was to exile oneself from friends and
community.

Washington officials could ignore such incidents; what they
could not disregard was the eagerness of the many that so in-
tensified the ignominy of the few. William McKinley decided
to accommodate as many volunteers as possible. "If you have
too many troops," he told Alger, "that is my fault. If you have
too few, that will be your fault." [42] Later he sent a reminder:

"Too many is just enough." [43] Alger, writing a friend of those "more than a million men [who] have offered their services," added his fear that "there is going to be more trouble to satisfy those who are not going than to find those who are willing to go." [44] Here, to the degree he believed that putting men in uniform would satisfy their desire for participation, the secretary of war miscalculated. It was combat, not military service, that the volunteers courted, and Alger soon discovered that they would object strenuously as all but a relative few found themselves barred from the road to San Juan Hill.

Designations of units to participate in the expeditions against Cuba, Puerto Rico, and the Philippines stood as the most dramatic dividers. Roosevelt recalled in a letter to his sister that he "could not help feeling very bitterly when it seemed that I would be left [behind in Tampa]." [45] Those who were excluded were often inconsolable. [46] Insistent on their conception of war, unwilling to permit the federal government to define for them what constituted patriotism, duty, or national emergency, volunteers rebelled as soon as they concluded that combat would be denied them. [47] Leonard Wood predicted correctly that unless Americans fought Spaniards, they would soon fight one another. [48] When "Grigsby's Cowboys" attempted to break into the theater at Camp Thomas, provost guards charged with bayonets, injuring a dozen men. [49] Though most volunteer units escaped violence, few avoided deterioration. Six hundred Pennsylvania boys at Camp Alger, Virginia, decided to go home for the Fourth of July; cavalry detachments pursued them. [50] A letter printed in a Toledo daily spoke to an almost universal condition: "Since there was no chance of the Sixth getting into actual war, things have grown very monotonous and desertions are of almost daily occurrence. . . . They claim they did not intend to desert, but skipped out from camp to take a run home for a few days and have a good time." [51] Clyde's volunteer company, protested the *Enterprise,* "fancies fighting but not loafing. . . . There ought to be some way to send these boys home until their services are needed." [52]

In describing the battle of Manila, Admiral George Dewey attempted to distinguish two varieties of discipline: while American crews might lack "the etiquette of discipline," such was immaterial "if the spirit of discipline exists." [53] In an Army of volunteer companies, hometown ties, as we have seen, made impossible the imposition of the etiquette of discipline. The resulting casualness of military operation might perturb professional officers, but combat companies were in little danger of losing the spirit of discipline as long as their members were able to retain their anticipation of the personal encounter with the enemy. Many training and garrison units compelled to remain behind approached the point of disintegration during the summer of 1898. "The increased Army had hardly been organized," Alger noted, "before the clamor for discharge from the service began." [54] A correspondent for the *Manchester Guardian,* John Black Atkins, was surprised in the spring of 1898 to find young Americans hurrying home from overseas just "to join in the scrap." [55] Had he not been busy covering the fighting in Cuba, he might have been equally surprised and less impressed by those who likely returned abroad before the war's end when the scrap proved elusive.

Even those whose chances of combat were bright found delay unbearable after the departure of Shafter's expedition. Augustus Gardner, then a captain on General James H. Wilson's staff, wrote to his wife that he feared "Santiago will fall before we get there." [56] Six days later he again subordinated national war aims to personal goals: "Every one here is frightfully dispirited at the sudden change in orders. You can't find a man who cares a damn whether there is yellow fever in Santiago or not, or who experienced any pleasure at the news of [that city's] surrender [to Shafter's army]." [57] On August 2, now closer to combat but constantly worried that it might still be snatched from him, he wrote from Puerto Rico: "The rumors of peace are thick, and every one is more disgusted than ever. I am not blood-thirsty; but I should like to see a little real fighting after all the farce." [58]

The volunteers of Hamilton, Ohio, transported from home to Camp Thomas and then, in Florida, from Tampa to Fernandina to Jacksonville, were even more unhappy with the news of an armistice. They "were naturally discouraged at the unexpected turn things had taken for, in their estimation, the United States had been altogether too hasty in concluding the war." They had had "no fair chance at the enemy." [59]

Home towns, reflecting the soldiers' anger and sense of betrayal, rallied to the support of their companies with maximum political pressure for early discharge. The final note, however, was sometimes different—a note of defense, almost apology, for the boys' failure to achieve their personal encounter with the enemy. Said the Toledo *Blade* on the eve of Company I's return from occupation duty in Puerto Rico: "They have had an arduous year of it. It is not their fault that they did not participate in the battles fought in Cuba and Porto Rico. Active life in the field would have been preferred by officers and men to the duties of the routine camp. . . . [Everywhere] the boys have proved themselves to be men. Northwest Ohio is just as proud of the boys of the Sixth as if they had fought before Santiago and had been with [General Nelson A.] Miles in Porto Rico. We all know they would have acted their part, no matter how trying the situation." [60]

Those chosen for the Santiago campaign—"a regiment here, a regiment there," Bigelow complained [61]—were of course elated and therefore willing to overlook much. The vessels that carried them to Cuba were foul, semi-converted animal and cargo carriers. Food was scanty and barely edible. There was practically no provision for medical care to the sick. Still, the anticipation of combat sufficed. Private Post spoke for those whose priorities remained unshaken: "No one could be really mad—hell, we were off to Cuba, weren't we?" [62]

Disillusionment, however, soon overtook those of Shafter's command who landed in southeastern Cuba in mid-June 1898 and fought the skirmish at Las Guasimas and the two battles of El Caney and San Juan that constituted the entire land campaign. The war took unanticipated forms. The climactic experience, grappling with the Spaniard, once more proved fugitive. The volunteer had calculated that the results of combat would not be random, that the distribution of living and dead would reflect the mettle of those engaged. His own fate would turn on the quality of his performance in battle. From the day of their landing at Daiquiri, however, Americans were regularly denied the ability to see their enemy, a vital element in the war of personal combat. The foliage was dense beyond the beaches. Adopting a tactic of the Cuban guerrillas, the enemy hid sharpshooters in the trees. The POP of the Spanish Mausers—"like a soda-water bottle being opened close to the ear," said Stephen Crane [63]—cut down Americans who had never glimpsed the enemy. The reporter Edward Marshall conveyed the suddenness and finality of the event: "The man lives, he is strong, he is vital . . . when suddenly, 'chug' he is dead." [64] Those hit regarded themselves "with astonishment rather than with despair," [65] shocked that decisions were being rendered with none of that moral involvement they were determined to invest.

During that first clash at Las Guasimas the enemy's invisibility produced as much stress as his bullets. "How helpless, oh, how helpless we feel." [66] Of the subsequent fight at El Caney a member of the Second Massachusetts said, "The buggers are hidden behind rocks, in weeds and in underbrush, and we just simply can't locate them; they are shooting our men all to pieces." [67] Roosevelt himself admitted bewilderment. It was a terrible test to be exposed to an enemy but unable to close with him or even return his fire. It was "astonishing" that there was such a "limited area of vision and experience . . . in the hurly burly of a battle." "Most of the land is covered with a dense tropical jungle. This was what made it so hard for us in the fight [at Las Guasimas]. It was very trying to stand, or advance slowly, while the men fell dead or wounded, shot down from we knew not whence; for smokeless powder renders it almost impossible to place a hidden foe." [68] Atkins caught the same reaction at San Juan: "To the private soldier the whole thing was mysterious, unnerving, baffling. Where was the fire coming from?" [69]

The impersonality of bullets fired by unseen assailants seared permanently some of the American participants. Private Post was one who set his preconceptions against his shock and decided that his experience mocked war as a test of individual virtue. "That killing of an enemy," he concluded, "was not a personal matter but rather a wholly abstract and necessary incident. We had seen but few Spaniards. But we had killed and been killed." He had, he thought, now moved beyond the days of a "frenzied civilianism." [70] The impatient Gardner finally found "a little real fighting" at Coamo in Puerto Rico, but felt none of the anticipated exaltation: "It is almost impossible to realize that it is you they are firing at. You feel like saying, 'You damn fools, don't point your confounded guns this way.' " And to his wife he wrote, "I can't help being glad the war is over. Any man who has been under a hot fire and says he was not afraid is either a fool or a liar. . . ." [71]

For soldiers like Roosevelt, caught in exposed positions, seen but not seeing, there was only one solution: press on and close with the enemy. "All simply knew," said Brigadier General William Auman, "that a mad drive must be made to the front and whatever might be encountered must be defeated." [72] Success awaited them. Since the Spaniards had constructed their main defense lines at El Caney and along the San Juan ridges in relatively open terrain, American charges did in the end restore some personal meaning to combat. They were chaotic affairs, in no sense responses to higher military direction.[73] Bigelow's experience may serve for many others. His Tenth Cavalry, a regular unit, "advanced without any command that I know of, and the men commenced firing of their own accord. I tried to stop the firing, as I thought it would dangerously retard the advance, and other officers near me tried also to stop it. I even pointed my pistol at the men. But it was no use. . . . As we approached the hill I asked an officer near me whether he did not think we should try to halt the men, and open a regular fire upon the top of the hill. He replied to the effect that we could not halt them, and that they might as well keep a-going. So on we went." [74] Wrote John R. Conn, a black trooper: "Men were crazy. Someone said, 'Let us charge' and someone sounded 'Let us charge' on a bugle. . . [and] that pack of demons swept forward. . . ." [75] Stephen Crane called San Juan a "soldiers' battle" fought by those who had no orders and those who disobeyed whatever orders they had. [76]

In what would become the most famous charge of the war Roosevelt led some of his Rough Riders, some from other units, up Kettle Hill, a small outcropping below and to the right of the principal Spanish fortifications on San Juan ridge. To see the enemy, to move at them, was relief and deliverance. One of Roosevelt's troopers, Edgar A. Knapp, revealed exaltation's triumph, still incomplete, over fear: ". . . we made our charge on the Hill . . . and it was a daisy, except for our terrible losses as men fell on all sides of us as we rushed up. A charge of this kind is a wonderful thing, as when you see a man leading you and all are rushing and cheering the biggest coward in the world could not resist rushing forward, even though he knew for a certainty that he would be shot." [77] It was, wrote Stephen Crane, "the best moment of anybody's life." [78]

Near the summit Roosevelt shot a Spanish officer with his pistol. Later he wrote home of this crucial experience: "Did I tell you I killed a Spaniard with my own hand." [79] His sister Corinne penetrated his attempt at understatement. " 'I' was revelling in victory. He had just 'doubled-up' a Spanish officer like a jack-rabbit, as he [the Spaniard] retreated from a block house. . . ." [80] Others felt similar fulfillment. Post met a wounded man who exulted, "Damn near stepped on the [Spanish] sonofabitch—then he got me. But I got him. I got mine. Now you go an' git yours." [81]

Not surprisingly, the Spanish sensed the personal quality of their opponents' antagonism. An American officer reported to the War Department: "It is understood that the Spanish object to the American style of fighting, as being a kind to which they were unaccustomed; their criticism being that the 10th (colored) United States Cavalry neither returned the Spanish fire nor retreated when fired upon from the heights, but just kept straight on up the hill. . . ." [82] A Spanish prisoner complained that the Americans did not observe the rules of the game, that "they tried to catch us with their hands." [83]

❖ ❖ ❖

With the seizure of San Juan, the land campaign in Cuba ended. Santiago surrendered on July 16, 1898. To the surprise of the men in Shafter's army, an even more harrowing ordeal lay ahead. No one had given much thought to sickness. It fit very awkwardly into a war of personal engagement; participants who assumed a link between moral force and physical vitality and thus perceived no need to precautionary measures, were likely to be disillusioned once serious sickness struck. The Army was not unaware of the dangers of tropical disease. The surgeon-general's circular of April 25 ordered elaborate safeguards. American soldiers were to boil water, sleep off the ground, protect themselves from the rain, and change clothes regularly. [84] That officer's intentions were laudable but his basic assumption—that instructions issued to units of the new Army would receive the attention given them in the constabulary—was inaccurate. He and others then proceeded to invite disaster by making preparations on the basis of strict compliance.

Reflecting the priorities of those around him, Shafter ordered all but seven ambulances left at Tampa to make space for more men. [85] So inadequate were the field hospitals that George Kennan, a writer and vice-president of the American Red Cross, cried out, "If there was anything more terrible in our Civil War, I am glad I was not there to see it." [86] Roosevelt found them so frightful that he would not send men to the rear "unless there was no escape." [87] Clara Barton's Red Cross

organization was told that it would be needed only to assist
Cuban reconcentrados. Even when Medical Corps facilities
were overwhelmed with sick and wounded soldiers, the surgeon in charge refused an offer of help from trained Red Cross
nurses. It was, he maintained until overruled by Washington,
not the place for women.[88]

Not even in battle did the American reluctance to subordinate the individual to joint undertakings prove more fateful.
After all, with the dense vegetation of southeastern Cuba rul-
ing out large-scale tactical movements, the lack of cooperation
within and between American units produced no decisive
military deficit. In mundane matters of hygiene, however, the
inability to organize effectively above the individual level became a critical matter. Who, intent on the chase after the
Spaniard, bothered to dig a drainage ditch, or a latrine? Who,
aching and tired, hesitated to accept the shelter of a fever-
infested hut that should have been burned? Who boiled a cup-
ful of water when he was thirsty?

Even where officers appreciated the danger and believed
they could command or persuade their men to health care, the
necessary equipment was lacking. "Orders were issued for us
to boil all our drinking water," recalled Captain Bigelow, but
"we had nothing to boil anything in but our tin-cups, which
held about one-third of the contents of a canteen." The
surgeon-general had also urged the soldiers to keep well fed:
"It was impossible to cook for the troop collectively," wrote
Bigelow, "as we had no kettles or other cooking-utensils, except the tin-cups and mess-pans carried by the men individually." [89]

The equipment shortage was another point of anguish and
later recrimination, another of those problems unanticipated
but predictable within the public's conceptualization of the
war. The editor Henry Watterson caught in an interesting way
the American subordination of technical to spiritual power:
"It was not the armor, the fortification, or the gun that was to

decide the contest; but the men behind the gun and the institutions behind the men." [90] Predictably, no one at first paid
any special concern to the gun. Although the regulars had new
.30 caliber Krag-Jorgensen rifles, National Guard units carried
Civil War Springfields that used black powder neatly marking
their position for the enemy's counterfire.[91] Against the troops
of a nation rapidly approaching first position in the world's
industrial index, the soldiers of a presumably degenerate European monarchy used modern Mauser rifles and smokeless
powder. Some Americans, perhaps more imbued with the
tenets of individual combat than the majority of their countrymen, were left undismayed by the disparity in weapons. General James Harrison Wilson noted the Ordnance Department's
conviction that Springfields were "good enough for fighting the
Spaniards." [92] Watterson himself welcomed the opportunity
offered American soldiers to demonstrate that their mechani-
cal skill could make the Springfields superior to the Mauser.[93]
Such sentiments came close to offering an inferior enemy
special odds in the game of war.[94]

Soldiers intent on personal goals whose achievement seemed
unrelated to the possibility of sickness; orders unenforced;
vital supplies undelivered: the result was illness of epidemic
proportion that overwhelmed the Fifth Corps. A week after
San Juan only four hundred of the nine hundred troopers
in Private Post's regiment were fit for duty. The buglers were
too sick to blow their calls.[95] On July 14 Captain Brown's
regulars counted forty men out of sixty-six; four days later
seventeen could stand.[96] Of the 456 black soldiers of the
Twenty-fourth Infantry who marched to Siboney, many to
serve as volunteers in hospitals, only 24 escaped illness.[97]
Atkins thought that at the time of Santiago's surrender only
10 percent of the Americans could have continued fighting.[98]
Drastic as that estimate appears, it found confirmation in an
authoritative source: Alger later admitted that 90 percent of
Shafter's men debarked at American ports sick or convales-

cent.[99] The toll was evident everywhere. William Paulding, who lost 90 of his 170 pounds, noticed that his hands were transparent to the light.[100] On their return to McKinley's home town, "young men twenty to twenty-five looked like old men."[101]

The United States suffered 345 battle deaths during the Spanish-American War; 5462 were lost to illness, a ratio 1:15.[102] Alger, pointing out that supposedly fever-immune Southern regiments suffered no less sickness, claimed that disease was uncontrollable, war's inevitable partner.[103] At Guantanamo, however, an isolated detachment of Marines under Lieutenant Colonel Robert W. Huntington survived ten weeks in terrain no different from that surrounding Santiago, with a two-and-one-half percent sick rate and no one lost to disease. Huntington insisted upon, and was able to enforce, the surgeon-general's instructions.[104] Widespread illness became *this* war's inevitable companion, not because of a medical science still inadequate to deal with the problem, but because of American attitudes toward the war. It is true, as Kennan charged, that United States troops were "not half equipped, not half fed, nor half cared for when they were wounded or sick."[105] It is equally true that the American public for whom combat carried the full meaning of the war did not comprehend until too late that supply and medical care might dispose of the fates of more men than the charge against the Spaniards.

Theodore Roosevelt was fortunate that his experience of battle so closely fitted his preconceptions—and that he achieved the personal encounter. There were even in his case, however, jagged fragments of experience that would have to be refitted or forgotten. That bewilderment before the enemy could be brought within sight; a fear close to panic; the realization of personal jeopardy and discomfort—these feelings overwhelmed the heroic in Roosevelt's letter to his friend Henry Cabot Lodge shortly after the climactic charge.

> Tell the President for Heaven's sake to send us every regiment and above all every battery possible. We have won so far at a heavy cost; but the Spaniards fight very hard and charging these intrenchments against modern rifles is terrible. We are within measurable distance of a terrible military disaster; we *must* have help—thousands of men, batteries, and *food* and ammunition. The other volunteers are at a hideous disadvantage owing to their not having smokeless powder. Our General [Shafter] is poor; he is too unwieldy to get to the front. I commanded my regiment, I think I may say, with honor. We lost a quarter of our men. For three days I have been at the extreme front of the firing line; how I escaped I know not; I have not blanket or coat; I have not taken off my shoes even; I sleep in the drenching rain, and drink putrid water.[106]

During the first days of August Roosevelt was a key figure in the composition and publication of the celebrated Round Robin that warned the American public, "This army must be moved at once or perish." [107] On August 7 main elements of the Fifth Corps sailed for home.

The fears of July, the alarm of early August receded quickly. Roosevelt had remained throughout "as big and as strong as a bull moose." [108] Physically unimpaired, he found it easier than most to reestablish the lineaments of his basic accomplishment: he had led his men with distinction; he had overcome frightening and unanticipated obstacles; he had met the enemy in personal combat and vanquished him. The personal-heroic lesson regained its luster. Roosevelt recalled an incident prior to the charge up Kettle Hill. Standing upright and exposed to Spanish fire, he had found a trooper skulking in the brush and had chided him for his cowardice. Seconds later, shots enveloped them both. The trooper, though lying prone, was shot through the body while Roosevelt was untouched.[109] The moral was clear. Only the brave were safe. War's decisions were purposeful, discriminating.

By September 15, the day the Rough Riders were mustered out of federal service at Montauk Point, Long Island, no phantom doubts remained. Roosevelt was already nostalgic: "Oh, well! So all things pass away. But they were beautiful days." [110] Thereafter the war experience became his wellspring of pride and reassurance. Admiring newspaper reporters and later his own pen gave it an important public dimension. The Rough Rider hat waved from numberless campaign platforms [111] spoke his awareness that an important part of his public allure derived from his success in realizing, as so few had done, American preconceptions of the Spanish-American War. Theodore Roosevelt was the assurance that war still meant what men expected it to mean.

The war experience was essential to Roosevelt's political career in a private as well as a public sense. Afflicted by a recurring sense of isolation, he often felt the presence of great forces marshaled against him, determined to crush him simply because he stood as a force for "right" and "decency." Whether as Civil Service commissioner, assistant secretary of the Navy, lieutenant colonel, governor, vice-president, or president, Roosevelt wrote of his own virtue isolated and impotent, of the perfect job he might have done had not opposing forces joined to block his projects.[112] Roosevelt never rid himself of what Owen Wister called his friend's "many darknesses." [113] Indeed they returned with special severity in his last years. But 1898 helped him endure the worst of these moods. The psychic return of the Santiago campaign was notable: Theodore Roosevelt had tested himself, had accomplished a personal feat of arms while leading a group of men representing his society. The virtues he demonstrated *had* drawn from the nation an approbation that seemed to promise emulation. He had fused the highest personal and social values in a single experience and had merged himself, temporarily at least, with his society.

A short time before his death he looked back and concluded, "San Juan was the great day of my life." [114]

CHAPTER V   *The Image of Enemy and Ally*

NINETEENTH-CENTURY LIFE seldom required Americans to think deeply on the nature of foreign peoples. The larger world rarely intruded. When a foreign crisis did penetrate the crust of their aloofness, however, Americans were not as unprepared as one might suspect of a people in only sporadic and superficial contact with other societies. Challenged from abroad, they did not halt and reflect afresh on the nature of a particular antagonist, for a complete characterization already existed. Americans automatically referred to a collective compendium of national images that assigned values to every overseas people.

Supporting such images were assumptions that, at best, lacked scientific rigor. The general belief was that, like the United States, other nations possessed histories unique to themselves, single streams that neither mingled with other flows nor converged into the larger waters of regional or world history. From each national experience Americans distilled what they deemed its critical events and dominant personalities. From these they extracted moral values that they believed would accurately characterize that people in every era. History, so interpreted, was the index to a people's vice and virtue.

In nineteenth-century America the single most important source of such images was the grammar-school reader.

No people fared worse in the schoolbooks than the Spanish. In the American view, Spanish history was a syllabus of barbarism that left both participants and their progeny morally misshapen. Such an image, moreover, did not exist only as an intellectual abstraction. With so few alternative sources of information available, it often set the lines of political debate. In the prelude to the Spanish-American War those who wished to resist American intervention in Cuba were handicapped by their inability to say anything in defense of the Spanish character. Those who urged American participation had the easier task of demonstrating that Spanish behavior was the simple extension of that Spanish history every American had memorized from his reader.

Americans at first hardly distinguished the image of the Cuban from that of the Spaniard. As anger against Spain mounted, however, it became necessary for them to differentiate, to convert to ally the enemy of their enemy. This was accomplished, but not through any objective examination of the conditions or attributes of the Cuban people. Instead, Americans of public consequence employed various and often contradictory historical analogies which, with scant reference to the Cubans themselves, had by 1898 persuaded most Americans that the Cubans were a moral, enlightened, and kindred race. The first physical contacts of American with Cuban and Spaniard would test these images of good and evil.

❖ ❖ ❖

In mid-December 1895 President Grover Cleveland and Secretary of State Richard Olney precipitated a diplomatic crisis over a fifty-year-old boundary dispute between Venezuela and Great Britain's colony of Guiana. Angry at London's rejection of earlier Washington suggestions that the controversy be submitted to arbitration, the president announced to Congress on December 17 his decision to appoint an American commission to determine the "true divisional line" between the two territories. Once the boundary was set, Cleveland warned, "it will . . . be the duty of the United States to resist, by every means in its power, as a willful aggression upon its rights and interests, the appropriation by Great Britain of any lands or the exercise of governmental jurisdiction over any territory which . . . we have determined of right belongs to Venezuela." [1] The United States, charging Britain with violating the Monroe Doctrine, threatened war.

The Venezuelan crisis, though generative of intense feeling, subsided within two weeks. Lord Salisbury's government, shocked by the vehemence of Cleveland's notes and struggling to meet another unanticipated emergency provoked by Doctor Jameson's raid into the Transvaal,[2] agreed to arbitration. Despite his resort to incendiary prose, the president did not desire war [3] and revealed that he too was receptive to compromise. Four years later all parties accepted the findings of an international investigating commission.

Of special concern here are the terms employed by Americans in debating the meaning of Britain's behavior.

Joseph Pulitzer—in 1864 an emaciated German-Hungarian immigrant without resources save for his own will to succeed, thirty years later the powerful publisher of the New York *World* whose extraordinary energies had already cracked the frail shell of his body—was one of those who led public opposition to Cleveland's policy. The president's bludgeon diplomacy, he told the *World's* half-million readers, was "a grave blunder" [4]; an Anglo-American war would be unpardonable folly. Into his antiwar editorials Pulitzer wove three themes. There was in the Venezuelan dispute, he insisted, no possible menace to the United States. He further denied Cleveland's contention that the controversy challenged, or that its outcome could affect, the validity of the Monroe Doctrine. Finally, he cautioned against what he judged to be the nation's state: "Let the war idea once dominate the minds of the

American people and war will come whether there is cause for it or not" [5]—an interesting hypothesis that Pulitzer himself did much to verify two years later.

Laced through these arguments were the lineaments of an image of a Britain benevolently disposed to American interests, of an admirable people friend rather than foe. England was a "friendly and kindred nation," [6] "the great naval and commercial and banking nation of the world" [7] whose political system was "essentially . . . of the people, more quickly and completely responsible to the popular will as expressed in the elections than our government is." [8] In Pulitzer's mind England and the United States stood together on grounds both religious ("the two representative Christian nations of the world") [9] and political ("the two great free nations of the world").[10] Racial affinity, similar levels of civilization and the past were other important ties. The *World* printed with approval a speech in which George F. Hoar summoned historical analogy to the aid of Pulitzer's argument. "The Pilgrims were Englishmen," said the Massachusetts senator. "Their children are, in the essentials, Englishmen still . . . English aptness for command, habit of success, indomitable courage, unconquerable perseverance have been, are and are to remain the American quality." [11]

In short, who the English were determined what the English did. By definition, kindred peoples would not harm one another's vital interests in Venezuela or anywhere else. War was incomprehensible when Anglo-American ties meant that it must be a species of civil war.

Supporters of the Cleveland-Olney ultimatum wove into their attack on the English a very different image. Henry Cabot Lodge charged that the British government, having already hemmed in the United States with a fortified line in the Pacific, was forging another ring in the Caribbean. London had recently fortified Santa Lucia, Trinidad, and Jamaica. The South American mainland was the next, but not the final, link. "If . . . [Britain] can do it successfully in Venezuela

she can do it in Mexico or Cuba; if she can do it other nations can also." [12]

Lodge found nothing remarkable in such notions of British
conspiracy. It was the thing to expect of a people no less
treacherous and hostile to American interests than any other
people. As he earlier told the Senate, "Since we parted from
England her statesmen have never failed to recognize that in
men speaking her language, and of her own race she was to
find her most formidable rivals. She has always opposed,
thwarted, and sought to injure us." [13] Lodge, too, summoned
historical analogy: Cleveland's critics "tell us that this territory [disputed by Venezuela and British Guiana] is remote
and worthless . . . [but] it matters not whether it is worthless
or valuable. The tea tax was trivial, but our forefathers refused to pay it because it involved a great principle, and the
attempt to collect it cost Great Britain her North American
colonies." [14]

Neither firebrand nor conciliator was fully immune to the
other's image of England. Amid the bristling indignation of
his message to Congress, Cleveland still conceded that it was
"a grievous thing to contemplate the two great English-
speaking peoples of the world as being otherwise than
friendly competitors in the onward march of civilization and
strenuous and worthy rivals in all the arts of peace." [15] On
the opposite flank Hoar argued for American recognition of
kinship with Englishmen "in spite of past conflicts and present
rivalry." [16] The absence of a strict polarity should not, however, disguise that Cleveland's supporters and detractors
marshaled their arguments around two competitive images of
the British. Partisans portrayed Britain as villain and presented the current crisis as a simple extension of that British
oppression antedating the Revolution. Cleveland's opponents
cited ties of ancestry, religion, and political structure to argue
that a Britain basically benevolent could intend no injury to
this country. Clearly, once Cleveland forced the matter on the
public's attention, the image of England supplied much of
the meaning of what England was doing in Venezuela.

Did England's behavior constitute a threat to the United States? One's answer had less to do with London's behavior in this particular controversy, still less with what was transpiring on the banks of the Orinoco, than on the image of England that Cleveland's message summoned to mind. The availability of alternative images set the lines of the American debate.

In a valuable study Ruth Miller Elson has suggested the influence of the stereotyped figures of foreign nationalities so prominent in the grammar-school readers one hundred years ago.[17] The belief that specific personality traits inhere in all members of designated nationality groups is still today a part of our intellectual baggage, but several factors added to the tyranny of nineteenth-century national images. Children, spending on average far fewer years in school, were deeply stamped by the long passages they were compelled to memorize. Moreover, American small-town life offered few of the experiences that today render rigid national stereotypes vulnerable to a more complex reality. Only the rich traveled abroad. Few European tourists or cultural organizations visited this country. Until the twentieth century transoceanic business contact was confined to a few large centers on the eastern seaboard. Immigrants were numerous in east and midwest, but native-born citizens assumed that all those of foreign origins were Americanizing. Favorable traits that seemed at odds with derogatory stereotypes could thus be ascribed to the recent acquisition of American characteristics, leaving the stereotypes intact. No media penetrated this cultural curtain.

A people buoyed by a sense of its own uniqueness, requiring no continuous relationships with other nationalities, and lacking bridges between its own and other cultures, was likely to find authoritative the lessons of the reader, "that first and only formal presentation of other nations." [18]

The world of the nineteenth-century schoolbook was almost static. Authors precipitated from each nation's history certain men and events on which they pronounced moral judgment and then offered the reader as the embodiment of a collective personality. The character traits thus extracted were often more censorious than complimentary, but almost every characterization combined the two categories. The English, as the rhetoric of the Venezuelan crisis made clear, could be both exemplar and oppressor, a parent solicitous, neglectful, or cruel. The Irish were ignorant, violent, uncivilized, and superstitious (the latter term often a nineteenth-century codeword for Catholic), but the Irish were also witty, warm, and hospitable. To judge by the readers, Americans admired the French as the people of Lafayette, a man of unalloyed virtue given a prominence in the books second only to George Washington. Napoleon was a man of undeniable force, on balance a respected figure to bring credit to his country. But there was also about the French another, less luminous aura: that of revolutionary terror; of un-American excess; of atheism and hyperrationality; of frivolity and even licentiousness. The image of the Italians was similarly skewed: Catholic, vengeful, effeminate, immoral, they were partially redeemed by their affability and artistic accomplishment.[19]

Only a few nationalities, Mrs. Elson discovered, merited unequivocal characterization. The images of Swiss and Scot were entirely complimentary. Praised almost as widely was the German, whose "military character" American authors recognized and regarded, at least until the early twentieth century, as a positive or at worst a neutral trait.[20]

By contrast, schoolbooks found almost nothing to praise in the Spanish. No other people was confined within such a narrow range of the authors' moral spectrum, or so limited to the dark bands. Others were granted some movement between the reprehensible and the laudable—the French record, as noted above, disclosed both a Terror and a Lafayette—but Spanish history apparently offered no alternation, no examples of the meritorious. Moreover, in the 1890s the range was narrowing even further.[21] Characteristics that drew American attention (though not necessarily praise) at midcentury—Spanish dignity, honor, military prowess—were subject to slow dilution, it seemed, as Spain disintegrated. That was nothing worthy, and much that was repugnant to Americans, in a conqueror grown indolent.

Harper's Pictorial History of the War with Spain, following the schoolbooks, saw Spanish history as an exposition of Spanish character. Spaniards, resisting the law of progress in which Americans believed, had never emerged from the dark ages. The Spanish character thus possessed an "inner core of cruelty." In Spanish history one could trace "this blood-red line of cruelty, entwined with a strand of golden greed, back through the black ages to . . . a remote ancestry." [22] *Harper's* historical "evidence" was standard: the Inquisition; Spanish conquistadores burning West Indian caciques or setting loose their dogs to tear apart hapless Indians; the garroting of the Inca Atahualpa; the betrayal of Montezuma; the cruelties the Duke of Alva inflicted on Hollanders. There was no variety, nor much charity, in the American view. Even the Spanish guerrilla war waged against Napoleon's soldiers, an episode that Americans might have applauded as the resistance of a brave people determined to protect its independence against a foreign tyrant, became instead another object-lesson in Spanish perfidy: "The French who fell into the hands of the Spaniards during the Peninsular War were invariably murdered." [23]

It was possible to push the indictment of Spanish cruelty a step further. Spanish methods were more than indefensible; they were unavailing. Unlike Napoleon, the Spanish produced no results that might mitigate their choice of means. "No single good thing in law, or science, or art, or literature . . . has resulted to the race of men . . . from Spanish domination in America. . . . I have tried to think of one in vain," announced Charles Francis Adams in 1897.[24] The same theme received scholarly treatment six months later when the president of the University of Wisconsin asked graduating seniors: "What has Spain ever done for civilization? What books, what inventions have come from Spain? What discoveries in the laboratory or in scientific fields?" His own answer was brief: "So few have they been that they are scarcely worth mentioning." He then returned in the climax of his address to the central American perception of Spain—changeless cruelty. "Examination of the Spanish character shows it to be the same as it was centuries ago. Wherever the Spaniard has endeavored to rule he has shown an unrivaled incapacity for government. And the incapacity was such and the cruelty was such that all their colonies and provinces have slipped away." [25]

Americans incorporated into this image individuals as well as events. William Dean Howells, a man very sensitive to the transformation of the 1898 war from one of Cuban liberation to one of colonial acquisition, visited Spanish prisoners of war at Portsmouth, New Hampshire. Those he saw seemed less evil incarnate than hapless Spanish peasants and fishermen. Describing his feelings in *Harper's Weekly*, he implored his countrymen. "When we remember Cortez, let us not forget Las Casas," [26] the Jesuit who protested Spain's exploitation of South American Indians. Such pleas were futile. The textbooks had not overlooked Las Casas and other Spanish humanitarians. But instead of presenting them as evidence that every people produces saints as well as rogues, authors offered them as the decisive argument in condemnation of the Spanish.[27] Las Casas had indicted his own countrymen for their cruelty. Who required additional proof?

Bastidas, the founder of St. Martha, New Granada, who was assassinated for objecting to Spanish exploitation of indigenous peoples, won no better literary fate. He was no expiator, concluded *Harper's*, but the "solitary exception which proves the rule." [28]

These textbook and periodical conceptions—a Spain stuck in its own history, frozen in her primitive stage, a people that had been and would be cruel—moved easily into the realm of political discussion. Henry Watterson wrote that from Cortez to Weyler the Spanish flag had been a symbol of "rapine and pillage." [29] Russell Hastings warned McKinley that "a Spaniard cannot buy a basket of eggs without intrigue." [30] Henry Cabot Lodge pronounced Spain "mediaeval, cruel, dying": Spaniards were "three hundred years behind all the rest of the world. What seems to us brutal treachery seems to them all right, and this is a fact well to remember in dealing with them." [31] Through the speeches of Ohio's Senator Joseph Benson Foraker runs this same simple thread: Spain was brutal and barbarous.[32] This was both incentive and justification for America's immediate intervention in Cuba.[33]

Foraker obviously countenanced immediate American action on the basis of this mental construct of the Spaniard. His image of the Spaniard was no abstraction, but the interpretive key to events elsewhere. Occasionally, the image was itself so strong that it replaced reality. James Creelman, a reporter for Pulitzer's *World*, interviewed General Valeriano Weyler Nicolau, the Spanish captain-general in Cuba. "Butcher" Weyler, "the most sinister figure of the nineteenth century," wore "a blood-red sash wound around his waistband." On his "smileless cruel face" was an expression of "brutal determination." He was "the fierce disciple of Cortez and Alva," "the incarnation of the surviving spirit of mediaeval Europe," and "the voice of the Middle Ages." [34] Creelman undoubtedly talked with Weyler, but when he came to write of the Spaniard, it was as if he had copied a page of his reader.

The image's ability to distort reality, to obscure the logic of particular situations, was most pronounced at the time of the *Maine's* destruction. Today, though neither proven nor disproven, official Spanish culpability seems unlikely: Spain had nothing to gain, and much to lose, by sinking the vessel. Today the American rush to condemn Spain appears a psychic aberration, a lapse into irrationality. At the time, however, the image of the Spaniard made any *other* explanation appear illogical. A sneak bombing against a background of treacherous assurances of Spanish goodwill; sleeping men plunged to watery graves—it was Spanish history come alive, this time with young Americans as its victims. Rough-shaped pieces of fact could be made to fit. When the Havana command offered the American survivors expressions of regret and every appropriate aid, Henry Watterson concluded that, while Cuban sadness was genuine, Spanish sympathy, so "ostentatious," must conceal an inward festiveness.[35]

The force of that same prejudgment is evident in the headlines of small midwestern newspapers:

The Fremont, Ohio, *Daily News* of October 8, 1897, headed a story on diplomatic relations:

> *The Dons Answer to Uncle Sam Will Probaby Be Evasive.*[36]

The Clyde, Ohio, *Enterprise* of May 10, 1895, headed as follows a story reporting that the Cuban rebels were "rapidly becoming discouraged":

> *This Is Probably Wrong* [37]

April 14, 1896:

> *MANY INSURGENTS KILLED*
> *At Least That Is The News Sent Out From Spanish Sources* [38]

May 19, 1896:

> *ANOTHER PROCLAMATION*
> *General Weyler Will Now Rob Cubans of All Their Corn* [39]

November 27, 1896:

> *WEYLER'S SYSTEM*
> *It Embraces Every Phase of Awful Cruelty* [40]

January 21, 1897:

> *THEY'RE PROUD OF IT*

Spaniards Talk About a "Great Victory" Near Havana
WAS A BRUTAL SLAUGHTER [41]

In no sense do such headlines represent an extension of big-city yellow journalism. Small-town editors shared little of Hearst's or Pulitzer's incendiarism. Their editorial policies remained conservative. Their aim was not to incite bellicosity but to convey the "facts" as they understood them.[42] The image of the Spaniard was accepted fact.

If there was near unanimity on the nature of the enemy, there remained considerable uncertainty regarding his capacity. The Spaniard was malevolent, all agreed, but what danger did he pose for Americans? On this point the image was ambiguous. Henry Cabot Lodge had spoken of Spain as "mediaeval, cruel, dying." How rapid was her decline? How much harm was she still capable of inflicting on others?

These questions produced speculation and considerable anxiety. Since there could be no definitive answers short of a test of arms, Americans anticipated war with ambivalent emotions. Those who often voiced the fear that the Spanish would not stand and fight could not always suppress the fear that they would. When Henry Watterson complained that Spanish courage was not the courage of "cool tenacity and hope," but that of desperation,[43] others sensed the unspoken corollary: desperate men could exact a high toll from their enemies.

No one caught better than Sherwood Anderson the American vacillation in definitions of Spanish prowess. At one moment he was confident war would be "a kind of glorious national picnic." [44] He could even indulge in a thin guilt that the job would be so easy, "like robbing an old gypsy woman in a vacant lot at night after a fair." [45] In other moments, however, the Spaniard as cyclonic evil seemed very near: "Dark cruel eyes, dark swaggering men in one's fancy." [46] Anderson dreamed of grappling with a Spanish commandant who, half drunk and surrounded by his concubines, plunged his sword into a serving-boy who had spilled the wine.[47] Americans like Sherwood Anderson, conceiving of themselves as moral vindicators, were given pause: was the Spaniard a still vigorous and thus dangerous evil-doer or only an unrepentant invalid?

This uncertainty may have had some bearing on the undulation of public emotion before and during the Spanish-American War. So often the objective situation seemed insufficient explanation for those roller coaster spurts up and down emotional inclines and through the curves. And, as at the amusement park, points of panic were numerous. The governor of Arizona had "not the slightest doubt" that Spanish sympathizers in Mexico would raid the territory and that "cattle thieves and desperados would . . . plunder and steal. . . ."[48] Businessmen in Bridgeport, Connecticut, believed that Hungarian immigrants in their midst were arming themselves and contemplating moves against the city's ordnance factories.[49] In the days of tension prior to the delivery of the president's war message, Minority Leader Joseph W. Bailey lost himself in the fear that William McKinley was scheming to force the House of Representatives into adjournment and would thereafter run the country on the $50,000,000 defense appropriation. Each member of the Democratic caucus swore to resist such an executive coup.[50] Never were oaths more solemn. Never was there less substance to charges of conspiracy.

Panic of greater magnitude developed shortly after the war began. American military intelligence lost contact with the Spanish Atlantic fleet as it lumbered from Old World harbor to New World grave. The east coast took alarm. Depositors transferred their savings to inland banks. Lessees insisted on provisions of redress in cases where Spanish gunfire destroyed shore properties. Towns demanded the protection of the American Navy. Assistant Secretary Theodore Roosevelt laughed and accurately called the affair a "comic panic,"[51] but the Navy Department continued to dispatch Civil War monitors to those towns whose representatives insisted on them.

Public tension before battles, public jubilation afterward, seems inordinate. The unprecedented celebration of Dewey's victory at Manila Bay suggests relief from the fear of disaster, disaster overtaking Americans in distant islands so exotic and unfamiliar. Dewey was deified. In the Caribbean campaign too there were wide swings of emotion. General Shafter, vacillating between the enemy as destroyer and as invalid, was never able to gauge clearly the danger that the Spanish Army posed for his own forces. Indecisive, he tried in the aftermath of the battle of San Juan to act so as to encompass both images. At the same moment that he telegraphed Washington that his Army was in such extreme danger that he was preparing to retreat, he sent an ultimatum to his opponent demanding the immediate surrender of Santiago. Americans certain of Spanish malevolence but unsure of Spanish power swung rapidly back and forth between an almost swaggering confidence and a deep-seated dread, between excessive celebration and excessive fear.

The image of the Cuban had at first none of the compelling emotional quality of the Spaniard. Indeed, since few Americans prior to 1895 counted the Cubans a distinct people, the image of the ally required simultaneously both separation from the image of the enemy and a delineation of its own.

The crafting of distinctions between Cuban and Spaniard did not begin with the arrival of the news of the Cuban revolt. Americans convinced of Spanish immorality assumed, correctly, that there had been considerable racial mixture in Cuba; Cubans must have thereby inherited every unlovely Spanish trait. Learning of the Cuban insurrection, Americans did not rush to embrace Cubans as kindred. There was no automatic assumption of Cuban virtue as there was of Spanish wrongdoing. Initial statements reveal both denunciation of the Spaniards *and* a deprecation of the *insurrectos* that hewed to Madrid's line. The Cubans were insignificant black rioters or

bandits who would be easily dispersed.[52] Richard Franklin Pet-
tigrew, a South Dakota senator who wished war because he
thought it would remonetize silver, cared nothing for Spaniard or Cuban: the best idea was to sink the island for twenty-
four hours "to get rid of its present population." [53] A prominent
Methodist clergyman thought the Cubans "indolent, seditious,
ignorant, superstitious and greatly useless." [54] Somewhat less
genteel was William Allen White: the Cubans were "Mongrels
with no capacity for self government . . . a yellow-legged,
knife-sticking, treacherous outfit." [55] Speaker of the House
Reed called them "yellow-bellies." [56]

No evidence suggests that Reed, with McKinley a last-
ditch opponent of the war, ever changed his mind about
Cuban deficiencies. There is, however, ample evidence for the
assertion that in the period 1895–97 the majority of Americans
began to view Cubans in a favorable, or at least a different,
way. It became increasingly difficult to deny sympathy to an
enemy of *the* enemy. How could the Spaniards so richly deserve chastisement if the Cubans were undeserving of freedom? How could American strength secure justice for the
weak if the weak were themselves malicious?

The solution was to refocus attention away from the Cubans,
avoiding any examination of them as a discrete people, and to
reinterpret the Cuban insurrection through a series of historical analogies that fostered emotional affiliation with the insurrectionists quite independent of their characteristics as Cubans.
Harper's Weekly was one of a few publications to grasp the
process. In their concern for "the cause of eternal justice"
and the immediate expulsion of the Spanish, the magazine complained, "Americans have not inquired as to the merits of the
Cubans." [57] An equally perceptive organization was the Cuban
Junta. Its policy was not to extol the Cuban but to tar the
Spaniard, letting Cuban virute emerge implicitly and by contrast.

To some Americans the Cuban rising became a latter-day
American Revolution. Richard Harding Davis, watching a

Spanish firing squad execute an "erect and soldierly" Cuban youth named Rodriquez, invoked for his many readers the death of Nathan Hale.[58] Governor John P. Altgeld of Illinois declared in public address that the Cubans' struggle was their American Revolution,[59] and Senator George G. Vest of Missouri drew out the moral: the insurrectionists deserved American support because they were emulating the American experience.[60] Senator William E. Mason of Illinois claimed a more substantial connection. Cuban boys had come to our colleges, learned about George Washington and returned home to tell their compatriots. Revolution was an inevitable result.[61] These judgments were based on a widespread but erroneous assumption that the Cubans had revolted to secure, not their own government, but good government on the American model.

Another prominent analogy was that of the Cuban as Southerner. Many former Confederates discovered in Spanish oppression echoes of the North's military occupation of the South during Reconstruction. Joseph Bailey's biographer assigns nine-tenths of the Texan's sympathy to empathy with those whom he thought resisting the same sort of military despotism he had opposed three decades before.[62] Similarly, Joseph Wheeler coupled his service as the youngest Confederate corps commander with his advocacy of the Cubans, "our brethren struggling for liberty."[63] Such Americans saw the Cuban as oppressed white. Others summoned an identical sympathy by picturing the Cuban as Negro. The Union League, for example, welcomed war as opening prospects for a new crusade against the abuse of black people.[64] Racist and racial liberal thus moved from opposite poles to join hands in support of the Cuban.

Other groups looked to European history for images to unlock the meaning of events in the Caribbean. To staunch Protestants, especially the clergy, the Cubans were another in a series of peoples who had risen against Catholic oppression. (Anti-clericalism was an insignificant factor in the revolt of the Cubans. It was prominent in the Philippines, but few Americans had heard that there was an simultaneous Filipino uprising.) American Catholic publications, unable to support either "brigands" or a revolt advertised by Protestants as anti-Catholic, found a quite different analogy: Cuba was suffering Spanish tyranny as Ireland endured English tyranny.[65] Its persuasiveness lay in the suggestion that the Cubans, like the Irish, were oppressed *because* of their religion, the faithful persecuted for their beliefs. Its weakness lay in the necessity to overlook the Catholicism of the Spaniards.

Henry Demarest Lloyd found another analogy both seductive and plausible. The Chicago socialist wrote that in the struggle of the Netherlands to win independence from Spain he had found the precise parallel to events in Cuba. William McKinley he cast as a second William of Orange.[66] Lloyd, staunch anti-imperialist that he became, apparently failed to consider that the slightest extension of his logic would have made appropriate William McKinley's rule over those same Cubans.

The Populists, like some Southerners, may have seen in the Cuban experience reflections of their recent past.[67] During the 1896 presidential campaign the most powerful segment of the American press had condemned Populists as revolutionaries, but there in Cuba was revolution made respectable, revolution compelling all to proclaim its virtue. And though the crusade of 1896 had failed, could not American justice prevail in Cuba, if not yet at home?

However confusing and contradictory, the various roles which Americans imposed on the Cuban had one element in common: support for American intervention on behalf of the Cuban. However divided at home on political, economic, or religious grounds, Americans found an appropriate interventionist argument in the grab bag of history. Only once do the Spaniards appear to have attempted a riposte by historical analogy. When in mid-1897 McKinley protested to Madrid the harshness of its reconcentration policy, the reply argued that reconcentration "was no worse than the devastation in the Civil War by Sheridan and Hunter in the Shenandoah Valley and by Sherman in Georgia." [68] The president's reaction is not recorded, but one can imagine his anger at this threat to revive sectional animosities.

With admiration for the way Cubans were repeating history, or with sympathy for the way Cubans were suffering history, Americans discovered new resemblances between themselves and the insurrectionists. Here the color problem seemed a serious barrier to Cuban-American cooperation. At least one-third of the Cuban population was black, and "nigger" was a powerfully derogatory category in North and South. White Americans of the 1890s were all but unanimous in their belief in black inferiority and the necessity of the social separation of the races. For prominent Americans to champion the aspirations of a mixed people—for a Joseph Wheeler, for example, to wage a viciously negrophobic campaign for the House of Representatives and then refer to Cubans as "our brethren"— required reappraisal of Cuban color and temperament. One avenue, the use of historical analogies that either exploited or circumvented the racial issue, has been discussed. A second, appropriate to Americans dedicated neither to the suppression nor the uplift of black people, involved the bleaching of the Cuban.

In his influential Senate speech of March 17, 1898, Vermont's Redfield Proctor assured his countrymen that better than three of four Cubans were "like the Spaniards, dark in complexion, but oftener light or blond." [69] The figure whom Americans came to accept as the prototypical victim of Spanish inhumanity, William Randolph Heart's most successful promotion, the rescued maiden Evangelina Cisneros, was described as possessing "a white face, young, pure and beautiful." [70] The Kansas soldier of fortune Frederick Funston, a volunteer smuggled to the island along underground routes maintained by the Cuban Junta's New York headquarters, wrote that "fully nine-tenths [of the insurrectionists] were white men." General

Gomez was himself "of pure Spanish descent." Most Cuban officers were former planters, stockmen, farmers, professionals, and businessmen—"the best men." [71] Later, when Gomez ordered General Garcia to join forces, Funston noted an important difference: rebel units from eastern Cuba contained a much higher proportion of Negroes.[72] Few other Americans were aware of the distinction. Correspondents, almost all of them strongly interventionist, made their way into rebel territory by working east from Havana. Few penetrated easternmost Santiago Province where black Cubans were most numerous. Their reports, like Funston's first letters, conveyed the impression that the Cuban Army was almost entirely white. This misconception would be corrected with abrupt and calamitous results when the Fifth Corps landed only thirty miles from the city of Santiago.

Another theme, Americanization, accompanied the stress on Cuban whiteness. This enlarged the basis of Cuban-American cooperation beyond bonds of color to include temperamental similarities. After a visit to rebel territory, Grover Flint wrote in *McClure's Magazine* that Gomez had shown an "Anglo-Saxon tenacity of purpose." The general's staff was "businesslike." [73] When Flint and others then praised the Cuban Army for its self-respect, determination, discipline, and concern for its wounded, the insurrectionary forces seemed an organization very similar to the United States Army. A plausible extension would suggest comparable fighting capacities. Here again Americans built unrealistic expectations. In fact they understood neither the Cuban Army nor the nature of the war it was fighting.

In restrospect, it is not difficult to discern that the Cuban insurrection was the first modern guerrilla war. The Cubans organized themselves in numerous small bands of soldiers only partially trained and equipped. They were unable to seize a single port or important inland town through the entire course of the rebellion. They could sustain no commissary operation, a weakness necessitating frequent dispersal of forces.[74] Their capital, if it was not New York City, traveled with them. Their government was solely a creation of paper. To their salvation, however, Gomez, a brilliant strategist, saw that Spain was vulnerable in her treasury. He stole Spanish stores; burned sugarfields, mills, and plantations on whose production Spanish revenues depended; tore up railroad track, telegraph lines, and bridges to compel costly repairs. He urged Cubans to withhold their services from the Spaniards and when exhortation failed, he terrorized collaborators, of whom there were many. He attacked Spanish forces only to seize weapons essential to prolong the insurrection, and then only after ensuring a local superiority in numbers.

Contrary to the realities of this war, pictures circulating in the United States showed Cubans meticulously uniformed and equipped, mounted and charging in impeccable column with flags flying.[75] Americans thereby assumed that roughly equivalent Spanish and Cuban Armies were testing one another in conventional warfare, an impression the Cuban Junta took pains to foster. It was far easier to pretend to the waging of a familiar war than to explain a new one, especially when the reality was unromantic, unregulated, expensive of noncombatant life and American-owned property.

The fiction of Cuban Army as conventional force could not have been maintained without Gomez's masterstroke: his incursion into western Cuba in late 1895 and early 1896. His intentions were limited—to deplete Spanish finances by burning cane, to demonstrate the *insurrectos'* strength to friend and foe. His advance was fluid. Men in small groups flowed westward through holes between plodding Spanish columns. Gomez's adversary, Captain General Martinez Campos, a humane but very orthodox soldier, was mystified. His men lacked sufficient training for conversion to new tactics. He could find no other solution than to call on Madrid for more and more reinforcements.

Not surprisingly, American reporters responded similarly, by trying to force a new war within old and comfortable terms.

Two examples of press coverage—one small-town, one large-city—demonstrate how a limited military success became a decisive propaganda victory.

Stories appearing in the Clyde *Enterprise* described Gomez's raid as if it were an invasion. The Cuban force, twelve thousand strong, marched westward in three columns (December 24, 1895), its movement a "steady push" (January 3, 1896) that reached to within eight miles of Havana (January 10). The Spanish Army abandoned the countryside to the insurgents, apparently without offering serious resistance. The *Enterprise's* headlines told this story:

January 10:

No Power Seems Adequate to Stop the Cuban Patriots

March 6:

THE DARING CUBANS
Spanish Troops Bottled Up in the Cuban Capital and Apparently Afraid to Go Out While the Insurgents Are Around [76]

At the same time the *Enterprise* and other small-town newspapers were printing reports both inaccurate and wildly optimistic, events in Cuba were producing a remarkable controversy fought out in the columns of the New York *World*. Pulitzer's man in Havana, William Shaw Bowen, possessed a stubbornness unusual to his profession in the 1890s. He insisted on uncompromising honesty in his own stories and protested inaccuracies in others' stories. On December 1, 1895, Bowen insisted that published reports of important battles fought during the preceding week were untrue.[77] The next day he flatly denied a *World* story, likely of Junta origin, reporting that Gomez and Maceo had combined their eight thousand troops to defeat ten thousand Spaniards at Jaguasco. He denounced "the programme of falsification being carried on by interested parties to humbug American readers." [78] On December 26 Bowen insisted that Gomez's movement was a raid confined to the destruction of sugar plantations.[79]

There followed the battle of communiqués. It was as if Pulitzer, in puckish humor, had decided to pair contradictory reports from the Junta and his temperate reporter, at least until he decided which he preferred. On December 28 Bowen reported that Gomez's advance had left Havana "singularly undisturbed." Immediately below his dispatch was another headed *HAVANA PREPARING FOR A SIEGE?* and claiming that "everything denotes the deepest anxiety." [80] On January 3, 1896, Bowen again complained of "startling fictions" that he was certain did not originate in Cuba. On the island there had been no great battles, no all-night struggles, no machete charges, no rebel artillery. In short, there had been "no action . . . worthy [of] the name of battle." The reported fear of a siege of Havana was "preposterous." [81] Two days later came the Junta's riposte. *HAVANA IS SURROUNDED,* proclaimed the headline crowning a report that Generals Gomez, Maceo, and Bandera were approaching the capital from three directions to complete their "triumphant march from the eastern end of Santiago de Cuba." [82] Undeterred, Bowen wrote on January 8 that *HAVANA IS NOT ALARMED* and again arraigned "wildly exaggerated stories." Equally uninhibited, the *World* printed below his story an item attributed to the Associated Press locating the Cuban forces eight miles from Havana and observing that "no movement apparently avails to check them." [83]

As early as January 7 an editorial revealed that the Junta's version of events was winning converts in high places. In announcing "the complete collapse of the Spanish campaign . . . made plainly apparent by the presence of the Cubans in Havana province itself, after marching almost the whole length of the island, practically without check," [84] the editorial forecast Bowen's defeat.

Not even a curiously candid letter from Gomez to the *World,* possibly sent at Bowen's instigation, arrested the drift to fantasy. The Cuban leader acknowledged that his aims were limited to spreading the revolution's influence and halting sugar-making, that he could neither take towns nor afford general engagements with the Spanish Army.[85] Such a letter might ordinarily have provoked some reconsideration of the nature of the struggle, but now the rush of events overtook it. Five days later Madrid recalled Campos and appointed in his place Valeriano Weyler, "The Butcher." This dramatic development sealed Gomez's victory. Largely unnoticed in the United States were the absence of an actual Cuban attack on Havana and Gomez's hasty withdrawal to the eastern provinces.

Soon Joseph Pulitzer became impatient with Bowen's demurrals or perhaps with the absence of action in his dispatches. He recalled Bowen and assigned to Havana the tempestuous and colorful James Creelman. If his employer had failed to understand his war, William Shaw Bowen had failed to grasp Joseph Pulitzer's journalism.

The American miscalculation was not the belief that the *insurrectos* had achieved a notable success. Bowen himself called the westward movement "a most remarkable military feat." [86] But Gomez's success was not that of defeating Spaniards, but of convincing Cubans and Americans that Spain could not crush his bands, that no one would easily dispose of this rebellion. The larger American error lay in missing that achievement, its ramifications and its originality. Lacking a realistic appreciation of Gomez's purposes and resources, Americans credited the Cubans with a traditional military prowess they never possessed. Gomez had moved to set the record straight, but overzealous Junta agents and drama-hungry editors and correspondents had created an image of Cuban strength without basis in reality.

Two years later American soldiers waded ashore in southeastern Cuba expecting to meet Cubans whose motives were to emulate the American historical experience, whose conventional fighting abilities were of a high order, whose color was white, or, at least, not black. On all three counts Americans were disappointed.

❖ ❖ ❖

Images of ally and enemy reversed rapidly, though not simultaneously. Members of the Fifth Corps reappraised the Cuban almost as they touched the beaches. The Cuban *insurrectos* who greeted them did not *look* like soldiers. Their clothes were in tatters, their weapons a strange assortment, their equipment woefully incomplete—"a crew," thought Theodore Roosevelt, "as utter tatterdemalions as human eyes ever looked on." [87] Earlier, the same appearance had seemed a virtue. Grover Flint, in an interpretation that gained wide currency in the United States, represented Cuban raggedness as a self-imposed gesture of sacrifice,[88] a Western Hemisphere equivalent of the patched cloaks of fanatical Sudanese Mahdists. One newspaper found the nobility of perseverance in those Cubans who continued to fight though "out of stores and ammunition, shoeless, coatless, gunless and discouraged." [89]

Personal contact converted admiration to disgust. The English correspondent John Black Atkins, noting that the insurgents looked "incredibly tattered and peaked and forlorn," thought "by far the most notable thing" about the American volunteers' reaction "was their sudden, open disavowel of friendliness toward the Cubans." [90] Unaware of the true nature of the Cubans' war, Americans were quick to generalize from appearance to fighting ability. Roosevelt immediately concluded that the Cubans would be useless in "serious fighting." [91] Captain John Bigelow's professional eye caught little more: "Bands of Cubans in ragged and dirty white linen, barefooted, and variously armed, marched past us, carrying Cuban and American flags. . . . The Cubans were evidently undisciplined. I thought from their appearance that they would probably prove useful as guides and scouts, but that we would have to do practically all the fighting." [92] George

Kennan of the Red Cross, perhaps the most judicious observer of events in Cuba, found himself struggling to reconcile his preconception of Cuban military prowess with an appearance that seemed to preclude fighting qualities. The *insurrectos* "may have been brave men and good soldiers," but "if their rifles and cartridge belts had been taken away . . . they would have looked like a horde of dirty Cuban beggars and ragamuffins on the tramp." [93]

If before white Americans had imagined Cuban complexions as pale as their own, now the darker shades seemed ubiquitous. Roosevelt thought Cuban soldiers "almost all blacks and mulattoes." [94] In a later letter to Secretary of War Alger, Leonard Wood elaborated the significance of color: the Cuban Army "is made up very considerably of black people, only partially civilized, in whom the old spirit of savagery has been more or less aroused by years of warfare, during which time they have reverted more or less to the condition of men taking what they need and living by plunder." [95] Americans abruptly opened, to include Cubans met for the first time, that popular domestic package of racial concepts—blackness, civilization-savagery, advance-reversion—that few had thought pertinent to the three-year debate over Cuba. Few were the observers like George Kennan who simply estimated that blacks and mulattoes comprised four-fifths of Gomez's force, without finding in *that* fact alone reason for mistrusting Cuban competence.[96]

Cuban behavior soon joined appearance as the next item in a lengthening indictment of the ally. American soldiers had accepted earnestly public declarations of their country's unselfishness in entering the war; they did, nevertheless, expect a return. Implicit in the dominant concept of the war—the disinterested relief of suffering Cubans—was the confidence that Cubans would view themselves as victims delivered from oppression and would be grateful. In reality, there was little Cuban gratitude.[97] No cheering greeted the American landings. The *insurrecto* accepted gifts of American rations but, thought Stephen Crane, "with the impenetrable indifference or igno-

rance of the greater part of the people in an ordinary slum."
"We feed him and he expresses no joy." [98] The volunteers
could not miss Cuban stolidity. At first surprised, they became
resentful and then angry.

Additional disillusionment was to come. Sharing his rations
in what he thought an act of charity,[99] the volunteer who went
unthanked was not likely to repeat the gesture, especially
when it was already obvious that the Army commissariat could
not keep his own stomach full. The hungry *insurrecto,* however, contrasting the supply bonanza on the beach with his
own meager resources, concluded that the Americans would
hardly miss what would suffice to feed him. He returned several times to his original benefactors, who were perplexed and
then indignant at the conversion of charity at lunch-time to
obligation by the dinner hour. When the Cubans found that
this method produced diminishing results, they began pilfering
from food stocks and picking up discarded items of equipment.
With each episode American contempt grew.

Other Cuban behavior antagonized the volunteers. The principal charge here, precisely that against the Spaniard, was
cruelty. Atkins reported the disgust of Americans watching
Cubans stab a bull to death and, later, decapitating a Spaniard
caught spying out American positions.[100] After the battle of
Santiago Bay, Captain Robley Evans, USN, was shocked by
Cubans shooting at Spanish sailors swimming ashore to escape
their burning vessels.[101] On such occasions few Americans
linked what they saw with the atrocities of "Butcher" Weyler
that had so enflamed public opinion at home. Fewer still understood the stresses of a guerrilla war. To keep their rebellion
alive Marti and Gomez had burned fields and factories, co-
erced some of their own compatriots, shot Spanish emissaries
who entered their lines with proposals falling short of full
independence. On either level a sense of the realities of guerrilla war might have offered some mitigation of Cuban "cruelty"—either that Cuban vengeance, while not pretty, was un-
derstandable, or that Cuban behavior must be viewed within

the frame of a bitter war of few rules. Americans instead concluded that there was another explanation for what they witnessed. Such behavior was intrinsic: Cubans were a cruel people.

Angry at what Cubans did, Americans were equally perturbed by what they would not do—act as labor forces for American fighting units. The Cubans "while loitering in the rear"—half of them feigning illness or simply lazing about, it was reported—refused to aid in building roads or cutting litter poles for the American wounded.[102] They would not act in mere logistical support of American units whose anxiety to close with the enemy would in any case have left little substantial role for the Cubans.[103]

The development of the military campaign did nothing to bridge growing estrangement. Preliminary arrangements were smooth enough. In response to a letter from Commanding General Nelson A. Miles, the Cuban leader in the Santiago area, General Calixto Garcia, agreed to assist the American debarkation and to block any reinforcements the Spanish might send to Santiago. On his own initiative, the effusive Garcia pledged that he would receive as commands all American suggestions for Cuban military action.[104]

The first trial of Cuban-American cooperation came at Guantanamo where just prior to the main landings a Cuban detachment assisted a unit of Marines under Lieutenant Colonel Robert W. Huntington. The Cubans, cabled Admiral Sampson to the president, were "of great assistance" in securing the beachhead and repulsing Spanish attacks.[105] Stephen Crane, one of the few Americans to see the landings at both Guantanamo and Daiquiri, was less complimentary. Conceding that the Cubans were at first efficient in supporting Huntington, he insisted that they soon traded the fight for food and a nap. Americans "came down here expecting to fight side by side with an ally, but this ally has done little but stay in the rear and eat Army rations, manifesting an indifference to the cause of Cuban liberty which could not be exceeded by some one who had never heard of it." [106]

Here Crane's indignation was manifestly misplaced. It was a vivid imagination that saw in exposure to American supplies the source of a sudden Cuban demoralization, as if the *insurrectos* had succumbed to canned food as Spanish energies, in the American view, had been sapped by surrender to the gold of South America. No more convincing is the charge of indifference. If there was a measure of Cuban passivity, it is much better explained as a response to dominant assumptions about the war. The Cubans were in no hurry. They had been battling Spaniards for more than three years. To employ haste implied a level of resources they had never achieved. They avoided decision because it could only go against them. A day well spent was one that prolonged the revolution. The American regret that the enemy had not fought on the beaches, the determination to pursue with the least possible delay, the fear the war might end without major combats—how strange must these have seemed to the Cuban. And if Americans were ignorant of insurrectionary war, Cubans were no better versed in conventional warfare. As Crane himself conceded, *insurrectos* could not leap overnight from a war of cunning to one rooted in the confidence of superior power.[107] They were alarmed by the American deficiency in woodcraft, unable to comprehend that the stealth of those whose aim was survival was superfluous to those whose aim was immediate victory.

When Garcia attempted to give effect to that imprudent agreement with the American command, the results were disastrous. To block six thousand Spanish reinforcements marching from Holguin to Santiago required a stand-up fight for which the Cubans had neither the numbers, the equipment, nor the training.[108] They failed to hold, and Americans grew even more contemptuous.

A short time later Shafter decided to exclude all *insurrectos* from the ceremony marking Santiago's surrender and to maintain largely intact the city's Spanish administration: "This war," he told Garcia, ". . . is between the United States of America and the Kingdom of Spain, and . . . the surrender . . . was made solely to the American Army." [109] In his protest the Cuban commander wrote:

> I have not been honored, sir, with a single word from yourself informing me about the negotiations for peace or the terms of the capitulation. . . . The important cere- monies of the surrender . . . and the possession of the city . . . took place . . . and I only knew of both events by the public reports. . . . A rumor, too absurd to be be- lieved, General, ascribes the reason of your measure and of the orders forbidding my Army to enter Santiago, to fear of massacres and revenges against the Spaniards. Al- low me, Sir, to protest against even the shadow of such an idea. We are not savages ignoring the rules of civilized warfare. We are a poor, ragged Army, as ragged and poor [as] was the Army of your forefathers in their noble war for independence, but as [did] the heroes of Santiago and Yorktown we respect too deeply our cause to disgrace it with barbarism and cowardice.[110]

It was a strong defense, touching on each major point of the American indictment of his forces and even summoning histor- ical analogy, but it came too late, as its author must have real- ized. Just as Americans began to suspect that they would soon fight Cubans,[111] Garcia withdrew his forces to the interior and resigned his command.

Disillusionment with America's ally reached those at home very quickly. Correspondents, often busier as participants than as observers, shared the soldiers' bitterness toward the Cuban. Confident of their objectivity and immune to appeals to higher statecraft, they filled their stories with their anger. Just as im- portant was the informal communications network. Visitors returning home from the war zone and uncensored letters pub-

lished by the hundreds in hometown newspapers spread the
news of Cuban villainy. The speed of the reversal was impressive. On June 30, 1898, an editorial in the Clyde *Enterprise*
referred to the Cuban Army, old style, as "a large and effective
fighting force of intelligent soldiers, who have already been
repeatedly complimented for bravery by the generals of the in-
vading [American] Army. Before this war is over it will be
found that the people who for three years have been opposing
Spanish tyranny . . . are as brave as any who wear the
blue." [112] It was the last such reference. On July 21 the *Enterprise* announced that the Cubans were "worthless allies."

Garcia's Soldiers Refuse to Fight or Work
Our Troops Despise Them [113]

An even faster reversal appeared in the pages of the Galesburg *Republican-Register*. In the fourteen days between June
25 and July 9 a sorely oppressed people worthy of American
aid became "murderous bands." [114]

An unanticipated result of this sudden reappraisal was a
sharp upswing in the popularity of William McKinley. The
president had worked vigorously and successfully to prevent
passage of a congressional resolution recognizing the rebel
organization as the de jure government of Cuba. Now Americans concluded that he was right: the Cubans were undeserving. "Thank God," exclaimed New York *Tribune* publisher
Whitelaw Reid, "McKinley didn't recognize the Cuban republic." [115]

Within a month of the landings the indictment of Cuban
was no less harsh than that of Spaniard. The correspondent
for *Leslie's Weekly*, Burr McIntosh, wrote that not one of the
Cubans "was ever seen to be guilty of an act which was not
selfish—and often criminal. . . . From the highest officer to
the lowliest 'soldier,' they were there for personal gain." [116]
Speaker Reed greeted the same estimate not with McIntosh's
disgust but with a tight satisfaction tinged with bitterness:

"The noble Army of Cuban martyrs had become an armed rabble as unchivalrous as it was unsanitary." [117]

❖ ❖ ❖

American soldiers concluded shortly after landing that Cubans were no better than Spaniards. The next revelation was equally unexpected: Spaniards were superior to Cubans.

Events quickly resolved, in a way welcome to the volunteers, that uncertainty at the core of the American image of Spanish malevolence. The enemy was not too enervated to fight. There would be battles. On the other hand those ferocious energies assumed to gird Spanish cruelty did not appear as omnipotence in combat. Americans would win the battles.

To be sure, the first days were somewhat deceptive. When the Spanish command did not contest the landings at Daiquiri and Siboney, American units charged beyond the beaches in eager pursuit of an enemy that seemed for a moment Sherwood Anderson's "old gypsy woman." But at Las Guasimas the Rough Riders, pushing through the brush with jokes, arguments, and babble, tripped upon a well-hidden, entrenched foe who inflicted seventy casualties before he withdrew. Guasimas was notable principally for the way it challenged American concepts of combat, but the very next battle forced a reconsideration of the nature of the enemy.

El Caney was a small crossroads hamlet of thatched huts and tileroof buildings dominated by a stone church. On the morning of July 1 Shafter sent units totaling six thousand men under the command of General Henry W. Lawton to seize the town. The resistance was much stiffer than the Americans had expected. Despite the fatalism of the Spanish high command, middle-grade officers and their men, conceding nothing, resisted stubbornly. The fighting lasted into the afternoon. When the church and a nearby fort were at last reduced, almost four hundred of the six hundred defenders were dead, wounded, or captured. The attackers suffered four hundred and forty-one casualties, including eighty-one dead.

At El Caney the stereotyped Spaniard dissolved. As soon as his men overran the final Spanish bastion, General Chaffee advanced to shake the hand of the Spanish lieutenant in charge.[118] In turn, a Spanish officer praised the courage of the Americans who had thrown themselves at Caney's trenches. George Kennan was sure that the "moral effect of this battle was to give each of the combatants a feeling of sincere respect for the bravery of the other." [119] A second battle that day on the San Juan ridges enlarged the volunteers' regard for Spanish valor. Americans whose commander calculated that they would sustain four hundred wounded suffered three times that number. When the crests were finally in American hands, Theodore Roosevelt felt a new esteem for a tenacious enemy. "No men of any nationality could have done better." The Spaniards were "brave foes." [120]

There was a similar, though not identical, turn in the war at sea. When Admiral Sampson hit on a scheme to block the channel from Santiago harbor by sinking the collier *Merrimac* in its midpassage, Lieutenant Richmond Pearson Hobson accepted the assignment. Enemy fire, however, disrupted the plan. Hobson and his crew were unable to scuttle the vessel at the critical spot or make their way to rescue craft. The next day, just as Americans were beginning to despair of Hobson's fate, Admiral Cervera sent a message to his blockaders: he had captured Hobson and his men and now offered assurances of their well-being. American officers were impressed. There was, said Captain Robley Evans, "never a more courteous thing done in war." [121]

A reconsideration of the enemy begun with Cervera's note ended with the destruction of the Spanish fleet. American naval officers who on July 4 inflicted terrible destruction on the Spaniards immediately felt a sympathy for foes crushed so decisively. Evans was sorry for Cervera, who was hauled from the water and then received with military honors and champagne.[122] There was an even greater measure of sympathy and respect when Americans soon discovered the abominable phys-

ical condition of the vessels in which the Spaniards had tried
to fight them. The ties of professional standards were ce-
mented; with wretched resources, the Spaniards had played
the game honorably.[123]

The Spanish, themselves victimized by caricatures of a re-
morseless enemy, responded to this treatment by offering their
captors that which Americans had expected from the Cubans:
gratitude.[124] Quite surprised that Americans were not vicious,
Spanish soldiers and sailors were immediately grateful that
they were not, as expected, to be killed. Even when life again
became an operating assumption, they continued to respond
with thanks to solicitous American care. Before long American
and Spanish enlisted men were exchanging greetings, then
stories and momentos. Fraternization became so intense that
General Shafter in a report to Alger described it as "something
remarkable." It was only with difficulty that he could keep
captives and captors apart.[125]

The parting of former foes was heavy with emotion on both
sides. To spur Spanish acceptance of his surrender terms,
Shafter offered to return Spanish soldiers to their homeland at
United States expense. Almost twenty-three thousand were
shipped from eastern Cuba at a cost of $513,860.[126] On the eve
of his departure for home one Spanish private addressed a
letter to the victors. He thanked them profusely for their kind
treatment and then went on to say, "You fought us as men, face
to face, and with great courage . . . a quality which we had
not met with during the three years we have carried on this war
against a people without religion, without morals, without conscience, and of doubtful origin, who could not confront the
enemy, but, hidden, shot their noble victims from ambush and
then immediately fled. . . . These people are not able to exercise or enjoy their liberty, for they will find it a burden to
comply with the laws which govern civilized communities." [127]

This letter, widely circulated, won American acclaim. Its
appeal was not only in its praise of Americans but in its dero-
gation on moral grounds of a war neither Spaniard nor Amer-

ican comprehended. Equally attractive was its vilification of
the Cuban, for here it gave expression to a de facto partnership of former foes against America's former ally. American
and Spanish officers, Leonard Wood said, were "drawn together by mutual respect and a common dislike for the cause
of their late estrangement, the Cubans . . . children, ignorant,
naive." [128] Here was a spiritual solidarity. In the Philippines,
where an essentially similar process was developing, rapport
took more momentous shapes. There American and Spanish
high commands agreed that neither the attack on, nor the defense of, Manila would be unstinting. The Americans wished
to minimize the loss of life. The Spanish commandant, General Fermin Jaudenes, required no more than a gesture that
would salvage his personal honor. Both sides joined in their
determination to arrange matters so as to deny Aguinaldo's
Filipino guerrillas access to the city.[129]

For many Americans the ally of early 1898 had become enemy and the enemy, ally.

In a 1912 article entitled "The Passing of San Juan Hill," Richard Harding Davis reported that on a return visit to Cuba he
had found changes "startling and confusing." The course of
the San Juan River had altered and obliterated the Bloody
Bend of such moment to the battle. More troubling was the
Cuban view of what had happened on that terrain fourteen
years earlier. The battlefield guide insisted that American
forces, arriving just as the Cubans were about to conquer the
Spaniards, had by luck alone received all the credit. He further reported that Cubans now ranked the fighting qualities
of their Spanish foes much higher than those of their American
allies.[130]

CHAPTER VI *The Popular Press and the War*

THE MANIFESTATION of an intense, inclusive sentiment for war with Spain was itself a signal of social transformation.

William McKinley's administration would be the last to reflect an American public opinion that had remained throughout the nineteenth century fragmented and narrowly parochial.[1] The president conceived of few of the problems reaching his desk as national problems. Until 1898 he devoted his work day to local issues, many similar in content, all susceptible to individualized solution but few central to local life: the appointment of a postmaster; a limited adjustment in a tariff schedule; the reception of a group from home; the granting of a pardon; the review of a decision handed down by the commissioner of pensions; the endorsement of relief measures, often private, to cushion the depredations of some natural disaster. Occasionally a president might confront issues with generalized implications—a Sherman Anti-Trust Act or a national monetary policy—but not until the twentieth century would a higher order of administrative action make their effects felt on the locale. Ordinarily there were few issues that compelled any reaction beyond localized response.

From the local perspective, limited need to resort to Washington as problem-solver encouraged, in a peculiar way, a reluctance to press local opinion on Washington. Small-town Americans, with the pride and confidence that their problems were amenable to local solution, understandably concluded that local knowledge was *the* requisite to solution. Those living beyond the county's limits, townsmen thought, lacked the full understanding on which valid opinions might be based. By such reasoning were local communities somewhat hedged in advancing the right accorded them by democratic theory, the right to shape decisions on the national level. Distance, they felt, denied them essential knowledge only personal contact could provide. Such beliefs reinforced the apathy of those at home toward distant developments in their own country and buttressed their obliviousness to problems overseas.

The reality of local power here sustained two elements vital to the social consensus dominant in post-Civil War America. It offered Washington administrations an immunity to all but the most compelling pressures for national domestic policies and, by extension, further insulated from currents of popular feeling those responsible for American diplomacy. At the same time, it upheld by default, by the absence of any necessity to test, a vital unifying tenet, the primacy of public opinion in the operation of American government at every level.

Americans assumed a priori both the existence of public opinion and its accurate and automatic translation into political decisions. The English observer James Bryce took as his own this confident creed. Opinions, he concluded, were cast on the level of the individual; each person—by thinking, by talking with others, by reading newspapers—converted "faint impressions" of apparently spontaneous generation into "definite positions." [2] Implicit here is a conception of the nation as a setting for autonomous individuals, each fashioning specific views for which his political representatives listen. Such a notion, though sanguine, was not entirely at odds with the realities of nineteenth-century life. As long as local issues remained the only ones vital to small-town America, they would prove manageable within each community's network of per-

sonal relationships; local opinion *could* command a high degree of political response. Should those citizens, however, begin to demand policies that could be effected only at the center
of government, they would risk discovery of a gap separating
political practice and democratic doctrine.

It was the Venezuelan Crisis of 1895 that best demonstrated
the corrosion of localism and the burgeoning of popular pressure for Washington action in international affairs. Such
results were not visible in the prelude. The first moves, undertaken by those accustomed to a foreign policy immune to
popular feeling, ran true to older forms. Though a former dip-
lomat had undertaken a campaign propagandizing in Venezuela's behalf and had been instrumental in the passage of a
joint resolution urging "friendly arbitration" on the British, the
Congress acted with the administration's blessing and without
rousing itself to special excitement.[3] Americans at large remained oblivious to antecedent developments. No significant
segment of the public had been mobilized when in mid-
December the executive provoked the crisis.

The clamorous excitement drawn from the citizenry by the
administration's ultimatum stunned Grover Cleveland and
Richard Olney. The president, hardly a popular figure in 1895,
was at first pleased by unaccustomed applause, but as he began to sense the public's underlying bellicosity, his gratification
slipped to suspicion and then alarm. Olney was "surprised by
the violence of the explosion of jingo feeling" and resolved to
say nothing more until the popular mood calmed.[4] By mid-
January 1896 the administration was able to begin the resolution of the dispute in the old style—slowly, carefully, quietly.[5]

The emotional effervescence of the Venezuelan crisis revealed the shattering of popular passivity on an issue thought
irretrievably remote from the daily concerns of the American
people. Popular emotion, easily hurdling the older insistence
on first-hand knowledge, leaped far beyond locale.

Twenty-five months later the situation in Cuba presented

another issue about which only a minute number of Americans possessed facts based on experience. Here the coalescence of public opinion in a matter of foreign policy was greater and more sustained than in 1895. Here the old forms were shattered rather than stretched. Unlike the Venezuelan matter, the crisis was not initiated by the executive branch, nor in the end could the White House control it. Cleveland and Olney had taken refuge in silence and the paroxysm had passed. The next president found no hiding place. The Cuban crisis sought him out and ruled him.

William McKinley's personal, temperamental inability to act should not obscure those nineteenth-century institutional limitations that, within the shaping social consensus, would have hobbled any president. The executive was unequipped to register broad public sentiment, to temper it in response to data pertinent to situations overseas and to translate the result into a national policy and program incorporating both public opinion's claim to consideration and the administration's own informed sense of the national interest. The center's problem, as Bryce saw, was that "[e]ach of . . . [the national government's] organs is too small to form opinion, too narrow to express it, too weak to give effect to it." [6]

Illustrative of Washington's weakness was the difficulty of assembling basic information. Facts, especially in the increasingly important realm of foreign affairs, were elusive. The federal government's processes for gathering data on situations overseas were irregular and unreliable. American consuls abroad—the party faithful, the businessman intent on his own commercial ventures, the occasional writer like Nathaniel Hawthorne hoarding consular fees against the day when they would suffice to support his art—only fitfully wrote dispatches home. The departments ordinarily lacked provision for the distribution of that intelligence which did arrive. There were few whose job it was to inform the public. Rarely did an official use information gathered by government to address the people on behalf of government.

William McKinley regularly revealed his own meager expectations of the executive branch as a source of information. The superintendent of the Coast and Geodetic Survey objected when he discovered the president following the movement of Dewey's fleet on a page torn from a school geography. McKinley was surprised, and pleased, to discover that someone in government could offer better maps.[7] Falling within this assumption that government did not generate essential information was McKinley's frequent resort to the fact-finder, the old and trusted friend who would explore specific problems and report directly to the president. Symptomatic of this problem, the American peace commissioners would hold negotiating sessions with Spain's delegates concurrently with hearings designed to elicit the most elementary facts about the conquered Philippine archipelago.

In 1898 aroused Americans began demanding of the federal government a program of broad national action for which neither presidential will nor institutional equipment was available. The result was a variety of vacuum, an insistent need without the means to meet it.

The popular press possessed four assets that made its attempts to fill the political vacuum far less ludicrous than we might assume a similar effort today.

There was, first, the residual deference derived from the role that the newspaper had played within the older social consensus. Politicians who carried the locale's mandate to their seats in Washington were sensitive to the problem noted by another English visitor, Beatrice Webb: the absence of organic connection between elector and representative, between local and central authority.[8] Even during the period of minimal local interest in, and pressure on, what transpired in Washington, there was tension rooted in their role. By what stan-

dard were office-holders to represent those who elected them?
With no possibility of constant contact with constituency and
with electors in any case reluctant to prescribe for problems
without bearing on their own lives, how were representatives
to judge each issue that came before them? A number apparently set for themselves the easy measure of personal enrich-
ment. The majority, however, felt the need of another guide,
one more frequent and comprehensive than the crossroads
meeting at election time, one of direct help in measuring their
actions against the ideal of public weal. Here the newspaper
played an essential role.

Politicians showed deference to the press. Their attention
seemed both a propitiation of, and an invitation to, public
opinion—conciliating the priest in worshipping the deity,
Bryce called it.[9] The politician's interest, however, was of a
special and limited kind. He viewed the newspaper less as a
source of information on what was happening, less as a finger
held to the public pulse, than as a support for the moral life.
He wanted to know that men whom he respected thought as
he did regarding the moral nature of the issues that confronted
him. He looked first not to the news pages but to the editorials.

Joseph Pulitzer and William Randolph Hearst frequently
risked their inheritance, this rooted assumption of the newspaper's morality and respectability. Both the *World* and the
Journal gambled and partially lost their standing as reputable
organs. In part this was a function of indelicate subject matter;
in part a function of the yellow press' appeal to groups assumed not to share middle-class moral precepts; in part a
function of the editors' backgrounds. Pulitzer, half-Jewish in
a day when anti-Semitism incurred little onus, arrived in New
York preceded by whispers condemning his role in a shooting
that involved the editor of his St. Louis newspaper. Even more
vulnerable was Hearst, whom West Coast society had cen-
sured for flaunting his mistress, a former waitress. To the
respectable people of New York he appeared the dilettante-
publisher lavishing momma's millions on crude pranks, the

journalistic equivalent of the chamber-pot incident that had
led to his expulsion from Harvard.[10] Nevertheless, both publishers periodically courted respectability and thereby recouped some social standing: their journals remained at least
the partial legatee of that older respect for the newspaper as
the enunciator of moral concerns.

A second, more potent asset lay in the fact that Joseph Pulitzer had already begun, as government had not, to build an
organization reflecting the shifting focus from individual to
mass, from locale to nation.

In the 1870s and 1880s that which the politician found in
the newspaper was not public opinion, though it called itself
that. It was instead the sentiment of the eastern, urban educated, the group that Bryce called the "active class" [11] and
Edwin Lawrence Godkin labeled the "reading class." [12] Editors
thought it their principal function to reinforce standards of
social conduct. In reality, they both shaped and reflected an
"ethical likemindedness," [13] a common outlook among small,
often otherwise unrelated groups of subscribers. Acting in this
capacity, editors seemed very powerful men. Before the extensive use of telephone, telegraph, and cable, newspapers
were small and personalized. New Yorkers referred to their
newspapers as "Dana's *Sun*" and "Bryant's *Post*." The appearance was that of giants of journalism creating private, powerful instruments of influence.

The reality, as Seymour Mandelbaum has shown, was less
flattering. In the New York City of the 1860s and 1870s tiny
groups of readers supported numbers of small newspapers.
Each journal's influence was ordinarily limited to a tight circle,
with the location of its office pointing the center and the reach
of local wagon transport, within perhaps a two-hour period,
setting its circumference. If he moved too far beyond the reflection of local interests and moral sensibilities, the editor
risked losing to numerous, nearby rivals that essential constituency.[14]

Newspaper editors shared the common view that the thinking individual was the critical unit of American society. In presenting materials, they were kept within rather narrow bounds by their personal commitments to upper middle-class ethical standards and, equally, by their belief that the respectable individual, capable of discerning truth for himself, would recognize falsity in a paper's pages and, refusing to buy, would immediately go elsewhere. This focus on high ethical content, accurately and coolly reported, was manifest in page appearance: small type; single-column tombstone headlines; accounts framed as tales, with the important at the end.[15]

Godkin spoke to the future when he asserted in 1898 that "the press is the nation talking about itself." [16] The press of the 1870s, 1880s, and much of the 1890s was more accurately the locale talking about its own, largely self-contained interests or, on the only level even slightly to transcend locale, the urban educated talking among themselves of the way Americans should behave.

It was Joseph Pulitzer, perhaps the quickest mind in the history of American journalism, who smashed this mold. He refused to accept traditional limitations on subject matter. He set out to enlarge constituency by offering materials that, though abhorrent to respectables, were exciting to a new readership. He chose a strategic location and there applied a broad vision, that of a newspaper speaking "not to a select committee," not even to all the people of a single city, "but to the whole nation." [17] An equally dramatic break with the past was his determination to realign the relationship of editor and reader. A childhood close to European poverty supplied both sympathy for those in the lower social ranges and immunity against the American middle-class conception of a society of discerning individuals. He would speak to the lower ranks, but not as respectable editors spoke to the urban educated. Instead of reflecting his readers' views, he would first catch their interest and then instruct them in his own views. His newspaper was to be a "daily schoolhouse" and a "daily teacher." [18]

By 1883, the year of Pulitzer's arrival in New York City, it had become possible for an innovative editor to break the confines of small, single-type constituencies approachable only through the appeal to reason. Technological advance was making his vision practicable. The trolley car enlarged a paper's compass from nine or ten to perhaps fifty miles.[19] The growth of regional advertising as corporate scale increased provided the essential alternative source of income. No longer need the editor remain chained to subscriptions. Reliance on advertising might at first appear to trade the rather diffuse control of class constituency for the tighter rein of the businessman, but advertisers, Pulitzer calculated, would be less interested than upper middle-class patrons in a paper's editorial policy and ethical content. Seeing in the larger public potential customers rather than threatening mob, they would look first to numbers. Pulitzer was the first to comprehend that a circulation large enough to attract and retain advertising opened the way to new influence.

Not only was there available a new source of funds, but by the mid-1880s a new and larger constituency—the immigrant masses—awaited tapping. With rapid increases in literacy came hunger for new reading materials. There would be in 1899 four times as many daily newspapers as in 1870. While population in cities of eight thousand or more would grow 52 percent between 1880 and 1899, daily newspaper circulation would rise 323 percent.[20]

Pultizer better than any other grasped the techniques necessary to win the loyalties of masses newly literate in English. In the twelve years between 1883 and Hearst's arrival in New York, Pulitzer, aided by Morrill Goddard and Arthur Brisbane, perfected his tactics: streamer headlines; huge line-cut illustrations; editorial cartoons; lead-sentence construction; simple words; short paragraphs.

His success no one would deny. Circulation rocketed. Half a continent away Jane Addams paid unknowing tribute to the swelling influence of Pulitzer's example:

If one makes calls on a Sunday afternoon in the homes of the immigrant colonies near Hull-House, one finds the family absorbed in the Sunday edition of a sensational daily newspaper, even those who cannot read, quite easily following the comic adventures portrayed in the colored pictures of the supplement or tracing the clew of a murderer carefully depicted by a black line drawn through a plan of the house and street.[21]

In 1900 Delos F. Wilcox concluded from measurements of illustrations, stories of crime and vice, and medicine and employment advertisements that forty-seven of one hundred and forty-seven newspapers were yellow.[22] Frank Luther Mott, the foremost historian of American journalism, included in this category such papers as the Chicago *Tribune*, the Chicago *Times-Herald*, the New Orleans *Times-Democrat* and the Atlanta *Constitution*.[23] Obviously many newspapers followed Pulitzer in striving to make the transition from class to mass audience.

The third asset available to the new journalism was its leaders' tactical flair in converting increased organizational and financial resources first into an enhanced power to influence the public and then into a new power of action.

William Randolph Hearst envied Pulitzer's success in declaring independence of a limited constituency by winning a mass audience. To the problem of securing for himself an equally strong circulation base he brought no new techniques. He did, however, possess a prankish and iconoclastic spirit [24] that happily pushed to extremes those that Pulitzer had developed. In 1896–98, attempting to make himself the mobilizer of national sentiment, he applied this tactic to the situation in Cuba.

Hearst's particular genius lay in his ability to reduce abstractions to the personalized language of locale, to convert distant, complex problems to easily grasped and emotionally appealing personal predicaments. The *Journal* developed a

major campaign around the fate of Doctor Ricardo Ruiz, a
Cuban who had emigrated to this country, taken out citizenship papers, and then returned to join the insurrection. When
the dentist died in a Spanish cell under mysterious circumstances, Hearst claimed without proof that prison officials had
beaten Ruiz to death. In Hearst's rendering Ruiz became sy-
nonymous with Spanish persecution of American citizens.

By far the most successful of Hearst's case studies was that
of Evangelina Cisneros, a young and attractive Cuban woman
whom the editor alleged the authorities had imprisoned for resisting the advances of a Spanish officer. In fact, Miss Cisneros
and her friends had assaulted a Spanish colonel in a futile
attempt to escape the island to which she and her father, a
ranking insurrectionist, were confined. Ignoring the episode's
political ramifications and concentrating on the theme of a
maiden's molestation, Hearst painted his story across the *Journal*'s front pages.[25]

Another Hearst theme was that of patriots unjustly executed, plain people killed without cause. Not only did the
Journal describe Spanish atrocities, it printed what it alleged
to be the names and addresses of the Cuban dead. Each story,
moreover, was lavishly illustrated to heighten the personal
appeal of the victims and the sense of Spanish inhumanity.
Willis Abbot later recalled a photograph of a Cuban beach
scene; *Journal* artists drew in Spanish soldiers who appeared
to be herding people into the water to drown.[26]

Through the wires of the Associated Press the more remote
corners of the country learned of such Hearst promotions.[27]
One can gain a rough measure of Hearst's success by noting
his impress on those whose interests should have rendered
them most resistant. Frequently moved by the misfortunes
of others, William McKinley was unable to steel himself
against the pitiable individual whose plight Hearst was ex-
ploiting. With greater sympathy than discretion, McKinley received Dr. Ruiz's widow at the White House. Following the
liberation of Evangelina Cisneros, when the *Journal* quoted

John Sherman as saying that "everyone would sympathize with the Journal's enterprise," the president was quoted as declaring that his secretary of state's words "correctly voiced the unofficial sentiment of the administration." No denial issued from McKinley's office. Indeed, Miss Cisneros was invited to talk with the president. Privately scorning the yellow press, banishing from the White House copies of both *World* and *Journal*, recognizing that Hearst was helping to set a collision course with Spain, McKinley nonetheless gave injury to Madrid, credence and respectability to Hearst by receiving a person he thought unjustly treated.[28]

Such manifestations of influence failed to satisfy William Randolph Hearst. Neither he nor Joseph Pulitzer was content with the older precept that the journalist's job was simply to set out his position and wait for reason to prevail. The new journalism insisted on action, both as a reflection of already-mobilized support and as an inducement to further support. Attempting first to persuade government *not* to act, attempting subsequently to incite others, including the agencies of government, *to* act, in the end the popular press itself began to act in government's stead.

While big-city journalism remained the province of the urban educated, newspapers generally stood sentinel against any government's urge to meddle with what upper middle-class readers assumed a beneficent status quo. Editors monitored the executive branch with special care, for it was thought especially prone to deleterious initiatives.

During the Venezuelan crisis Joseph Pulitzer's role was this traditional one, the sentry alert to check executive encroachment. Angered by what he assumed administration bellicosity, he cabled British political and religious leaders, eliciting from almost all, including the Prince of Wales and former Prime Minister William E. Gladstone, gracious and conciliatory replies that were immediately printed in the *World* in the cause of peace. He cast his reading of the outcome in genteel fashion. "Publicity had done its work": [29] the power of the press had compelled Cleveland and Olney to desist from government initiatives of a most dubious character.

This customary role, however, should not disguise Pulitzer's efforts to forge a new relationship for journalism vis-à-vis government. He wished to embody the popular will, and that required a conception far beyond the enforcement of laissez faire. He was not content with occasional chastisements of federal initiatives. Coveting recognition that the *World* spoke with the voice of the whole people, he demanded that Washington act in ways *he* thought reflected the popular will. If the federal government failed to respond, Pulitzer himself might mobilize resources to act in its place. He did so with an air of the nag, the person moving with a show of reluctance as if to shame another into accepting a clear responsibility.

Though his target seemed to be the rich rather than the government,[30] Pulitzer as early as 1885 began to test his ability to mobilize action. When a private drive failed to collect sufficient funds to construct the pedestal for Frederic Auguste Bartholdi's Statue of Liberty, the *World* took the project in hand. "The World is the people's paper, and it now appeals to the people to come forward and raise the money. The $250,000 that the . . . statue cost was paid in by the masses of the French people—by the workingmen, the tradesmen, the shop girls, the artisans . . . Let us respond in like manner. Let us not wait for the millionaires to give money . . . Let us hear from the people." [31] The crusade begun in March produced $101,091 by August: 120,000 people sent in sums ranging from five cents to Pulitzer's $250. A reporter caught his employer's spirit: "It is a grand thing to see a paper leading the sentiment of a nation. That is what The World is doing today." [32]

During the Venezuelan dispute Pulitzer reached out beyond New York City and beyond the nation and, by enlisting the support of those figures important to English public life, brought undeniable pressure on what he deemed miscreant government. Although Venezuela stole the drama, it was in

an almost simultaneous confrontation—the debate over the
sale of government bonds—that Pulitzer with great boldness
pushed far beyond the concept of the newspaper as sentinel.
Here Pulitzer disputed not the fact of federal action but the
method. He castigated as "further costly dickers with a bond
syndicate" negotiations between J. P. Morgan and a small
group of government officials headed by the president.[33] He
insisted that the government offer its bonds directly to the
public. "The World," he said, "offers in advance to take
one million dollars of the new bonds at the highest market
price. . . . It will *compel a public loan*. . . . The voice of
the country will be heard. . . ." [34] The fact that a public
sale had failed two years earlier required action to establish
the practicability of Pulitzer's alternative. The *World* sent
telegrams and prepaid reply forms to 10,370 banks throughout the nation asking them to support a public issue. Fifty-
three hundred replies, breaking Western Union's one-day
record for messages sent to a single address, pledged purchases of $235,000,000.[35]

As the *World* chided Washington, it became evident that the
syndicate was only a secondary target. "The needless waste
of ten or fifteen millions . . . [in brokers' commissions] is not
the only or even the chief objection . . . [to this transaction].
It involves something of immeasurably greater worth than any
number of millions. It involves popular confidence in the integrity of the Government . . . Secrecy of negotiation . . .
awakens, unjustly, suspicions against the honor of the Government itself. . . . Trust the people, Mr. Cleveland!" [36] On January 6, 1896, the secretary of the Treasury announced that he
had authorized sale to the public. The issue was quickly over-
subscribed. Attacking a government initiative, Pulitzer had
moved on to prise open an alternative rejected by the executive, to mobilize opinion to compel government to abandon
its preferred route.

William Randolph Hearst adopted Pulitzer's notion of the
newspaper as an instrument of action vis-à-vis government.

He quickly moved to persuade or, when necessary, to compel government to act in ways he urged. Again, however, there was the Hearst impulse to the extreme. Implicit in many of his actions was the portrayal of the newspaper as surrogate government.[37] His was a journalism that in limited categories of action would rival and occasionally displace government.

Such a conception was not mere flatulence, for Pulitzer's innovative response to new technological capabilities permitted the newspaper to gather financial and organizational capacities that were, at certain points, superior to those of the federal government.

Information-gathering stands as a case in point. With government not yet providing an alternative source of information, political leaders accepted the newspaper as authoritative. Hearst's most famous reporter, James Creelman, claimed that the newspaper alone had access to the changing facts, and congressmen, who regularly cited newspaper stories in support of points made in debate, appeared to agree. Senator Mason called such articles "the only means of getting information." Senator Hoar employed his hometown newspaper as a private reference service, telegraphing for desired facts. As W. A. Swanberg concluded of the Cuban situation, "the United States administration . . . knew scarcely more than was printed in the newspapers." [38]

To politicians watching Pulitzer and Hearst fling out their news networks, the *World* and the *Journal* seemed especially useful. While still one of the Senate's most powerful members, John Sherman quoted the *Journal* on the floor. The Senate's Foreign Relations Committee sought out *Journal* reporters Lawrence and Lainé for advice on the situation in Cuba.[39]

Pulitzer and Hearst recognized the potential purchase in sources of information superior to Washington's. Wagering that indispensability might scour some of sensationalism's tarnish, they raced to relay to office-holders news that was barely creeping through official channels. Ten days after the *Maine*'s destruction the *World* sent to the secretary of war a dispatch in which correspondent Sylvester Scovel described the progress of the official American inquiry then underway in Havana. Scovel's report, the *World* assured Alger, "contains information of the highest importance, and will prove useful to you." It would have, had the secretary paid it attention, for it told him, accurately in both cases, that "all the Board are now convinced that the *Maine* was blown up externally" and that Washington could not expect to receive the "secret" report before the following Wednesday.[40] Alger and other administration officials, including the secretary of the Navy, first learned of Dewey's victory at Manila Bay when they opened telegrams from the *World*.

As the popular press moved to fill this information vacuum, so did Hearst exploit the void created by government's reluctance to act. Pulitzer's action tactics—urging the people to contribute money, to purchase government bonds, to sign petitions—did not encroach on government's sphere, but Hearst set for himself no such limit. In the Cisneros affair, for example, Hearst at first ordered more than two hundred reporters to knock on the doors of some of the nation's most respectable families. The widows of Ulysses Grant and Jefferson Davis, the wife of the secretary of state, even the mother of the president joined thousands of other women in signing petitions entreating the Pope's intervention and the Queen Regent's clemency. Lady Rothschild was prominent in the collection of two hundred thousand English signatures. Evangelina Cisneros, nonetheless, continued to languish in a Havana prison; in Hearst's reading, the government thereby revealed itself unwilling to meet its duty to translate public opinion into policy. Thus, before the popular frenzy had opportunity to subside or the Spanish had time to divest themselves of this acute embarrassment, Hearst sent reporter Karl Decker to Havana under orders to spirit the "Flower of

Cuba" from her cell. Bribery rather than daring or ingenuity sufficed. Disguised as a sailor, Evangelina Cisneros was smuggled to New York for mammoth celebrations organized by Hearst to mark her deliverance.

Later, during the Spanish-American War, Hearst ordered Creelman to scuttle a vessel in midpassage of the Suez Canal in order to bar a Spanish fleet sailing for the Pacific.[41] Though in the end of the outcome of the battle of Santiago Bay caused Madrid hastily to recall Admiral Manuel de la Carvara's squadron, Creelman was undismayed. Like Hearst, he had thought the United States government incapable of taking the essential step at Suez and, though his own aid had here proven unnecessary, he continued to uphold Hearst's belief in the indispensability of journalistic interjection: "There are times when public emergencies call for the sudden intervention of some power outside of governmental authority." [42]

Equally as important as these actions was Hearst's constant resort to an imagery of surrogate government. As early as 1896, in a poll of the governors, he solicited opinion favorable to American intervention in Cuba and estimates of the numbers of volunteers each state would supply; he printed the results as if the *Journal* were an official organization whose capsulization of popular sentiment should lead automatically to its translation into government policy—specifically a war against Spain. Subsequent steps offered a picture of editor as powerful public servant. With no heed to Washington's possible diplomatic discomfiture, Hearst dispatched reporter Ralph Paine to deliver to the Cuban rebel general, Gomez, a diamond sword that, from its description, would seem a suitable gift from one potentate to another. He referred to his correspondents as "special commissioners." He designed a *Journal* flag to be flown from his buildings and vessels. He engaged a group of Congressmen to inspect conditions in Cuba under the *Journal*'s auspices. Speeches and articles issuing from this "Congressional Commission" were both fiercely interventionist and unabashedly laudatory of the accuracy of Hearst's reportage on Cuba.[43]

Predictably, the *Journal*'s war organization was elaborate: between seventy and eighty correspondents; at least ten dispatch boats; extensive wire facilities and instrument depots. After offering the Navy his yacht and the Army a half-million dollar cavalry regiment—and securing no commission in return—Hearst entered the war zone as a journalist. Private Post, marching in column, noticed the editor at the roadside, drawn up as if to review the passing troops. Hearst later exposed himself to the enemy's fire and in his culminating adventure waded onto a beach to take as prisoners of war twenty-nine Spanish survivors of the naval battle of Santiago Bay.[44]

Such activities must of course be weighed for serious substance against Hearst's penchant for self-advertisement. Whether he was moved by an aversion to discipline, by a particular form of social pretension, or by a truly radical vision is unclear, but there is evidence that he did see his own role as one of mobilizing power that would rival, and eventually supersede, the federal government's. The intent implicit in the pattern of his actions prior to and during the war was made explicit at the conflict's close. In a signed editorial appearing in the *Journal* on September 25, 1898, he wrote:

The force of the newspaper is the greatest force in civilization.

Under republican government, newspapers form and express public opinion.

They suggest and control legislation.

They declare wars.

They punish criminals, especially the powerful.

They reward with approving publicity the good deeds of citizens everywhere.

The newspapers control the nation because THEY
REPRESENT THE PEOPLE.[45]

❖ ❖ ❖

William Randolph Hearst alone could not have offered so comprehensive a challenge. Vital was the popular press' final asset,
a cadre of reporters who shared his philosophy of expansive
journalism.

The dynamic uniting in the popular press technology and
circulation too often obscures the emotional dynamic that
persuaded newspapermen that their actions on behalf of the
people were at least as important as those of government.
Many who worked for Pulitzer and Hearst, far from the
stereotypical city-room cynic, were charged with an almost
electric idealism. To them the old journalism had voiced
only the interests of class or commercial constituencies. They
brought to their battle to enlarge journalism a fervor that
seemed to foreshadow that of the young settlement workers of
the following decade. Their sense of journalism as a calling to
public service was apparent in Arthur Brisbane of the *World*
who, his friend Charles Edward Russell slyly and reluctantly
conceded, "was willing to sacrifice himself for the cause of
the common people." [46] The leading motive of the yellow
press, insisted James Creelman, was "moral responsibility." [47]
The newspaper would speak the needs of all the people,
particularly the distressed. So heavily did enthusiasm armor
these subalterns of the new journalism that one, the *Journal's*
Willis Abbot found selflessness even in his editor. Hearst, he
reported, was entirely sincere in his sympathy for the masses.[48]
Even that supreme misanthrope Ambrose Bierce found excitement in the great numbers of people to whom the yellow
press would carry his words.[49]

These journalists of the second echelon were increasingly
important for, in a result ironic to a movement undertaken to
enlarge editors' influence, power was seeping from front

offices. In December 1895 the circulation of the *World* stood at 583,000, an increase of almost 100,000 in twelve months. In the year following its purchase by Hearst, the *Journal's* sales rose from 77,239 to 430,410. The defect concealed in such success was the passing of one-man management. No editor, however talented, could maintain control of such huge, multi-faceted operations.

Equally telling was the way in which the techniques of the new journalism, notably shouting headlines and magnetic illustrations, diminished the authority of the editor's own voice by drawing the reader from editorial to news pages.[50] Despite his pivotal role in devising the new typography, Pulitzer retained an old-fashioned respect for the editorial page; he superintended editorial policy just as if careful reasoning continued to move his readership far more than those breathless and gaudy news columns. Hearst, more realistic, held the *Journal's* editorial page in contempt.

A new kind of journalist waited to exploit these developments. As late as 1890 President Eliot of Harvard is reported to have denounced reporters as "drunkards, deadbeats and bummers"; five years later college graduates were already the rule in eastern newspaper offices.[51] They were confident young men unwilling to assume that the editor's interests defined their own. They had a first glimpse of themselves as "professionals" whose standards would be rooted not in editorial dictation but in press clubs and in schools of journalism. Prizing the new typography, they discovered in the crusade and the human-interest story ideal vehicles both of their social idealism and its individualized expression. Again Hearst showed himself more adaptive than his rival. Pulitzer apparently overlooked the point that defections from the *World's* staff might hinge less on lavish salary increases than on Hearst's offer of by-lines denied Pulitzer employees. To characterize yellow-press correspondents solely in terms of a mock moralism intended to camouflage either cynicism, commercialism, or infantile adventurousness is to miss the wellspring of many of their actions.

Thus, in a James Creelman, the belief that he was serving others before self dictated a new relationship between newspaper and government. Professing to care about those whom he called "the distressed," he was at home with the notion of the newspaper as the appropriate agency to relieve victims, whether of Spaniards or politicians, criminals or rascals. When Spanish Premier Canovas noted during a conversation with the reporter that "the newspapers in your country seem to be more powerful than the government," Creelman offered no demurral on grounds of principle or practice. Yes, he replied, newspapers are "more in touch with the people." [52]

Others shared this conception of the newspaper as an agency of action supplemental to, but at least commensurate with, the federal government. When General Shafter issued an order excluding correspondents from the ceremony marking Santiago's surrender, Sylvester Scovel announced himself from a rooftop overlooking the town square. Hauled down at Shafter's command, he insisted that he be included in official photographs of the surrender in recognition of the press' role in the war. When Shafter revealed that he found Scovel's proposition less than self-evident, the incensed reporter marred the dignity of the occasion by swinging at the general's nose.[53]

Correspondents generally thought of themselves as full military participants,[54] and the Army had no greater success in demarcating the line between soldier and newsman than between officer and enlisted volunteer. During the battle of El Caney, Creelman located a hidden route and then led General Chaffee's men in a bayonet charge against the Spanish position. Clambering atop the fort, he seized the Spanish flag —not for self, not for country, but as "a glorious prize for my newspaper." [55] Those who have commented on the ensuing scene—Hearst arriving to tell the wounded Creelman, "I'm sorry you're hurt, but wasn't it a splendid fight? We must beat every paper in the world" [56]—emphasize the editor's misplaced anxiety for the story rather than the survival of his correspondent. Overlooked is the fact that in relating the episode Creelman himself had no word of criticism for Hearst's reaction. He assumed, optimistically, that for Hearst too the cause transcended individual profit or puffery.

Because correspondents would act where government hesitated, because newspapers were "more in touch with the people," Creelman concluded that the newspaper must serve as their direct agent. Circulation rather than ballots would provide the measure of popular endorsement. To buy the newspaper was to vote its editor a "moral regency"; hence circulation figures would serve as referenda on a paper's specific actions "when it attempts to usurp the functions of the police, the courts, the legislature or even the President." It was to be—neither Hearst nor Creelman flinched from the ultimate logic of the argument—a system of "government by newspaper." [57]

James Creelman was to be disappointed in his happy anticipation of the new journalism's assumption of power, and here Hearst and Pulitzer must bear partial responsibility. They delighted in exposing, denouncing, and demeaning one another, to the sole profit of an Associated Press whose ethics were not noticeably superior to their own. Hearst moreover drove on to the ultimate excess. When William McKinley was assassinated, many Americans connected the deed with the *Journal's* earlier publication of Ambrose Bierce's quatrain

> The bullet that pierced Goebel's breast
> Can not be found in all the West;
> Good reason, it is speeding here
> To stretch McKinley on his bier

and an editorial suggesting that "If bad institutions and bad men can be got rid of only by killing, then the killing must be done." [58] Many then concluded that Hearst was indeed a menace. Irate citizens burned bundles of the *Journal,* hanged the publisher in effigy, and forced advertisers to withdraw their patronage.

Hearst might have recouped the revenue and reputation lost in this setback, were not other developments revealing fundamental flaws in original yellow-press calculations. The gravest error lay in the basic economic assumption. While both *World* and *Journal* gained huge circulations, in neither case did advertising and revenue grow commensurately. Both newspapers lost money in 1898. Too many of the new readers either lacked purchasing power or were otherwise resistant to advertising; too many of the old, more prosperous readers defected to other dailies. The advertisers themselves began to organize, the better to resist rate increases by playing paper against paper.[59] The Hearst-Pulitzer rivalry, in pursuing larger and larger numbers, had revealed unexpected limits to the circulation-advertising-profits equation.

The yellow press' thrust to power encountered yet another check. Both publishers had pressed the federal government to take various actions, but each was torn between urging government to act and acting as government. As Washington did respond to public pressure (most notably in mobilizing for war), it immediately reestablished itself as the focus of loyalty. The *Journal* and the *World,* with no claim on popular allegiances comparable to that of the state, found their area of maneuverability shrinking. A newspaper that conceded an identity between "the public interest" and administration policy invited eclipse, but to continue to court attention by championing the public interest *against* official policy and behavior in wartime required the most delicate calculations.

It was on this exposed flank that Hearst caught Pulitzer when the *World* printed a dispatch by Stephen Crane reporting that the 71st New York had wavered during the battle of San Juan. The *Journal* rushed into print a righteous denunciation of the *World's*:

SLURS ON THE BRAVERY OF THE
BOYS OF THE 71ST

Attempting to absolve itself, the *World* established a memorial fund for the regiment's dead, but so severe was public censure that it was compelled to return the money it had collected.[60] Government rather than newspaper embodied patriotism and though Hearst here invoked such sentiment to his tactical advantage, he at the same time reduced his own leverage vis-à-vis government.

To the first of these unforeseen problems Pulitzer and Hearst had no choice but to respond similarly. The cumulative effects of economic miscalculation so weakened the *World* and reduced the publisher's options that only a return to the status quo ante seemed feasible. Pulitzer opened negotiations with his rival, agreed to a truce and again admonished the *World's* staff to practice journalism of only the highest character.[61] Hearst, after probing with no success the possibilities of a newspaper cartel, was compelled by similar stringency to accept Pulitzer's armistice.

To the second problem Hearst and Pulitzer responded from very different ultimate aims. One cannot read Joseph Pulitzer's correspondence in the years 1896–98 without feeling shafts of sympathy. Those brilliantly innovative energies of the 1880s had cost him his health. He had lost his eyesight, and so fragile was his nervous system that a loud noise produced shattering pain.[62] Traveling almost constantly in an unsuccessful quest for relief, Pulitzer visited the *World* office only three times after 1890.[63] It was his greater misfortune that his nemesis appeared and, in pushing to its limits each of Pulitzer's propositions, revealed the unresolved tensions in his thought.

Pulitzer held initial impact essential. He prized format that seized readers' emotion, riveting their attention and rendering them receptive to his instruction. As he said of the *World:*

It's read by, well, say a million people a day; and it's my
duty to see they get the truth; but that's not enough. It's
got to be put before them briefly so that they will read
it; clearly so they will understand it; forcibly so they will
appreciate it; picturesquely so they will remember it;
and, above all, accurately so that they may be wisely
guided by its light.[64]

Pulitzer may have been wholly sincere, but the *World's* pursuit of brevity, clarity, vividness, and especially force frequently terminated in gross simplification alien to accuracy.
In large measure this grew from Pulitzer's inability to separate
spheres of titillation and instruction. The basic concept, as
Swanberg has noted, was that of a "hula dancer performing
in front of a cathedral in order to attract the crowds," [65] but
Pulitzer never entirely purged himself of the temptation to
summon those larger crowds that would flock to see the girl
dance on the altar. The urge to attract readers often rendered the urge to instruct the victim of deferred purpose.
    Nevertheless, his ultimate aims (however limping many of
his efforts to achieve them) were essentially didactic. No
longer nurturing the political ambitions of his youth—"I can
never be president because I am a foreigner, but some day
I am going to elect a president" [66]—he still aspired to recognition as a moral force of national consequence. He assumed
that whatever the day-to-day techniques employed to attract
an expanding readership, he would be able to identify issues
of moment to the nation and then, with the voice of reason,
educate and mobilize the people to enlightened positions. He
pursued power, but he never doubted that, when he chose,
he could express that power as service to his fellow men.
Never did he better approach this ideal than during the
Venezuelan crisis: never did he move further from it than
during the preliminaries to the Spanish-American War.
    Hearst avoided the snare of Pulitzer's thought because he
found it unnecessary to separate hula dancer and cathedral:

Find out what your readers want and give it to them.[67] The ultimate appeal, he thought, was to be found in what Arthur McEwen called "gee-whiz emotion." [68] It followed that only through sensation could one speak to the entire nation, and Hearst too sought a national voice. His aims, however, lacked any pedagogical cast. They were purely manipulative. His goal in these years was specific, personal power. His method was that of fastening the *Journal* to any issue that would aid in forging a national political constituency.

Thus, with their efforts to establish a quasi-governmental power blocked by the intransigency of patriotism, it is not surprising that the two attempted to apply contrary solutions. Joseph Pulitzer retreated in some relief to that older role of sentinel: within a year he was denouncing that which he had helped to create, the "enormous expansion" of presidential power.[69] Hearst, to the contrary, continued to press ahead. As the nation emerged from that extraordinary emotional climate of the 1890s, however, he was able to find no new way to bring mass circulation to bear on the political process. To hook the newspaper to still greater power only one route remained open: to unite newspaper, public interest, and government in the person of William Randolph Hearst. He stood for the nation's highest office and there his ultimate ambition met its defeat.

So disappeared the publishers' hopes for government by newspaper. The power of the yellow press was short-lived in part because economics and patriotism showed themselves less malleable than expected. In greater measure the transiency of its influence reflects the belated willingness of Washington itself to move into the political vacuum. Under Theodore Roosevelt the federal government began to respond to those entering and enlarging the center's political processes, those for whom only the *World* and the *Journal* had spoken.

Epilogue

AMERICANS celebrated the Spanish-American War as a signal success. The collective memory of the conflict quickly incorporated the substance of John Hay's "splendid little war" and Redfield Proctor's "new birth"—and just as swiftly expunged Private Post's "I survived." Only World War II can challenge its claim as the most popular of America's wars.

Granting that American idealism in early 1898 was no less restrained than in early 1917, one would look for a comparable disillusionment moving to penetrate the undeniable gap between commitment and realization. In fact, there was little. Though a small minority of Americans vigorously contested McKinley's colonial acquisitions policy and a handful spoke their distress that Valeriano Weyler was the apparent author of the American Army's tactics in suppressing the Philippine Insurrection, neither issue roused the public at large. General approbation of the war itself remained undented. There was none of the post-1918 period's searing sense of deception and betrayal, whether by allies abroad or businessmen at home, fusing with retrospective repugnance for a president's idealistic leadership; what disenchantment appeared in 1898 was no more than a sadness flecked with anger that the Cubans and Filipinos had proven unworthy of American humani-

tarianism. Such sentiment generated minimal domestic stress
—indeed, it worked to rehabilitate McKinley's reputation—and
somehow allowed Americans to sustain simultaneously the
nobility of the effort and the ignobility of its beneficiaries.
By popular reckoning, the conflict remained, in Lodge's
phrase, the "wonderful war."

Not even the Spanish-American War, however, could repay
all of the hopes invested in it.

As long as he was able to maintain that by a broad restoration of individual character war would strengthen his society,
Theodore Roosevelt could ignore the problem of power. He,
with William McKinley, Pierpont Morgan, and others of the
old consensus, assumed that character automatically controlled power. The decisions of self-regulating men of character would be right, socially beneficent, indeed altogether
irreproachable, whether the issue were a vote, a war, an industry, or a canal. Character, and the common moral sentiment for which it stood, were their own safeguards against
any abuse of power.

On Kettle Hill Roosevelt had escaped temporarily the stress
of those border situations in which a person—not least the
American office-holder in a time of flux—is compelled to
choose between evils. He had gloried in combat purged of
moral ambiguity. Indeed, he had there achieved an apotheo-
sis of individualism. The war, nonetheless, "was not a great
war." Though powerful in some lives, it had failed to touch
sufficient numbers of lives. It had been neither long enough
nor strenuous enough to release the requisite cleansing energies. It had not worked that restoration of society on which
Theodore Roosevelt had counted.

The Indian summer of consensus thus slipped away. Almost
as soon as he entered the White House, Roosevelt found his
society again pressed by the problem of business power.

If the declaration of war had served as a victory of humanitarianism over commercial influences, it was a triumph
without substance. Whatever the emotional satisfaction it
offered in appearing to vanquish material values, it lacked
practical result. As they concluded that hostilities were inevi-

table, businessmen supported the war effort no less than others, and Americans at large immediately suspended their criticism of the money power. Indeed, one might speculate that the war's absorption of antibusiness sentiment may have vitiated the emotional force behind antibusiness aspects of Progressive reform. In any case, the movement toward corporate consolidation continued. Mergers occurred in record numbers in the four years immediately following the war.

In those measures with which he responded to this situation Roosevelt linked old and new systems. In the minds of his countrymen he continued to epitomize the values of nineteenth-century individualism. Yet it was he who moved early in the twentieth century to strengthen those structures of government "too small to form opinion, too narrow to express it, too weak to give effect to it." His actions gave to the executive branch a new voice and influence that left no interstices for publishers anxious to act in quasi-official capacities. He adopted the rhetoric of the journalistic crusade, conveying to those he called the "half-educated reading public" a sense of government's new moral concerns. More important, he conceded that economic aggregates had grown so large that one could no longer assume that the values of individualism, independent of institutional force, shaped them to the public interest. Under Roosevelt's direction, Washington first came to consider the application of power as one of the routine processes of governence. The initial dimensions were modest—not before the 1930s would the center's power enter directly the lives of those in Clyde and Galesburg, New York and Chicago—but even Roosevelt's halting attempts to limit the size of corporate units and to apply regulatory acts signaled government's departure from the old system.

"I believe in a strong Executive," he said. "I believe in power."

Conceding that character no longer controlled commerce, linking presidency and power, Theodore Roosevelt acknowledged the disintegration of the social consensus that had shaped post-Civil War America.

Notes

CHAPTER I

1. Herbert N. Casson, *The History of the Telephone* (Chicago, 1910), pp. 202–3. See also Richard T. Loomis, "The White House Telephone and Crisis Management," *United States Naval Institute Proceedings*, XCV (Dec. 1969), 64–65.
2. See Albert K. Weinberg, *Manifest Destiny: A Study of Nationalist Expansionism in American History* (Baltimore, 1935), p. 270. Weinberg quotes Dr. Frank W. Gunsaulus from Harry F. Atwood, *Keep God in American History* (Chicago, 1919): "From the point of view of theological determinism, 'statesmanship is seeing where almighty God is going and then getting things out of his way.'"
3. Quoted in Larzer Ziff, *The American 1890s: Life and Times of a Lost Generation* (New York, 1966), p. 71.
4. *Speeches and Addresses of William McKinley, From March 1, 1897 to May 30, 1900* (New York, 1900), p. 166.
5. Charles S. Olcott, *William McKinley*, 2 vols. (Boston and New York, 1916), I, 23. See also the remarks of William McKinley Osborne quoted in the unsigned article "President William McKinley. Main Events in His Life," *Ohio State Archaeological and Historical Society Quarterly*, X (July 1901), 233. "On our way back to Poland [Ohio] that night we discussed the matter together and decided that it was our duty to volunteer, and we thought that the man who staid [*sic*] would be despised by the community. . . . Our enlistment was

in cold blood, and not through the enthusiasm of the moment."
6. Olcott, *McKinley*, I, 33.
7. *Ohio State Archaeological and Historical Society Quarterly*, p. 234.
8. Olcott, *McKinley*, I, 37, 45–46.
9. Margaret Leech, *In the Days of McKinley* (New York, 1959), p. 8.
10. Ibid., pp. 58–60; H. Wayne Morgan, *William McKinley and His America* (Syracuse, New York, 1963), pp. 169–74.
11. W. A. Swanberg, *Citizen Hearst, A Biography of Willian Randolph Hearst* (New York, 1961), p. 86.
12. Thomas Beer, *Hanna* (New York, 1929), p. 103. Anna Maus, visiting at the White House the wife of the president's military aide, was introduced to Ida McKinley. "A few minutes after our arrival, President McKinley passed across the far end of the hall, and she called him to come to her. He protested that two Senators were waiting for him. 'Let them wait,' she said, 'I want you so much.' The gentle, dear man came down . . ." Anna Page Russell Maus, "Reminiscences of the Wife of an Army Surgeon," typescript with pages unnumbered, in the Halsted Maus Family Papers, United States Army Military History Research Collection, Carlisle, Pennsylvania. (Hereafter cited as USAMHRC.)
13. Walter B. Stevens, "William McKinley, the Beloved Among Presidents," *Commonwealth*, I (Nov. 1901), 214. "The natural and pure devotion to the invalid wife was beautiful. It had its practical side. In the making of a character fit for the White House, it had no small part." See also Julia B. Foraker, *I Would Live It Again, Memories of a Vivid Life* (New York and London, 1932), p. 257. The author, wife of the powerful Ohio Senator, wrote that the American public wove "a halo for . . . [McKinley] out of his devotion to his invalid wife. . . . Whatever the qualities, the circumstances, that led him to the highest pinnacle of fame, the thing that endeared McKinley to the nation was his slavish protectiveness towards the woman to whom the best had been given—and taken away. The unbroken guard he kept, his patience and gentleness in circumstances of the most trying nature, affected Washington, affected the whole country as nothing coming from the White House ever had done."
14. Olcott, *McKinley*, II, 361.

15. Edward Thornton Heald, *The William McKinley Story* (Canton, Ohio, 1964), p. 43.
16. *Speeches and Addresses of William McKinley, From his Election to Congress to the Present Time* (New York, 1893), p. 2.
17. Vincent De Santis, "American Politics in the Gilded Age," *The Review of Politics*, XXV (Oct. 1963), 556. James E. Pollard, *The Presidents and the Press* (New York, 1947), p. 552. The author notes that newspapers in the 1890s did not yet consider the White House a sufficiently important news source to cover it thoroughly or even regularly.
18. Shelby M. Cullom, *Fifty Years of Public Service* (Chicago, 1911), p. 275.
19. Oscar Doane Lambert, *Stephen Benton Elkins* (Pittsburgh, 1955), p. 227.
20. Ibid., p. 225.
21. Samuel Gompers, *Seventy Years of Life and Labor, An Autobiography*, 2 vols. (New York, 1925), I, 522–23.
22. Ida M. Tarbell, "President McKinley In War Times," *McClure's Magazine*, XI (July 1898), 213. Miss Tarbell believed that the "great majority" of unofficial visitors received McKinley's personal attention.
23. Henry L. Stoddard, *As I Knew Them: Presidents and Politics from Grant to Coolidge* (New York and London, 1927), p. 231. See also Joseph L. Bristow, *Fraud and Politics at the Turn of the Century* (New York, 1952), p. 25. McKinley "could shake hands with thousands, apparently without great fatigue, and would never listen to the suggestion that he meet the people formally without handshakings. . . . He seemed to love to meet the public in cordial face-to-face greeting."
24. Leech, *McKinley*, pp. 441–42.
25. "William McKinley, An Address by William F. Burdell before the Buz Fuz Club, Dayton, Ohio, April 19, 1902," pp. 12–13, in the Papers of George B. Cortelyou, Library of Congress.
26. Stoddard, *As I Knew Them*, p. 231. Bristow, *Fraud and Politics*, p. 79. "This round of perplexing interviews is repeated day after day and year after year."
27. Olcott, *McKinley*, I, 298. See also Stanley L. Jones, *The Presidential Election of 1896* (Madison, Wisconsin, 1964), pp. 111–12.
28. Heald, *McKinley Story*, p. 53. Bristow, *Fraud and Politics*, p. 23. Bristow, as McKinley's Fourth Assistant Postmaster Gen-

eral an important patronage dispenser and trouble-shooter, described the President's voice as "neither musical nor especially strong . . . [but] peculiarly sympathetic and very effective," though McKinley "was not, in the popular sense, a great orator."

29. Cullom, *Fifty Years*, p. 276.
30. Leon Burr Richardson, *William E. Chandler, Republican* (New York, 1940), pp. 539, 542.
31. George F. Hoar, *Autobiography of Seventy Years*, 2 vols. (New York, 1903), II, 315, 317.
32. Albert Halstead, "The President At Work—A Character Sketch," *The Independent*, LIII (Sept. 5, 1901), 2084. "More than any recent President he has caused his political opponents to find it a pleasure to call." Bristow, *Fraud and Politics*, p. 76, notes McKinley's ability to refuse favors and create admirers at the same time.
33. James H. Moynihan, *The Life of Archbishop John Ireland* (New York, 1953), pp. 151, 258.
34. Henry Adams, *The Education of Henry Adams: An Autobiography* (Boston and New York, 1918), p. 374. Julia Foraker, *I Would Live It Again*, p. 257, believed that McKinley possessed a "genius for winning the regard of men."
35. Halstead, "The President at Work," p. 2085. "It is remarkable that in so many instances the President has some knowledge of the candidate [for an appointment], due to his own long public service and wide acquaintance."
36. William Barnes and John Heath Morgan, *The Foreign Service of the United States: Origins, Development, and Functions* (Washington, D.C., 1961), p. 151.
37. A. Bower Sageser, *First Two Decades of the Pendleton Act* (Lincoln, Nebraska, 1935), pp. 218–20. See also Leech, *McKinley*, pp. 371–72.
38. John Bassett Moore, quoted in Charles Ulysses Gordon, *William McKinley Commemorative Tributes* (Waterloo, Wisconsin, 1942), p. 26.
39. Cullom, *Fifty Years*, p. 276.
40. Quoted in Bess Furman, *White House Profile: A Social History of the White House, its Occupants and its Festivities* (Indianapolis and New York, 1951), pp. 258–59.
41. Stoddard, *As I Knew Them*, p. 253.
42. Lyman J. Gage, *Memoirs* (New York, 1937), p. 91.

43. Frederick Lewis Allen, *The Big Change* (New York, 1952), p. 91.
44. Bristow, *Fraud and Politics*, p. 32. "No man has ever been President who got such a firm hold on the affections of those with whom he came into close personal relations."
45. Olcott, *McKinley*, I, 61. For a contradictory view, see Ernest R. May, *Imperial Democracy, The Emergence of America as a Great Power* (New York, 1961), p. 114. May believes that McKinley possessed "traces of virtue but few of character." It was, however, precisely for the latter that the president's contemporaries appear to have valued him.
46. In *The Autobiography of Lincoln Steffens* (New York, 1931), pp. 245–46, the author tells of a distraught old woman of the Lower East Side who, pulling him upstairs and into her one-room tenement flat, points to her three young daughters watching from a window as a prostitue nearby services client after client. Steffens suggests drawing the curtain; the woman has none. "Ask the . . . [prostitute] to pull her blind." "I have. Oh, I have begged her on my knees, and she won't." Steffens then crosses to the prostitute and there discovers that the old woman earlier had her raided, "and now I have to pay—big—to stay here." In her anger the prostitute is determined to ruin the old one's daughters. New threats, however, reduce her to tears, and she ultimately agrees to pin a blanket across her window. Returning to the street, Steffens meets a patrolman. "I have fixed it," he tells him. "Don't do anything. It's all right now." Steffens concludes his account: "It wasn't, of course. Nothing was all right. Neither in this case, nor in prostitution generally, nor on the strikes—is there any right—or wrong. . . . It was, it is, all a struggle between conflicting interests, between two blind opposite sides, neither of which is right or wrong." This moral relativism, symptomatic of the disintegration within the urban setting of those older, very tidy categories of right and wrong, did not until after 1900 gain sufficient force to compel most middle-class Americans to give more sympathetic definition to such social problems.
47. Interest in the Cuban insurrection diminished markedly during the presidential campaign of 1896.
48. Irwin Hood (Ike) Hoover, *Forty Two Years in the White House* (Boston and New York, 1934), p. 22.
49. McKinley to freight agent of Pennsylvania Railroad, Jan. 24,

1895; McKinley to presidents of chambers of commerce in Cleveland, Cincinnati, Columbus, Toledo, and Dayton, Feb. 15, 1895; McKinley to M. W. Whitney, Chairman, Committee of Trades Assembly, Nelsonville, Ohio, July 11, 1895, McKinley Manuscript Collection, Ohio Historical Society, Columbus. Copies in Stark County Historical Center, Canton, Ohio.

50. John Addison Porter to Joseph G. Darlington, Jan. 8, 1898; Porter to Governor Daniel Hastings of Pennsylvania, Jan. 10, 1898, Papers of William McKinley, Library of Congress.

51. Richard W. Leopold, *The Growth of American Foreign Policy, A History* (New York, 1962), p. 173.

52. Heald, *McKinley Story*, p. 89.

53. James B. Morrow in the Washington *Post*, Mar. 22, 1908, quoting a former Secretary of the Interior under McKinley, Cornelius N. Bliss: "President McKinley walked back and forth in the wide path behind the White House, enduring in silence and alone another 'agony of the garden.' "

54. Lawrence Shaw Mayo, ed., *America of Yesterday as Reflected in the Journal of John Davis Long* (Boston, 1923), p. 165. On April 2 Long again noted the president's "weariness and nervous strain" (p. 175). John Hay later observed that in his efforts to avert war McKinley "strained almost to breaking" relationships with many of his friends. Quoted in Gordon, *McKinley Commemorative Tributes*, p. 77.

55. H. H. Kohlsaat, *From McKinley to Harding: Personal Recollections of Our Presidents* (New York, 1923), p. 67.

56. *Speeches 1897–1900*, p. 129. "Your voice," McKinley told the people, "when constitutionally expressed, is commanding and conclusive. It is the mandate of law. It is the law to Congress and to the Executive."

57. Chauncey M. Depew, "Memorial Address on President McKinley at the Lincoln Anniversary Banquet of the Republican Club of New York, February 12, 1902," Cortelyou Papers.

58. Mark Hanna as quoted in the Washington *Post*, Sept. 28, 1901: "The one absorbing purpose in William McKinley's political career was to keep closely in touch with the people . . ."

59. Bristow, *Fraud and Politics*, p. 89.

60. Horatio S. Rubens, *Liberty, The Story of Cuba* (New York, 1932), pp. 336–37. "In the month preceding this [war] message [to Congress] popular opinion had turned against McKinley. His picture was hissed in theatres, he was hung in effigy in several towns." See also Edward Thornton Heald, McKinley

Biography (Unpublished MS, Stark County Historical Society, Canton, Ohio), chapter 26, p. 64. For an extreme example of the animus building against McKinley see W. D. Sloan to John D. Long, Dec. 8, 1897, in the Papers of John D. Long, Massachusetts Historical Society, Boston, Massachusetts. "The men of the Cabinet are of excellent reputation but McKinley will everlastingly damn every one of them by his cowardly [,] heartless [,] unamerican action. When he accepted the nomination . . . he agreed to use his . . . power to secure freedom to Cuba. His action and words . . . have branded him a liar and a fraud—and every man in Ohio [,] Indiana and Kentucky condemns his Cuban utterances. His administration will stink worse than that mercenary scoundrel that preceded him. . . . This country is not far from insurrection. No man has the right to put the brand of cowardice on this people. We will not stand it. . . . *The limit of patience has been reached.*"

61. Frederick Merk, *Manifest Destiny and Mission in American History, A Reinterpretation* (New York, 1970), p. 250. "But his philosophy was that a President obeys, does not resist, public opinion."

62. Edmund Wilson, *Patriotic Gore: Studies in the Literature of the American Civil War* (New York, 1962), pp. 750–53.

63. Ibid., pp. 758–59.

64. Mark DeWolfe Howe, comp., *The Occasional Speeches of Justice Oliver Wendell Holmes* (Cambridge, Massachusetts, 1962), p. 80.

65. Quoted in Hermann Hagedorn, *Leonard Wood: A Biography,* 2 vols. (New York, 1931), I, 141. See also Charles W. Fairbanks, *Address by Charles W. Fairbanks at the Unveiling of the McKinley Monument, Toledo, Ohio, 14 September 1903* (Indianapolis, 1903), p. 7. (Copy in Cortelyou Papers.) The vice-president recalled that McKinley remarked just prior to the war, "I do not care for the property that will be destroyed, nor the money that will be expended . . . but the thought of human suffering that must enter many households almost overwhelms me."

66. General Stewart L. Woodford, "McKinley and the Spanish War," *Yearbook of the Oneida Historical Society,* X (1905), 142.

67. Leech, *McKinley,* p. 177. McKinley forwarded the official report to the Congress with no comment of his own. See also Henry Watterson, *History of the Spanish-American War*

(Boston, 1898), p. 41; Henry Cabot Lodge, "The Spanish-American War: II—The Coming of War," *Harper's New Monthly Magazine*, XCVIII (March 1899), 505.

68. James Ford Rhodes, *The McKinley and Roosevelt Administrations, 1897–1909* (New York, 1922), pp. 27–28; Leech, *McKinley*, pp. 95–96.

69. Olcott, *McKinley*, I, 323–24. The author estimates that one hundred and twenty million documents were distributed by the McKinley campaign organization. See also Jones, *Election of 1896*, p. 279. The Chicago office alone deployed two hundred and fifty speakers.

70. Pollard, *Presidents and Press*, p. 552. As president, McKinley "had no special sense of publicity nor did he feel any need of it."

71. Mayo, *Long*, p. 165.

72. Tarbell, "President McKinley," p. 214.

73. Gamaliel Bradford to John D. Long, no date but probably written during the first week of April 1898, Long Papers. The "trouble is that . . . [the immense majority of the country] has no direct contact with . . . [the president]. All sorts of reports and rumors are flying as to what he says and does. One paper says this and another that, so that there is nothing authentic. Meantime Congressmen say they are overwhelmed with messages from their constituents urging war. . . . The President does not owe his position to Congress. He owes it to the people of the United States and they have the right to hear from him. A dozen lines given out under his signature, merely asking for time and patience [,] would be printed in every newspaper in the country, and give them something to talk of besides the jingoism in Congress."

74. Olcott, *McKinley*, II, 53–54; Telegrams to McKinley from A. Hewitt, Women's Christian Temperance Union, Oscar S. Straus, Apr. 11, 1898; Thomas Wilson to McKinley, Apr. 18, 1898; Cyrus Huling and E. N. Higgins to McKinley, Apr. 19, 1898; letters from various formal and informal military units and veterans organizations; White House form letter sent in reply to above, Apr. 7–18, 1898, McKinley Papers.

75. Arthur Wallace Dunn, *From Harrison to Harding, A Personal Narrative, Covering a Third of a Century, 1888–1921*, 2 vols. (New York and London, 1922), I, 231.

76. Mark Hanna to McKinley, Apr. 3, 1898, McKinley Papers.

77. Dorothy Ganfield Fowler, *John Coit Spooner, Defender of Presidents* (New York, 1961), p. 228.

78. William Henry Smith, *The Life and Speeches of Hon. Charles Warren Fairbanks* (Indianapolis, 1904), p. 69. For another statement of this view, see "Speech by Honorable Thomas H. Anderson, Associate Justice, Supreme Court," *Memorial Service to William McKinley, Late President of the United States, under the Auspices of the Ohio Republican Association of Washington, D.C. in Chase's Theater, October 6, 1901* (Washington, D.C., 1902). Copy in Cortelyou Papers. Also Harry Thurston Peck, *Twenty Years of the Republic, 1885–1905* (New York, 1906), pp. 544–45. McKinley and his advisors "knew that war was unavoidable, yet they were desirous of gaining time for preparation." The best recent statement of this position is found in Timothy G. McDonald, "McKinley and the Coming of the War with Spain," *Midwest Quarterly*, VII (Spring 1966), 225–39, in which the author holds that the president paced his diplomatic and political steps to match the speed with which the Pacific fleet could be prepared for combat.

79. John A. S. Grenville, "Diplomacy and War Plans in the United States, 1890–1917," *Transactions of the Royal Historical Society*, Series 5, II (1961), 4; Margaret Long, ed., *The Journal of John D. Long* (Rindge, New Hampshire, 1956), pp. 216–17; Mayo, *Long*, p. 157.

80. John D. Long to Theodore Roosevelt, Feb. 25, 1898, Papers of Theodore Roosevelt, Library of Congress.

81. Marvin A. Kreidberg and Merton G. Henry, *History of Military Mobilization in the United States Army, 1775–1945* (Washington, D.C., 1955), p. 152. As late as March 9 McKinley was stipulating that the $50,000,000 be used solely for military projects of a defensive nature. James A. Huston, *The Sinews of War: Army Logistics, 1775–1953* (Washington, D.C., 1966), pp. 275–76. McKinley "applied such a strict interpretation of the term 'national defense,' that he permitted none of these funds to be used for any other purpose than the improvement of coast defenses and fortifications." The quartermaster, subsistence, and medical departments were "permitted to do nothing outside their old routine" until the day the war began.

82. Russell A. Alger to McKinley, Apr. 15, 1898, McKinley Papers.

83. Henry Cabot Lodge to McKinley, Mar. 21, 1898, McKinley

Papers. See also Lodge to George (Lyman?), April 4, 1898, Papers of Henry Cabot Lodge, Massachusetts Historical Society, Boston, Massachusetts. "Congress is already [*sic*] to follow and behave as it has done since the blowing up of the Maine if the right lead is only given. Whether that lead will be given is the crucial question. If it is not we shall go to pieces with bitter debates in Congress, party divisions and the consequent ruin of the party. What is far worse it will present us in an awful light to ourselves and the other nations of the earth. . . . If the break comes . . . we shall all go down in the wreck, Senator[s] and Representatives alike." Lodge to John (Morse?), Apr. 15, 1898. "Congress . . . has been compelled to strike out a policy, a task which should never have devolved upon it."

84. Statement of Congressman C. A. Boutelle of Maine in Boston *Herald* of Oct. 23, 1898, cited by Rhodes, *McKinley and Roosevelt Administrations*, p. 60.

85. David Magie, *Life of Garret Augustus Hobart* (New York and London, 1910), p. 174. See also Mrs. Garret A. Hobart, *Memories* (Privately Printed, 1930), p. 60.

86. Public figures sensed that McKinley remained uncommitted to war. Henry Cabot Lodge, "The Spanish-American War," p. 509. Many "felt that the message was too gentle, and that the President really did not desire as yet decided measures." Indeed, one as close to events as the secretary of the navy refused even to consider the statement a war message. John D. Long to Mrs. J. H. Robbins, Apr. 12, 1898, in Long Papers. "I trust now that . . . [it] has gone in that the situation will be less exacting, and I am today more hopeful for peace than I have been for some time." See also Mayo, *Long*, p. 178. Carl Russell Fish, *The Path of Empire, A Chronicle of the United States as a World Power* (New Haven, Connecticut, 1919), p. 102. "To the very moment of crisis, McKinley was opposed to a war with Spain." Walter Millis, *The Martial Spirit* (Boston and New York, 1931), p. 145. Millis, too, seems to believe that McKinley remained resistant to the end; he suggests that in fact McKinley hoped that the American naval blockade recommended in his message might still prevent, rather than incite, the conflict.

87. Russell A. Alger, *The Spanish-American War* (New York and London, 1901), pp. 48 and 61. The war's crucial strategy conferences were held at the White House with the president

presiding. McKinley overruled Miles' bid to give primacy to the Puerto Rican expeditionary force and to postpone the sailing for Santiago. See also William Allen White, *Masks In a Pageant* (New York, 1928), p. 178. One of McKinley's most acerbic critics, White nonetheless concedes that the president conducted the war "with precision and vigor."

88. *Speeches 1897–1900*, pp. 125–26.
89. Ibid.
90. Ibid., p. 160.
91. James Boyle quoted in the New York *Times,* Sept. 1, 1912. See also Henry S. Pritchett, "Some Recollections of President McKinley and the Cuban Intervention," *North American Review,* DCXL (Mar. 1909), 400. In May 1899 McKinley told Pritchett that, had he been left alone, he could have concluded an arrangement with the Spanish government without war. Lambert, *Elkins,* p. 239. Senator Elkins thought McKinley would have required no more than an additional thirty days. John D. Long to Henry L. Higginson, Apr. 18, 1898, Long Papers. "My own judgment is that if Congress had followed the suggestion of the President and left the matter in his hands the independence of Cuba would have been secured without a drop of bloodshed." See also Long to Professor James B. Thayer, Apr. 18, 1898, and to Edwin A. Hill, Apr. 21, 1898.

CHAPTER II

1. Proctor's Senate speech is printed in *Congressional Record,* 55 Cong., 2 Sess. (Mar. 17, 1898), Vol. 31, pp. 2916–19. Unless otherwise noted, Proctor quotations in the following passages are to be found there.
2. Washington Gladden, *Recollections* (Boston, 1909), p. 386; (Watterson) New York *Tribune,* Mar. 18, 1898; Harry J. Sievers, ed., *Benjamin Harrison, 1833–1901, Chronology–Documents–Bibliographical Aids* (Dobbs Ferry, New York, 1969), p. 75.
3. Washington *Post,* Mar. 22, 1908.
4. "Biography of Redfield Proctor," Aug. 1903, in the Papers of Redfield Proctor, Proctor (Vermont) Free Library. Unless otherwise noted, letters cited hereafter are to be found in this collection.
5. David C. Gale, *Proctor, The Story of a Marble Town* (Brattleboro, Vt., 1922), pp. 115 and 117.

6. Proctor to Messrs. Noyes and Company, Washington *Evening Star,* Jan. 15, 1898.

7. Proctor to Hon. Harry S. Foster, M.P., Dec. 26, 1898. Profits in 1897 and 1898 were respectively $350,000 and $400,000. See Proctor to Foster, Jan. 23, 1899.

8. Philadelphia *Telegraph,* Mar. 5, 1908; Washington *Star,* Mar. 5, 1908; Springfield *Republican,* Mar. 6, 1908.

9. Dunn, *From Harrison to Harding,* I, 234. See also the New York *Times,* Mar. 5, 1908. "[On] one occasion while debating with one of his colleagues his opponent dubbed him the 'Tombstone Senator.' This name came to be a standing joke, and whenever Senator Proctor appeared at the War Department . . . word was passed around that there had been another skirmish, and the Senator of Vermont had come around to take orders for a few more tombstones."

10. Proctor to Captain Clyde D. V. Hunt, Apr. 25, 1898; New York *Herald,* Mar. 14, 1898; Proctor to Fletcher Proctor, Mar. 29, 1899.

11. (*Wall Street Journal*) Quoted in Alexander DeConde, *A History of American Foreign Policy* (New York, 1963), p. 344; (*American Banker*) Julius W. Pratt, *Expansionists of 1898* (Baltimore, 1936), p. 247; "Senator Proctor on Cuba's Desolation," *The Literary Digest,* XVI (Mar. 26, 1898), 361.

12. New York *World,* Mar. 18, 1898.

13. See, for example, Cordell Hull, *The Memoirs of Cordell Hull* 2 vols. (New York, 1948), I, 26. "I became so consumed with a desire for the fullest information obtainable regarding conditions in the nation and the operation of the governmental machinery at the national capital that when my Congressman . . . came through . . . on his [1890] fall campaign . . . I, by much effort, got hold of enough money to engage a span of horses and a buggy . . . and drove him for seven days across the almost impassable sections of the Cumberland Mountains primarily to ask him questions. I defrayed the entire expenses of the trip. It was for me an opportunity to secure much valuable information that I greatly desired."

14. Tom L. Johnson, *My Story* (New York, 1911), p. 48; Carl Lorenz, *Tom L. Johnson, Mayor of Cleveland* (New York, 1911), p. 12.

15. (Hanna) New York *World,* Mar. 25, 1898; (churches) Pittsburgh *Times,* Mar. 29, 1898; Chicago *Post,* Mar. 18, 1898.

16. Proctor to John S. Mosby, Nov. 25, 1897. See also the Cincin-

nati *Inquirer*, Feb. 20, 1898; McDonald, "McKinley and the Coming of the War with Spain," p. 232; Walter La Feber, *The New Empire* (Ithaca, New York, 1963), p. 391.

17. "Biography," p. 11; Washington *Post*, Mar. 22, 1908 (". . . but I was in the Senate and preferred to stay there.").

18. Proctor to Governor W. P. Dillingham of Vermont, Dec. 20, 1897; to Hobart, Oct. 19, 1897; to Hanna, Oct. 19, 1897; to Alger, Sept. 5, 1898.

19. (McKinley) *Congressional Record*, p. 2916; (escort) Proctor to Lt. H. R. Lemley, Feb. 8 and 15, 1898; (letter) Day to Fitzhugh Lee, Feb. 15, 1898, in the Proctoriana Collection, Vermont Historical Society, Montpelier, Vermont.

20. Boston *Advertiser*, Feb. 25, 1898; Cincinnati *Inquirer*, Feb. 20, 1898; New York *Times*, Feb. 27, 1898; (quotation) *Advertiser*, Feb. 25, 1898.

21. Proctor to Alger, Oct. 4, 1897; to James Manchester, Nov. 6, 1897; to Alger, Nov. 11, 1897; to Sir William Van Horne, Nov. 20, 1897; to George F. Baird, Nov. 29, 1897 and Jan. 6, 1898; to Alger, Jan. 13, 1898; to Horne, Feb. 12, 1898; to Hobart, Mar. 29, 1898; to Horne, Apr. 12, 1898. The Boston *Transcript* of March 5, 1908, reported that the project was ultimately "deferred . . . by claims of property owners."

22. Washington *Post*, Mar. 22, 1908. See also Proctor to John D. Long, Oct. 6, 1897, and, in the Long Papers, Long to Proctor, Oct. 8, 1897, and Long to W. E. Chandler, Oct. 12, 1897.

23. Proctor to John T. Burnet, Dec. 1, 1898.

24. New York *Times*, Feb. 27, 1898; Boston *Advertiser*, Feb. 25, 1898.

25. Springfield *Republican*, Mar. 6, 1908; Washington *Star*, Mar. 5, 1908; Philadelphia *Telegraph*, Mar. 5, 1908.

26. New York *Evening Journal*, Mar. 18, 1898; New York *Press*, Mar. 18, 1898; Boston *Herald*, Mar. 18, 1898.

27. Philadelphia *Evening Telegraph*, Mar. 18, 1898.

28. Foster Rhea Dulles, *Prelude to World Power, American Diplomatic History, 1860–1900* (New York, 1965), p. 160. "A jingo! and it is a relief to see a man who can't be touched by the timid people of wealth." Theodore Roosevelt, *Autobiography* (New York, 1913), p. 235. Cullom, *Fifty Years*, p. 283.

29. Proctor to Paul Brooks, Feb. 14, 1898. The Cincinnati *Inquirer* reported on February 20 that Proctor believed the United States government should intervene to stop the war. See also the Ludlow (Vt.) *Tribune*, Feb. 25: "There is a good deal of

fight in Col. Proctor and he has been free to say that it is quite time that the inhumanities practised by Spain should be stopped."

30. Proctor to Senator Francis M. Cockrell, Nov. 11, 1898; to H. L. Stillson, Nov. 10, 1898; to Senator William P. Frye, Nov. 11, 1898; to McKinley, Nov. 11, 1898.

31. For a detailed treatment of the American reversal of views, see chapter 5. (Description) Proctor to General Guy V. Henry, Dec. 19, 1898; ("firmness") Proctor to General H. W. Lawton, Sept. 6, 1898; (dissimilarity) Proctor to Henry, Dec. 19, 1898; (annexation) Proctor to G. G. Benedict, Mar. 10, 1902.

32. Proctor to R. A. Perkins, Nov. 17, 1898.

33. Proctor to Fletcher Proctor, June 27, 1898; to General M. C. Butler, Dec. 26, 1898; to Hunt, Feb. 25 and Mar. 29, 1899.

34. Proctor to James A. Smith, Jan. 3, 1898; to Charles H. Aldrich, Jan. 10, 1898; to Lemley, Feb. 8 and 15, 1898; to Aldrich, Feb. 15, 1898.

35. George Dewey, *Autobiography* (New York, 1913), p. 228; Proctor to Alger, Aug. 24, 1898 ("Will be very glad . . . if you will invite me . . . I will keep distinctly in the background."); to Hunt, Aug. 31, 1898; to Capt. Thomas F. Barr, Nov. 10 or 11, 1898; to Senator George G. Edmunds, Dec. 22, 1898; to Col. A. B. Carey, Dec. 28, 1898. Proctor to Alger, Feb. 4, 1899, in the Papers of Russell A. Alger, William L. Clements Library, Ann Arbor, Michigan.

36. Washington *Post*, Mar. 22, 1908.

37. Alger to Proctor, Aug. 13, 1898, in the Vermont Historical Society; Proctor to Alger, Aug. 15, 1898, in the Alger Papers; ("tremendously stirred") Proctor to Fitzhugh Lee, Mar. 19, 1898; ("take wonderfully") to Fletcher Proctor, Mar. 21, 1898; (depreciation of own role) to General Julius J. Estey, Mar. 21, 1898; to Perkins, July 2, 1898; to Leavitt J. Hunt, June (?), 1898.

38. (Hoar) Quoted in the Burlington (Vt.) *Daily Free Press*, Mar. 5, 1908; Lyman Abbott, *Reminiscences* (Boston and New York, 1914), p. 437; New York *Commercial Advertiser*, Mar. 18, 1898; Sacramento *Bee*, Mar. 18, 1898; Pittsburgh *Times*, Mar. 29, 1898; Boston *Journal*, Sept. 24, 1898; Chicago *Record*, Oct. 20, 1898; Washington *Star*, Mar. 5, 1908.

39. "The Point of View," *Scribner's Magazine*, XXIV (July 1898), 124.

40. Washington *Star,* Mar. 5, 1908; Watterson, *Spanish-American War,* p. 46.

CHAPTER III

1. Lieutenant Colonel Arthur L. Wagner and Commander J. D. Jerrold Kelley, *Our Country's Defensive Forces in War and Peace, The United States Army and Navy, Their Histories from the Era of the Revolution to the Close of the Spanish-American War, With Accounts of Their Organization, Administration, and Duties* (Akron, Ohio, 1899), pp. 40–41.
2. Kreidberg and Henry, *Mobilization,* p. 153. "Only the Civil War veterans had ever seen a force much larger than a regiment." Indeed, even regimental formations were a rarity. See, for example, the statement of Theophilus G. Steward, a black chaplain attached to the Twenty-fifth Infantry: ". . . the whole regiment met together [in April 1898] for the first time since 1870, in the Union Depot at St. Paul." Willard B. Gatewood, Jr., *"Smoked Yankees" and the Struggle for Empire: Letters from Negro Soldiers, 1898–1902* (Urbana, Illinois, Chicago, and London, 1971), p. 25.
3. Alger, *Spanish-American War,* p. 7. See also Major C. Joseph Bernardo and Eugene H. Bacon, *American Military Policy: Its Development Since 1775* (Harrisburg, Pennsylvania, 1955), p. 280.
4. Alger, *Spanish-American War,* p. 7; Alger to Lew Wallace, April 6, 1898, Alger Papers.
5. *Report of the Commission Appointed by the President to Investigate the Conduct of the War Department in the War with Spain* (Washington, 1899), p. 13.
6. Wagner and Kelley, *Country's Defensive Forces,* p. 99.
7. Bernardo and Bacon, *American Military Policy,* p. 250.
8. Ibid.; Jim Dan Hill, *The Minute Man in Peace and War* (Harrisburg, Pennsylvania, 1964), pp. 129–30.
9. Edward Thornton Heald, " 'McKinley's Own' and the Spanish-American War," typescript of radio address broadcast Feb. 12, 1950 over WHBC/WHBC-FM. Copy at Stark County Historical Center, Canton, Ohio.
10. "Army War College Study No. 20, Resources of the United States-Men," p. 38. Copy in War Department Historical, Spanish-American War, Miscellaneous Data and Information,

National Archives, Washington, D.C. (Hereafter cited as War Department Historical.)

11. Hull, *Memoirs,* I, 34.
12. Kreidberg and Henry, *Mobilization,* pp. 161–63; "Report of the Adjutant General, USA, 1899," p. 11 as quoted in "Army War College Study No. 20," p. 40, War Department Historical; Nelson A. Miles, *Serving the Republic* (New York and London, 1911), p. 270.
13. Tanner to Corbin, May 19, 1898, in "Muster In War With Spain," The Office of the Adjutant General, National Archives, Washington, D.C. (Hereafter cited as AGO Records.) Close political calculus is evident in Shelby Cullom's telegram to Adjutant General Corbin; the senator asked "whether it is possible for me to prevail upon the Gov't to accept a battery from Galesburg . . . Gov't has accepted a battery from Danville on east side of state. This one is on the west and are [*sic*] exceedingly anxious to be accepted." Cullom to Corbin, May 3, 1898, ibid. In his reply of May 4, Corbin refused Cullom's request.
14. William Allen White, "When Johnny Went Marching Out," *McClure's Magazine,* XI (June 1898), 199. See also Hill, *Minute Man,* p. 126: "He [the National Guardsman] and his comrades were small people from farms, villages and main street stores."
15. See Lewis E. Atherton, *Main Street on the Middle Border* (Bloomington, Indiana, 1954), pp. 217–33.
16. Karl W. Heiser, *Hamilton in the War of '98* (Hamilton, Ohio, 1899), p. 137.
17. William Oates, *The Fifteenth Alabama in Civil War and Spanish-American War* (New York, 1900), p. 236.
18. Constance Gardner, ed., *Some Letters of Augustus Peabody Gardner* (Boston and New York, 1920), pp. 6–7.
19. Hobart, *Memories,* p. 27.
20. Sherwood Anderson's enlistment in the local National Guard company, one of his biographers reports, was recognized as "a boost socially." William Alfred Sutton, "Sherwood Anderson's Formative Years (1876–1913)" (Ph.D. dissertation, Ohio State University, 1943), p. 84.
21. Carl Sandburg, *Always the Young Strangers* (New York, 1952), p. 404.
22. A. Maurice Low, "Amateurs in War," *Forum,* XXVI (October

1898), 166. For additional information on the pattern of company activities see Wagner and Kelley, *Country's Defensive Forces*, p. 99. For the same emphasis on the ceremonial and social in a Negro militia company, see George Brown Tindall, *South Carolina Negroes, 1877–1900* (Columbia, South Carolina, 1952), p. 288.

23. W. Selden Gale and George Candee Gale, eds., *Historical Encyclopedia of Knox County and Illinois* (Chicago and New York, 1899), p. 683.

24. Clyde *Enterprise*, Nov. 1, 1895; March 3, 1898.

25. William Allen White, *The Autobiography of William Allen White* (New York, 1946), pp. 74–75. I am also here indebted to ideas that Robert Wiebe has shared with me in several conversations.

26. Atherton, *Main Street*, pp. 100–105.

27. Sandburg, *Young Strangers*, p. 404.

28. Maurice Matloff, ed., *American Military History* (Washington, D.C., 1969), p. 291.

29. Walter Millis, *Arms and Men, A Study in American Military History* (New York, 1956), p. 178; Roosevelt, *Autobiography*, p. 244.

30. For an interesting discussion of the growth of military professionalism during this period see Samuel P. Huntington, *The Soldier and the State, The Theory and Politics of Civil-Military Relations* (Cambridge, Mass., 1957), pp. 226–30.

31. John D. Long to Major George A.J. Colgan, May 5, 1898, Long Papers. ". . . all the world wants a commission."

32. John P. Dyer, *From Shiloh to San Juan: The Life of "Fightin' Joe" Wheeler* (Baton Rouge, Louisiana, 1941), p. 226.

33. Roosevelt, *Autobiography*, p. 265.

34. Alger, *Spanish-American War*, p. 33.

35. Benedict Karl Zobrist, "How Victor Lawson's Newspapers Covered the Cuban War," *Journalism Quarterly*, XXXVIII (Summer 1961), 330–31.

36. Richard Harding Davis, "Our War Correspondents in Cuba and Porto Rico," *Harper's New Monthly Magazine*, XCVIII (May 1899), 938.

37. Galesburg *Evening Mail*, Apr. 28–Sept. 19, 1898. See also the *Evening Mail's* story on George Martin, Sept. 21, 1898. For the similarity of patterns elsewhere in the country see Josephus Daniels, *Editor in Politics* (Chapel Hill, 1941), pp. 277–78.

Daniels' correspondent with North Carolina troops wrote of their illnesses, rules infractions, complaints of slow pay, and similar matters.

38. Thomas Leslie McGirr in the Galesburg *Republican-Register,* June 11, 1898.

39. Ray Stannard Baker, "How the News of the War Is Reported," *McClure's Magazine,* XI (Sept. 1898), 492.

40. For hometown organization in support of local military companies see Heiser, *Hamilton in the War,* pp. 75–80; Charles Johnson Post, *The Little War of Private Post* (Boston, 1960), p. 3; Clifford P. Westermeier, *Who Rush to Glory, The Cowboy Volunteers of 1898: Grigsby's Cowboys, Roosevelt's Rough Riders, Torrey's Rocky Mountain Riders* (Caldwell, Idaho, 1958), pp. 137–38, 140; *Enterprise,* Apr. 28, 1898; *Evening Mail,* June 27, 1898.

41. Heiser, *Hamilton in the War,* p. 70.

42. Roosevelt to Alger, July 17, 1898, Alger Papers, See also Roosevelt to Henry Cabot Lodge, Dec. 6, 1898, Elting E. Morison, ed., *The Letters of Theodore Roosevelt,* 8 vols. (Cambridge, Mass., 1951–1954), II, 892.

43. *Enterprise,* Apr. 27, 1899.

44. *Evening Mail,* July 11, 1898. George Martin wrote in a letter published in the July 12 edition, "Company C boys hope to behave with honor to themselves and to their beloved city."

45. *Republican-Register,* Apr. 23, 1898. Millis, *Martial Spirit,* pp. 156–57, quotes Congressman Oscar Underwood of Alabama addressing his colleagues: "There is hardly a man on this floor who has not received letters from his constituents stating that they would be glad to volunteer, glad to fight for their country, if they can be officered by their home men. They want to know their officers and be officered by men who have been raised [,] and who have lived [,] among them."

46. *Evening Mail,* May 10, 1898.

47. *Enterprise,* June 16, 1898.

48. Ibid., May 19, 1898; Sept. 15, 1898.

49. *Evening Mail,* May 14, 1898.

50. Sandburg, *Young Strangers,* p. 404.

51. Millis, *Martial Spirit,* pp. 158–59; Gregory Mason, *Remember the Maine* (New York, 1939), pp. 75–76.

52. See Chapter IV.

53. Sherwood Anderson, *Memoirs* (New York, 1942), p. 125.

54. Fremont *Daily News,* May 9, 1898.

55. Quoted in *Report of the Secretary of War* (Washington, D.C., 1898), p. 153.
56. *Evening Mail,* May 14, 1898.
57. Sherwood Anderson, *A Story Teller's Story* (Garden City, New York, 1924), p. 284.
58. Ibid., pp. 281–82.
59. Ibid., pp. 284–85.
60. Ibid., p. 282.
61. Sandburg, *Young Strangers,* p. 409.
62. Ibid., p. 422; *Republican-Register,* Oct. 1, 1898; *Evening Mail,* Sept. 20, 1898. Dissension in similar form appeared in Anderson's company. Captain Rydman, of whom the boys were "tired," did not speak at the Clyde homecoming. *Enterprise,* Mar. 2 and June 8, 1899.
63. Post, *Little War of Private Post,* pp. 145, 252.
64. Ibid., p. 257.
65. *Evening Mail,* June 9, 1898.
66. Hagedorn, *Leonard Wood,* I, pp. 150–51.
67. Theodore Roosevelt, *The Rough Riders* (New York, 1899), p. 31.
68. At Tampa Wood dispatched a trooper to locate ammunition for the regiment's Colt machine guns. Meeting General Adna R. Chaffee, the volunteer blurted out, "Say, Colonel Wood wants the cartridges for the Colt guns a heap pronto. We are a-going aboard the ship." Shot back Chaffee, "Don't you know enough to be a soldier? You should dismount, salute, and stand at attention until I notice you." Saying little but speaking volumes, the soldier replied, "I ain't no soldier. I'm a Rough Rider." Virgil Carrington Jones, *Roosevelt's Rough Riders* (Garden City, New York, 1971), p. 62.
69. John Bigelow, Jr., *Reminiscences of the Santiago Campaign* (New York and London, 1899), p. 164.
70. Willis J. Abbot, *Watching the World Go By* (Boston, 1933), pp. 228–29. Bryan's regiment was "largely a neighborhood organization, recruited in Nebraska, and its men to a surprising number were known to their colonel." See also Merle Curti, "Bryan and World Peace," *Smith College Studies in History,* XVI (April–July 1931), 118, and Paolo E. Coletta, *William Jennings Bryan, Political Evangelist* (Lincoln, Nebraska, 1964), p. 226.
71. Louis W. Koenig, *Bryan, A Political Biography of William Jennings Bryan* (New York, 1971), p. 279.

72. Anna Maus, "Reminiscences," USAMHRC. Nurse Maus was puzzled by the determination of an ill soldier to leave her recuperation hospital, one the men called "the best place on earth," and to return to Bryan's unit. He "said that nothing could take the place of his Colonel. 'We sit around him every evening and he tells us how to live and how to die.' "

73. *Evening Mail,* Aug. 18, 1898.

74. Roosevelt to New York Governor Levi Parsons Morton, Mar. 19, 1895, and to C. Whitney Tillinghast, Jan. 13, 1898, in Morison, *Letters,* I, 436 and 758.

75. Hagedorn, *Leonard Wood,* I, 154.

76. Roosevelt, *Rough Riders,* pp. 29–30.

77. Hagedorn, *Leonard Wood,* I, 153.

78. Ibid., p. 148.

79. Dixon Wecter, *When Johnny Comes Marching Home* (Cambridge, Mass., 1944), p. 9.

80. There is fragmentary evidence that some regular officers believed that black enlisted men better approached their soldierly ideal than did the more recalcitrant white volunteers. Wrote N. C. Bruce, a black North Carolinian, "It is freely admitted that . . . for . . . an implicit obedience to orders, for imitativeness and aptness to time and tune, and for holding together in the midst of danger, the Negro is a superior man for making the true soldier." N. C. Bruce to *The News and Observer* (Raleigh), May ?, 1898, quoted in Gatewood, *Smoked Yankees,* p. 106.

81. Alger, *Spanish-American War,* p. 100; *Investigating Commission,* p. 119.

82. *Investigating Commission,* pp. 207–8.

83. William Carey Brown, *The Diary of a Captain* (Richmond, Virginia, 1927), p. 17.

84. Quoted in *Report of the Secretary of War, 1898,* p. 70.

85. It is no surprise that those commended for heroism often seemed to combine courage in the face of the enemy with resistance to the orders of their officers. Two of three Rough Riders whom Roosevelt recommended for Congressional medals of honor fell in this category. (Theodore Roosevelt to William H. Carter, Mar. 20, 1899, Roosevelt Papers.) Disobedience appeared to give a fillip to heroism.

86. Stephen Crane, "Virtue in War," in *Wounds in the Rain: A Collection of Stories Relating to the Spanish-American War of 1898* (London, 1900), pp. 158–59.

87. Ibid., p. 173.
88. "Army War College Study No. 13, Study of the Laws Relating to the Organization of the Militia and Volunteer Forces of the United States, With a History of the Operations and Efficiency of These Forces in Our Several Wars," Part IV, 1905–1906, p. 45, in War Department Historical.
89. "Report of the Inspector General," in *Report of the Secretary of War, 1898*, p. 152.
90. *Investigating Commission,* p. 118. Emphasis added.
91. Richard W. Leopold, *Elihu Root and the Conservative Tradition* (Boston, 1954), p. 40.
92. "Military Policy of the United States," p. 51, War Department Historical.
93. Kreidberg and Henry, *Mobilization,* pp. 199–201.
94. Ibid., p. 150; Edward M. Coffman, *The War to End All Wars, The American Military Experience in World War I* (New York, 1968), pp. 17, 61, 65.
95. Miles was the last commanding general of the Army; the bureaus retained for a longer period their independent powers but finally yielded in 1918 to the centralized control of Chief of Staff Peyton C. Marsh. Russell F. Weigley, *History of the United States Army* (New York, 1967), p. 559; Coffman, *War to End Wars,* pp. 49, 51, 162.
96. Anderson, *Story Teller's Story,* p. 278.
97. Brom Weber, *Sherwood Anderson* (Minneapolis, 1964), p. 9.
98. Coffman, *War to End Wars,* p. 67.
99. Henry Jervey, "Mobilization of the Emergency Army," Lecture presented at General Staff College, Jan. 3, 1920. Copy in Army War College Library, Washington, D.C.

CHAPTER IV

1. "The Soldier's Faith, An Address Delivered on Memorial Day, May 30, 1895, at a Meeting Called by the Graduating Class of Harvard University," quoted in Howe, *Speeches,* p. 75.
2. Millis, *Arms and Men,* p. 175.
3. Roosevelt to Francis Cruger Moore, Feb. 9, 1898, in Morison, *Letters,* I, 771. Roosevelt to William Wirt Kimball, Nov. 19, 1897, ibid., 717.
4. Roosevelt to Henry Cabot Lodge, Dec. 27, 1895, ibid., 504: "The clamor of the peace faction has convinced me that this country needs a war."

5. Roosevelt to Henry White, Apr. 30, 1897, ibid., 606: "I wish to Heaven we were more jingo about Cuba and Hawaii! The trouble with our nation is that we incline to fall into mere animal sloth and ease, and tend to venture too little instead of too much." Roosevelt to Cecil Arthur Spring Rice, May 29, 1897, ibid., 621: "It certainly is extraordinary that just at this time there seems to be a gradual failure of vitality in the qualities . . . that make men fight well and write well."

6. Roosevelt to Frederick Jackson Turner, Apr. 10, 1895, ibid., 440: "I have always been more interested in the men themselves than in the institutions through and under which they worked."

7. Norman Thomas, *War: No Glory, No Profit, No Need* (New York, 1935), p. 29.

8. Burton J. Hendrick, *The Training of an American: The Earlier Life and Letters of Walter H. Page* (Boston and New York, 1928), p. 257.

9. Sandburg, *Young Strangers,* p. 409.

10. G. Wallace Chessman, *Theodore Roosevelt and the Politics of Power* (Boston, 1969), pp. 7, 9.

11. Howard K. Beale, *Theodore Roosevelt and the Rise of America to World Power* (Baltimore, 1956), p. 4.

12. Chessman, *Politics of Power,* p. 7. One might have expected that Roosevelt's family history, his social class, his writing interests and his Washington post would have inclined him to enlist in the Navy. Why he did not he left unclear. He was, however, fully aware of the Navy's reliance on new, massive, technologically complex battle vessels, and he may have realized that the resort to such engines of war would further circumscribe the role of individual performance.

13. Beale, *Rise of America,* p. 36.

14. Roosevelt to General Bradley T. Johnson, Mar. 14, 1898, Roosevelt Papers.

15. Roosevelt to General Bradley T. Johnson, Mar. 7, 1898, Roosevelt Papers. Roosevelt to Anna Roosevelt Cowles, Mar. 30, 1896, in Morison, *Letters,* I, 522.

16. In an address titled "Washington's Forgotten Maxim" and delivered at the Naval War College in June 1897, Roosevelt said that "no triumph of peace is quite so great as the supreme triumphs of war" and that "peace is a goddess only when she comes with sword girt on thigh." Quoted in David H. Burton, *Theodore Roosevelt: Confident Imperialist* (Philadelphia,

1968), pp. 44–45. Beale, *Rise of America,* p. 36, notes Roosevelt's conviction that "there was something dull and effeminate about peace."

17. Roosevelt, *Autobiography,* p. 275.

18. Ibid., pp, 577, 524.

19. Suggestive here is the fact that the enemy was so often referred to in the singular. See Corinne Roosevelt Robinson, *My Brother Theodore Roosevelt* (New York, 1921), p. 174: "Theodore has sure made his mark on the Spaniard"; and on p. 175 she quotes her brother: "I was near the line, with my men, nearest the Spaniard." Fiction, too, was replete with such references. See, for example, John Fox, Jr., *Crittenden: A Kentucky Story of Love and War* (New York, 1914), p. 51: "coming face-to-face with the Spaniard"; p. 115: "Nobody thought the Spaniard would fight."

20. Ernest Howard Crosby, *War Echoes* (Philadelphia, 1898), p. 3.

21. Roosevelt, *Autobiography,* pp. 250, 269.

22. Roosevelt, *Rough Riders,* p. 23.

23. Westermeier, *Rush to Glory,* p. 56. The "select party" with which Roosevelt left Washington to join the western recruits at San Antonio included fifteen Yale and Harvard students, three mounted policemen from New York City, three members of the United States Cavalry, three Southerners with cowpunching experience, and seven "swells" from the Knickerbocker and Somerset clubs.

24. Roosevelt, *Rough Riders,* p. 12.

25. Gerald Langford, *The Richard Harding Davis Years: A Biography of a Mother and Son* (New York, 1961), pp. 195–96.

26. In one of the regiments comprising the Puerto Rican expeditionary force more than three hundred of the men had never fired a gun. Telegram from Nelson A. Miles to Secretary of War, June 5, 1898, in *Report of the Secretary of War, 1898,* p. 24. See also Richard Harding Davis, *Notes of a War Correspondent* (New York, 1912), p. 66.

27. Roosevelt, *Rough Riders,* p. 33.

28. Heald, "McKinley's Own," II, 66: "Every member of Company K of Alliance signed a pledge of total abstinence."

29. Owen Wister, *Roosevelt: The Story of a Friendship* (New York, 1930), p. 38; White, "Johnny Marching Out," p. 205; (Allen) quoted in Galesburg *Republican Register,* Jan. 30, 1897; (Ware) quoted in Ray Ginger, *Age of Excess: The United*

States from 1877 to 1914 (New York, 1965), p. 188; (Bierce) quoted in Richard O'Connor, *Ambrose Bierce, A Biography* (Boston and Toronto, 1967), p. 176; (William James) quoted in Robert L. Beisner, *Twelve Against Empire: The Anti-Imperialists, 1898–1900* (New York, 1968), pp. 41, 43; (Henry James) quoted in Wilson, *Patriotic Gore*, p. 663.

30. Roosevelt to James Brander Matthews, Dec. 7, 1894, in Morison, *Letters*, I, 410–11.

31. "While . . . 223, 235 volunteers enlisted in the war, only about 18,000 were brought against the enemy in Cuba or Porto Rico. . . ." "Communication to the Secretary of War from the Chief of Staff regarding a Military Policy April 20, 1910," p. 7, War Department Historical. See also Huston, *Sinews of War*, p. 277. Less than one-fifth of the total Army force of 274,700 saw campaign service of any kind.

32. Dunn, *From Harrison to Harding*, I, 261.

33. Roosevelt, *Autobiography*, p. 245; Westermeier, *Rush to Glory*, pp. 42, 67.

34. Miscellaneous Reports (Operations), War Department Historical. Telegrams from the White House to Shafter on June 7, 1898, included the following: "You will sail immediately" and "Since telegraphing you an hour since the President directs you to sail at once with what force you have ready."

35. J. D. Miley, *In Cuba with Shafter* (New York, 1899), p. 283.

36. *Report of the Secretary of War, 1898*, p. 25.

37. Burr McIntosh, *The Little I Saw of Cuba* (New York and London, 1899), p. 2.

38. "The Military Policy of the United States and a Comprehensive Scheme for the Organization of the Armed Forces on Land, Report of a board of officers convened at Washington, D.C., under verbal instructions from the Chief of Staff, to consider and report upon the above subject. December 11, 1908," War Department Historical.

39. *Evening Mail*, May 14, 1898; May 6, 1898.

40. *Enterprise*, May 5, 1898.

41. Fremont *Daily News*, May 6, 1898.

42. Alger to Grenville M. Dodge, May 21, 1898, Alger Papers.

43. Alger to Nelson A. Miles, July 23, 1898, Alger Papers.

44. Alger to Lew Wallace, Apr. 6, 1898, Alger Papers.

45. Robinson, *My Brother*, p. 168.

46. "Our disappointment in not getting to participate in action in Cuba was great. . . . How we envied those guys who covered

themselves with glory in the charge up San Juan Hill." John F. Couch, "The Boys of 1898 in Cuba and J. D.'s Rags to Riches Career in the Philippines," pp. 2–3. The Deisher-Couch Papers, USAMHRC. Regulars were not immune to such reactions, though the focus was more often on separation from unit than on denial of combat. Recalled one confined to garrison duty, "I saw the beautiful colors marching to join the regiment. It was too much for me. I fled my quarters and sought the . . . most secluded place. . . . The scar was permanent." Charles Gerhardt, "Memoirs," p. 21, The Charles Gerhardt Papers, USAMHRC.

47. Some evidence suggests that black volunteers were willing to tolerate a higher level of racial mistreatment *until* the chance of combat disappeared. See Winslow Hobson to *The Gazette* (Cleveland), ca. October 15, 1898, and J. Madison Pierce to *The Gazette,* Aug. 23, 1898, in Gatewood, *Smoked Yankees,* pp. 118, 114.

48. Hagedorn, *Leonard Wood,* I, 149.

49. Westermeier, *Rush to Glory,* p. 209.

50. *Evening Mail,* July 6, 1898, p. 4.

51. Toledo *Sunday Commercial,* reprinted in *Enterprise,* Aug. 18, 1898.

52. *Enterprise,* Sept. 15, 1898.

53. Dewey, *Autobiography,* p. 229.

54. Alger, *Spanish-American War,* p. 39. See also *Report of the Secretary of War, 1898,* p. 9.

55. John Black Atkins, *The War in Cuba: The Experiences of an Englishman with the United States Army* (London, 1899), pp. 3–4.

56. Gardner, *Letters,* p. 19. In April, while still a civilian, Gardner had written his father-in-law, "Do not forget [,] if there is any actual fighting [,] that I want to have a chance at the game. . . ." Augustus Peabody Gardner to Henry Cabot Lodge, Apr. 16, 1898, Lodge Papers.

57. Gardner, *Letters,* p. 22.

58. Ibid., p. 28.

59. Heiser, *Hamilton in the War,* pp. 41–42.

60. Toledo *Blade,* reprinted in *Enterprise,* Mar. 16, 1899.

61. Bigelow, *Reminiscences,* p. 22.

62. Post, *Little War of Private Post,* p. 88.

63. Stephen Crane, "The Red Badge of Courage Was His Wig-Wag Flag," New York *World,* July 1, 1898, quoted in Olov W.

Fryckstedt, *Stephen Crane: Uncollected Writings* (Uppsala, 1963), p. 337.
64. Quoted in Frank Freidel, *The Splendid Little War* (Boston, 1958), p. 113.
65. Atkins, *War in Cuba*, p. 125.
66. Freidel, *Splendid Little War*, p. 135.
67. Ibid., p. 133. The Army's inspector-general, J. C. Breckinridge, later conceded that the volunteers had "found it difficult to contend with an invisible enemy pouring in an effective fire from a position impossible to determine." *Report of the Secretary of War, 1898*, p. 156.
68. Roosevelt to Corinne Roosevelt Robinson, June 27, 1898, in Morison, *Letters*, II, 845. See also Roosevelt, *Rough Riders*, p. 105, and Augustus Peabody Gardner to Henry Cabot Lodge, June 27, 1898, Lodge Papers.
69. Atkins, *War in Cuba*, p. 124.
70. Post, *Little War of Private Post*, p. 257.
71. Gardner, *Letters*, pp. 31, 34.
72. Quoted in the Buffalo *Illustrated Express*, June 1898 (?). Copy in the William Auman Papers, USAMHRC.
73. Ambrose Bierce's imagination later offered this encounter between Clio and the Historian. Begged the Muse, "Ask me who really built the Great Pyramid, and why. . . . Ask me who was the man in the iron mask. . . . Ask me anything in reason, but don't ask me who commanded the American Army in the Yanko-Spanko War." On Clio's advice, the Historian decides to spin a coin to determine whether Shafter or Miles was in charge. Discovering, however, that the coin is smooth on both faces, he writes, "The Army before Santiago had no commander." Ambrose Bierce, "The Ordeal," in *The Collected Works of Ambrose Bierce*, 12 vols. (New York and Washington, D.C., 1909–12), XII, 227–28.
74. Bigelow, *Reminiscences*, pp. 124, 126.
75. John R. Conn to Mrs. J. W. Cromwell, Aug. 24, 1898, quoted in Gatewood, *Smoked Yankees*, p. 69.
76. Stephen Crane, "Stephen Crane's Story of the Battle of San Juan," New York *World*, July 14, 1898, quoted in Fryckstedt, *Uncollected Writings*, pp. 356–57.
77. Edgar A. Knapp to Madge Olmsted, Aug. 6, 1898, Roosevelt Papers.
78. Quoted in Jones, *Rough Riders*, p. 181.

79. Roosevelt to Henry Cabot Lodge, July 19, 1898, in Morison, *Letters*, II, 853.
80. Robinson, *My Brother*, p. 173.
81. Post, *Little War of Private Post*, pp. 120–21.
82. Alger, *Spanish-American War*, p. 113.
83. Langford, *Richard Harding Davis Years*, p. 199.
84. Alger, *Spanish-American War*, pp. 287, 412–14; George Kennan, *Campaigning in Cuba* (New York, 1899), p. 261; Atkins, *War in Cuba*, p. 167.
85. Alger, *Spanish-American War*, pp. 290–91; Kennan, *Campaigning*, p. 238; *Investigating Commission*, p. 71. Of the seven, only three were available to medical officers for use during the fighting of July 1.
86. Kennan, *Campaigning*, p. 133.
87. Roosevelt, *Rough Riders*, p. 197.
88. Kennan, *Campaigning*, pp. 5, 84–86.
89. Bigelow, *Reminiscences*, pp. 85, 100.
90. Watterson, *Spanish-American War*, p. 74.
91. Inspector-General Breckinridge, quoted in *Report of the Secretary of War, 1898*, p. 156: "Often we fought for hours against an invisible enemy who was firing fatally upon us all the time. The volunteers, as soon as the Springfields were fired, at once revealed their position and drew the fire of the enemy. . . ."
92. James Harrison Wilson, *Under the Old Flag*, 2 vols. (New York and London, 1912), I, 441.
93. Watterson, *Spanish-American War*, p. 75.
94. Faith of this magnitude may help to explain why, lacking the pressures of military necessity, there was so little resistance to committing to combat volunteer units that "as a rule, were almost wholly unprepared for field service . . . [and were] deficient in numbers, in arms, equipment, uniform, underclothing, shoes, and wagon transportation and . . . [in large part] were lacking in discipline, drill and target practice." Army War College Study No. 20, p. 46, War Department Historical.
95. Post, *Little War of Private Post*, pp. 260–61.
96. Brown, *The Diary of a Captain*, pp. 22, 24.
97. Major A. C. Markley to Adjutant-General, Sept. 18, 1898, War Department Historical.
98. Atkins, *War in Cuba*, p. 205.
99. Alger, *Spanish-American War*, p. 426.

100. William Paulding, "A Few Words on My Army Life," p. 93, The William and Grace Paulding Papers, USAMHRC.

101. Heald, *McKinley Era*, pp. 70–71. See also unsigned letter to Editor, *Illinois Record*, Aug. 29, 1898, in Gatewood, *Smoked Yankees*, p. 72.

102. "Annual Report of the Adjutant-General to the Secretary of War, 1 November 1898," in *Report of the Secretary of War, 1898*, p. 273: Twenty-three officers and 257 enlisted men were killed in battle; four officers and 61 enlisted men died of wounds. Prior to the onslaught of disease, the number of dead was so small that each of the fallen became the focus of wide civic and even statewide homage. When early in the war Ensign Worth Bagley became the single naval officer to be killed by the enemy, the "funeral was held in . . . Capitol Square [of Raleigh, North Carolina], attended by two thousand soldiers in training and by the whole community and hundreds from all over the state, with tributes of flowers from Washington and Annapolis. He was buried with the honors of a brigadier general" and a statue was erected to his memory. Daniels, *Editor In Politics*, p. 271.

103. Alger, *Spanish-American War*, p. 283.

104. Kennan, *Campaigning*, p. 264.

105. Ibid., p. 215.

106. Roosevelt to Henry Cabot Lodge, July 3, 1898, in Morison, *Letters*, II, 846.

107. Kennan, *Campaigning*, p. 219. See also Roosevelt, *Autobiography*, pp. 266–68, and Millis, *Martial Spirit*, pp. 350–53.

108. Quoted in Jones, *Rough Riders*, p. 265; Roosevelt, *Rough Riders*, p. 202.

109. Roosevelt, *Rough Riders*, p. 127.

110. Jacob Riis, *Theodore Roosevelt: The Citizen* (New York, 1903), p. 200.

111. Editorial, New York *Times*, Oct. 14, 1898. "We should like, in entire friendliness to Col. ROOSEVELT, to suggest . . . that he is not promoting his election by the prominence he allows his admiring companions in the Rough Rider regiment to take in his canvass, and especially by permitting them to appear so often and so conspicuously in their war-worn uniforms. Whatever else may be, neither the war in Cuba nor the gallantry and efficiency of Col. ROOSEVELT is [*sic*] in question. . . . The extreme use of men in kahkis [*sic*], as part of

the stage setting for Col. ROOSEVELT's speeches, implies the contrary."

112. Roosevelt to Cecil Arthur Spring Rice, Aug. 5, 1896, in Morison, *Letters*, I, 554. Roosevelt to Henry Cabot Lodge, Mar. 30, 1897, ibid., I, 592. Roosevelt to William Sheffield Cowles, Mar. 30, 1898, ibid., II, 804. Roosevelt to Lodge, July 7, 1898, ibid., II, 850.

113. Wister, *Roosevelt*, p. 68.

114. Dixon Wecter, *The Hero in America: A Chronicle of Hero Worship* (New York, 1941), p. 378. See also Kennan, *Campaigning*, p. 100. Roosevelt, the author records, said that he would not have missed the fight at Las Guasimas "for the best year in his life." See also Roosevelt to Henry Cabot Lodge, July 31, 1898, in Morison, *Letters*, II, 863. "This has been, aside from Edith, *the* time of my life."

CHAPTER V

1. James D. Richardson, ed., *A Compilation of the Messages and Papers of the Presidents, 1789–1897*, 10 vols. (Washington, D.C., 1900), IX, 658.

2. Joseph J. Matthews, "Informal Diplomacy in the Venezuelan Crisis of 1896," *Mississippi Valley Historical Review*, L (Sept. 1963), 196–97. James L. Garvin, *The Life of Joseph Chamberlain*, 3 vols. (London, 1932–34), III, 66, recalls "with what stupefaction the Venezuelan ultimatum was received. . . ."

3. Nelson M. Blake, "Background of Cleveland's Venezuelan Policy," *American Historical Review*, XLVII (Jan. 1942), 276. The author (p. 259) describes Olney's note of July 20 and Cleveland's special message of December 17 as "among the most crudely assertive ever issued by responsible American statesmen."

4. Editorial, The New York *World*, Dec. 18, 1895.

5. Editorial, *World*, Dec. 21, 1895.

6. Editorial, *World*, Dec. 22, 1895.

7. Ibid.

8. Editorial, *World*, Dec. 21, 1895.

9. Editorial, *World*, Dec. 22, 1895.

10. Ibid.

11. *World*, Dec. 22, 1895.

12. Henry Cabot Lodge, *Monroe Doctrine. Speech of Hon. Henry Cabot Lodge, of Massachusetts, in the Senate of the United States, December 30, 1895* (Washington, 1896), pp. 15–16.

13. Quoted in John A. Garraty, *Henry Cabot Lodge: A Biography* (New York, 1953), p. 152.

14. Lodge, *Monroe Doctrine*, p. 16.

15. Richardson, *Messages and Papers*, IX, 658.

16. *World*, Dec. 22, 1895.

17. Ruth Miller Elson, *Guardians of Tradition: American School-books of the Nineteenth Century* (Lincoln, Nebraska, 1964).

18. Ibid., p. 103.

19. Ibid., pp. 105–27, 147–50.

20. Ibid., pp. 104, 143–45.

21. Ibid., p. 151.

22. *Harper's Pictorial History of the War with Spain* (New York and London, 1899), p. 2.

23. Ibid., p. 8.

24. Charles Francis Adams, *"Imperialism" and "The Tracks of Our Forefathers," Paper Read to Massachusetts Historical Society, 20 December 1898* (Boston, 1899), p. 6.

25. Baccalaureate address of President Adams, quoted in *Republican-Register*, June 25, 1898.

26. William Dean Howells, "Our Spanish Prisoners at Portsmouth," *Harper's Weekly*, XLII (Aug. 20, 1898), 827.

27. Elson, *Guardians of Tradition*, p. 119.

28. *Harper's Pictorial History*, p. 3.

29. Watterson, *Spanish-American War*, vi.

30. Russell Hastings to McKinley, Aug. 10, 1898, McKinley Papers.

31. Garraty, *Lodge*, pp. 189–90; Henry Cabot Lodge to John (Morse?), Feb. 25, 1898, Lodge Papers. See also Lodge to Henry (White?), Apr. 6, 1898: "Don't you think it is worth-while to stop this talk about *two* civilized nations, and remember with whom we have to deal?"

32. Joseph Benson Foraker, *Notes of a Busy Life*, 2 vols. (Cincinnati, 1916), II, 19.

33. There was substance to the complaint of the French ambassador that many Americans thought modern Spain and sixteenth-century Spain identical. Jules Cambon, *Le Diplomate* (Paris, 1926), pp. 34–35. See, for example, the statement of a Washington columnist quoted in the *Republican-Register*, Mar. 19, 1898. For 1000 years "the history of Spain has been a turbulent and sanguinary record of bloody and cowardly assassination, infamous treachery and cruel oppression."

34. James Creelman, *On the Great Highway: The Wanderings and Adventures of a Special Correspondent* (Boston, 1901), pp. 158–60.

35. Watterson, *Spanish-American War,* p. 34.
36. *Daily News,* Oct. 8, 1897.
37. *Enterprise,* May 10, 1895.
38. Ibid., Apr. 14, 1896.
39. Ibid., May 19, 1896.
40. Ibid., Nov. 27, 1896.
41. Ibid., Jan. 21, 1897.
42. On the basis of a survey of editorial comment in more than forty midwestern newspapers, George Auxier concluded that journalistic influence was effected not through sensationalism but through emphasis on such basic factors as fundamental American interests in the Caribbean, etc. (George Auxier, "Middle Western Newspapers and the Spanish-American War, 1895–1898," *Mississippi Valley Historical Review,* XXVI [Mar. 1940], 524). To ascribe to such newspapers an essentially detached and reasoning expression of views is, however, to miss the frequent contradiction between the sentiments of news and editorial columns. Conservative editorial policies and grossly provocative news stories often appeared together in ways the modern reader might think ludicrous. One example is that of the Galesburg *Plaindealer,* Feb. 18, 1898. A news story on page 3 described the *Maine* as an "object of intense hatred at the hands of the Spaniards." Conceding that the truth of the tragedy was unknown, the article nonetheless concluded that, "It is safe to wager that there is no accident about it." As for the request that Americans refrain from hasty judgments, that was "asking a great deal." The day's editorial on page 4, however, urged that until the official inquiry was complete and the truth revealed, "all should withhold expressions of opinion." A study of editorial comment alone would here reveal only a part of the journal's impact.
43. Watterson, *Spanish-American War,* p. 76.
44. Anderson, *Story Teller's Story,* p. 279.
45. Ibid., p. 277.
46. Ibid., p. 275.
47. Ibid., pp. 280–81.
48. Myron H. McCord to McKinley, Apr. 22, 1898, AGO Records.
49. Secretary of War to Honorable L. A. Cooke, governor of Connecticut, Apr. 29, 1898, conveying memorandum of previous day prepared by Assistant Secretary of War Meiklejohn, AGO Records.
50. Sam Acheson, "Joseph W. Bailey and the Spanish War," *Southwest Review,* XVII (Winter 1932), 151.

51. Roosevelt, *Autobiography*, p. 234.
52. See, for example, Sister Mary S. Connaughton, "The Editorial Opinion of the Catholic Telegraph of Cincinnati on Contemporary Affairs and Politics, 1871–1921" (Ph.D. dissertation, Catholic University of America, 1943), p. 47.
53. Dunn, *From Harrison to Harding*, I, 232.
54. Reverend Arthur Edwards, editor of the *Northwestern Christian Advocate*, quoted in Kenneth M. MacKenzie, *The Robe and the Sword: The Methodist Church and the Rise of American Imperialism* (Washington, 1961), p. 49.
55. Quoted in Walter Johnson, *William Allen White's America* (New York, 1947), p. 110.
56. William A. Robinson, *Thomas B. Reed, Parliamentarian* (New York, 1930), p. 369.
57. *Harper's Weekly*, XLII (Apr. 16, 1898), 363.
58. Davis, *Notes*, pp. 7, 9.
59. Ray Ginger, *Altgeld's America: The Lincoln Ideal vs. Changing Realities* (New York, 1958), p. 184.
60. Quoted in Rubens, *Liberty*, p. 225.
61. *Republican-Register*, Oct. 2, 1897. See also Henry Cabot Lodge to John (Morse?), Feb. 25, 1898, Lodge Papers. The Cuban "upper classes have been largely educated in the United States, and they are a good deal more civilized than the Spaniards and less brutal."
62. Acheson, "Bailey," p. 142.
63. Dyer, *From Shiloh to San Juan*, p. 216.
64. May, *Imperial Democracy*, pp. 71–72.
65. Frank P. Reuter, *Catholic Influence on American Colonial Policies, 1898–1904* (Austin, Texas, 1967), p. 6.
66. Chester McA. Destler, *Henry Demarest Lloyd and the Empire of Reform* (Philadelphia, 1963), p. 448.
67. See Richard Hofstadter, *Age of Reform* (New York, 1955), pp. 85–90.
68. John Spencer Bassett, *Expansion and Reform, 1889–1926* (New York, 1926), pp. 72–73.
69. *Congressional Record*, 55 Cong. 2 Sess. (Mar. 17, 1898), vol. 31, p. 2918.
70. Quoted in *Harper's Pictorial History*, p. 7. Similarly, George Clarke Musgrave, *Under Three Flags in Cuba* (Boston, 1899), p. 93.
71. Frederick Funston, *Memories of Two Wars: Cuban and Philippine Experiences* (New York, 1911), pp. 28–31.

72. Ibid., p. 65.
73. Grover Flint, "In the Field with Gomez," *McClure's Magazine,* XI (June 1898), 193–94.
74. Rubens, *Liberty,* p. 132.
75. See, for example, *Harper's Pictorial History,* pp. 46–47.
76. *Enterprise,* Dec. 24, 1895; Dec. 27, 1895; Jan. 3, 1896; Jan. 10, 1896; Mar. 6, 1896.
77. *World,* Dec. 1, 1895.
78. Ibid., Dec. 2, 1895.
79. Ibid., Dec. 26, 1895.
80. Ibid., Dec. 28, 1895.
81. Ibid., Jan. 3, 1896.
82. Ibid., Jan. 5, 1896.
83. Ibid., Jan. 8, 1896.
84. Editorial, *World,* Jan. 7, 1896.
85. *World,* Jan. 13, 1896.
86. Ibid., Dec. 26, 1895.
87. Roosevelt, *Rough Riders,* p. 75.
88. Flint, "Gomez," pp. 195–96.
89. Detroit *Journal,* Nov. 5, 1895, quoted in George W. Auxier, "The Cuban Question as Reflected in the Editorial Columns of Middle Western Newspapers (1895–1898)" (Ph.D. dissertation, Ohio State University, 1938), p. 5.
90. Atkins, *War In Cuba,* pp. 98–99.
91. Roosevelt, *Rough Riders,* p. 75.
92. Bigelow, *Reminiscences,* p. 84.
93. Kennan, *Campaigning In Cuba,* p. 92.
94. Theodore Roosevelt, "The Fifth Corps at Santiago," in *The Works of Theodore Roosevelt,* 24 vols. (New York, 1923), XIII, 221.
95. Leonard Wood to Alger, Oct. 22, 1898, Alger Papers.
96. Kennan, *Campaigning In Cuba,* p. 92.
97. O. O. Howard, "The Conduct of the Cubans in the Late War," *The Forum,* XXVI (Oct. 1898), 155.
98. Stephen Crane, "Hunger Has Made Cubans Fatalists," *World,* July 12, 1898, quoted in Fryckstedt, *Uncollected Writings,* pp. 349–50.
99. Freidel, *Splendid Little War,* p. 94.
100. Atkins, *War in Cuba,* pp. 100–101.
101. Mason, *Remember the Maine,* p. 248.
102. *Enterprise,* July 21, 1898; Report of Major M. E. Webb to Brigadier General Henry M. Duffield, July 5, 1898, included

in Duffield's letter to Lt. Colonel E. J. McClernand, Dec. 7, 1898, War Department Historical. Such observations were frequent until the Americans' days of debilitation.

103. Howard, "Conduct of Cubans," p. 153.

104. *Report of Secretary of War, 1898*, p. 28; Miles, *Serving Republic*, p. 280; Unsigned Telegram to McKinley, n.d., McKinley Papers; Calixto Garcia to W. R. Shafter, July 12, 1898, War Department Historical.

105. Sampson to secretary of the Navy, June 18, 1898, McKinley Papers.

106. Stephen Crane, "Stephen Crane's Vivid Story of the Battle of San Juan," *World*, July 14, 1898, in Fryckstedt, *Uncollected Writings*, pp. 364–65.

107. Crane, "Hunger," in Fryckstedt, *Uncollected Writings*, p. 350.

108. Garcia to Shafter, July 10, 1898, War Department Historical.

109. Shafter to Garcia, July 20, 1898, War Department Historical.

110. Garcia to Shafter, July 19, 1898, War Department Historical.

111. Lieutenant J. W. Heard to Adjutant-General, Aug. 21, 1898, in "Report of Major-General Commanding the Army," War Department Historical. It should be noted that American soldiers ordinarily expected that the *Cubans* would initiate hostilities.

112. Editorial, *Enterprise*, June 30, 1898.

113. *Enterprise*, July 21, 1898.

114. *Republican-Register*, June 25, 1898; July 9, 1898. Similarly, Warren Harding's Marion *Star*. On June 20, the newspaper spoke of Cubans who were at least good guerrillas and scouts; on July 21 it thought it might be necessary to "whip the Cubans." Randolph C. Downes, *The Rise of Warren Gamaliel Harding, 1865–1920* (Columbus, Ohio, 1970), pp. 68–69.

115. Whitelaw Reid, "Problems Flowing from the Spanish War," *Century Magazine* (Sept. 1898), quoted in Whitelaw Reid, *American and English Studies*, 2 vols. (New York, 1913), I, 109.

116. McIntosh, *Little I Saw of Cuba*, p. 74.

117. Robinson, *Reed*, p. 369.

118. Roosevelt, "Fifth Corps," p. 239.

119. Kennan, *Campaigning In Cuba*, p. 123.

120. Roosevelt, "Fifth Corps," p. 239; Roosevelt, *Rough Riders*, p. 156.

121. Robley D. Evans, *A Sailor's Log: Recollections of Forty Years of Naval Life* (London, 1901), p. 437.

122. Ibid., pp. 451, 455.

123. Editorial, *Republican-Register,* July 9, 1898. "The Spanish soldiers have done all that they could for their native country. America admires a courageous foe . . ."

124. Stephen Crane, "Spanish Deserters Among the Refugees at El Caney," *World,* July 8, 1898, in Fryckstedt, *Uncollected Writings,* p. 368; Rubens, *Liberty,* p. 374; George G. Lewis and John Mewha, *History of Prisoner of War Utilization by the United States Army, 1776–1945* (Washington, D.C., 1955), p. 44.

125. Alger, *Spanish-American War,* p. 279.

126. Ibid.

127. Ibid., pp. 280–81.

128. Hagedorn, *Leonard Wood,* I, 185, 193. See also Heard, War Department Historical. In a report critical of Cubans, the author observed that "Spanish troops have the greatest contempt for the Cubans, a common slang expression being that the 'Cubans fire four shots and run.' "

129. Dewey, *Autobiography,* p. 27; House Document No. 2, 55 Cong., 3 Sess., vol. 3, p. 46. The attack was not fully a sham; six Americans were killed.

130. Davis, *Notes,* pp. 116, 132–33.

CHAPTER VI

1. Kent Cooper, *Kent Cooper and the Associated Press, An Autobiography* (New York, 1959), p. 4. The author believes that interest in vicinage news remained dominant until 1893.

2. James Bryce, *The American Commonwealth,* 3rd edition, 2 vols. (New York, 1895), II, 248–49.

3. See John A. S. Grenville and George Berkeley Young, *Politics, Strategy, and American Diplomacy, Studies in Foreign Policy, 1873–1917* (New Haven and London, 1966), chapter 5. Also, Leopold, *Growth of American Foreign Policy,* p. 162. The resolution, adopted unanimously in the House, passed the Senate without debate.

4. Henry James, *Richard Olney and His Public Service* (Boston and New York, 1923), p. 123.

5. An arbitration commission finally announced its award (largely in Britain's favor) on October 3, 1899. Leopold, *Growth of American Foreign Policy,* p. 164.

6. Bryce, *Commonwealth,* II, 268.

7. Pritchett, "McKinley," pp. 398–99.

8. David A. Shannon, ed., *Beatrice Webb's American Diary, 1898* (Madison, Wisconsin, 1963), pp. 36–37.

9. Bryce, *Commonwealth*, II, 273.

10. Swanberg, *Hearst*, p. 33. Hearst had chamber pots delivered to a number of his Harvard professors.

11. Bryce, *Commonwealth*, II, 253.

12. Edwin Lawrence Godkin, "The Growth and Expression of Public Opinion," *Atlantic Monthly*, LXXXI (Jan. 1898), 11–12.

13. Franklin H. Giddings, *Democracy and Empire* (New York, 1900), p. 10.

14. Seymour J. Mandelbaum, *Boss Tweed's New York* (New York, 1965), pp. 21–24.

15. Julian S. Rammelkamp, *Pulitzer's Post-Dispatch 1878–1883* (Princeton, New Jersey, 1967), p. 124, notes a striking example of the old journalism. The *Post-Dispatch*'s account of the 1880 Republican convention, covering the crucial session chronologically, buried in the third column its first mention of Garfield's nomination on the thirty-sixth ballot.

16. Godkin, "Public Opinion," p. 6.

17. Quoted in James Creelman, "Joseph Pulitzer—Master Journalist," *Pearson's Magazine*, XXI (Mar. 1909), 246. Though Edward W. Scripps also sought a new readership and broke with prevailing standards of propriety, he retained the traditional notion of reader as rational, autonomous, decision-making individual. Scripps' task, as he saw it, was to present *all* the facts, however indelicate, and then "after discharging . . . [his] duty as a witness," leave the jury—the public—to find its verdict. Though Scripps' newspapers would thus reach a new readership, the editor's role would remain unchanged. Negley D. Cochran, *E. W. Scripps* (New York, 1933), p. 51. Scripps, moreover, feared and often rebuffed advertisers; that advertising revenue in which Pulitzer saw a new freedom was to Scripps the threat of bondage. Edmond D. Coblentz, *Newsmen Speak, Journalists on Their Craft* (Berkeley and Los Angeles, 1954), p. 25.

18. Pulitzer Cablegram to *World*, Oct. 10, 1889, quoted in Coblentz, *Newsmen Speak*, p. 11.

19. Delos F. Wilcox, "The American Newspaper: A Study in Social Psychology," *Annals of the American Academy of Political and Social Science*, XVI (July 1900), 59.

20. Frank Luther Mott, *American Journalism: A History, 1690–*

1960, 3rd edition (New York, 1962), p. 507; Alfred McClung Lee, *The Daily Newspaper in America: The Evolution of a Social Instrument* (New York, 1937), p. 65. Percentage increases derived from data on p. 725.

21. Jane Addams, *Twenty Years at Hull-House* (New York, 1910), p. 433. Another reverberation helped to produce the "magazine revolution" of the 1890s. Frank A. Munsey, determined to publish a general magazine whose appeal would extend beyond the upper class, a magazine "of the people and for the people," admitted that he had learned much from the Sunday papers. Theodore P. Greene, *America's Heroes, The Changing Models of Success in American Magazines* (New York, 1970), pp. 59, 67.

22. Wilcox, "American Newspaper," pp. 77–78.

23. Mott, *American Journalism*, p. 532.

24. John Tebbel, *The Life and Good Times of William Randolph Hearst* (New York, 1952), p. 57. Visiting Rome as a boy, Hearst wished to put out a light that he was told had burned for one thousand years.

25. For a detailed treatment of the Cisneros adventure, see Swanberg, *Hearst*, pp. 119–29.

26. Abbot, *Watching the World Go By*, p. 215.

27. Heald, "McKinley Biography," chapter 26, p. 57; Mott, *American Journalism*, p. 533; Swanberg, *Hearst*, p. 121; Marcus M. Wilkerson, *Public Opinion and the Spanish-American War, A Study in War Propaganda* (New York, 1932), pp. 91, 102.

28. Wilkerson, *Public Opinion*, p. 85; *Journal*, Oct. 11, 13, 16, 1897, quoted ibid., p. 91; Bristow, *Fraud and Politics*, p. 89.

29. Editorial, *World*, Dec. 29, 1895. Some celebration may have been justified. Secretary of State Olney paid angry tribute to Pulitzer's influence by threatening to invoke a 1799 statute subjecting any citizen convicted of addressing a foreign government to a $5000 fine and five years in prison. James W. Barrett, *Joseph Pulitzer and His World* (New York, 1924), p. 207. The assessment of Colonial Secretary Joseph Chamberlain was less grudging: "The *World* led public thought when it secured expressions . . . from leading men of America and Great Britain and performed an inestimable service to the English-speaking people of the whole world . . . [and] a patriotic service to its country. It did not wait for a leader, but led the people."

Quoted in Don C. Seitz, *Joseph Pulitzer: His Life and Letters* (New York, 1924), p. 207. Five British peace organizations selected Pulitzer for special honor. Barrett, *Pulitzer*, p. 160.

30. Homer W. King, *Pulitzer's Prize Editor, A Biography of John A. Cockerill, 1845–1896* (Durham, North Carolina, 1965), p. 135.

31. *World*, Mar. 16, 1885, quoted in W. A. Swanberg, *Pulitzer* (New York, 1967), p. 104.

32. John R. Reavis to Joseph Pulitzer, June 16, 1885, quoted ibid., p. 105.

33. Ibid., p. 200.

34. George Cary Eggleston, *Recollections of a Varied Life* (New York, 1910), pp. 329–30.

35. Swanberg, *Pulitzer*, p. 201.

36. *World*, Jan. 3, 1896, quoted ibid.

37. The "press sometimes acted as though it were the government." Charles H. Brown, *The Correspondents' War, Journalists in the Spanish-American War* (New York, 1967), vii.

38. Creelman, *On the Great Highway*, 191; (Mason) Wilkerson, *Public Opinion*, p. 54; (Hoar) Solomon Bulkley Griffin, *People and Politics Observed by a Massachusetts Editor* (Boston, 1923), p. 369; Swanberg, *Hearst*, p. 118.

39. Brown, *Correspondents' War*, pp. 57, 59, 137.

40. *World* to Alger, Feb. 25, 1898, Alger Papers.

41. Creelman, *On the Great Highway*, p. 190.

42. Ibid., p. 190. Hearst apparently concocted preliminary plans for Alfred Dreyfus' liberation from Devil's Island. Musgrave, *Under Three Flags*, p. 104.

43. (Poll) Ibid., p. 91, and Joseph E. Wisan, *The Cuban Crisis as Reflected in the New York Press (1895–1898)* (New York, 1934), p. 231; (Sword) Ralph D. Paine, *Roads of Adventure* (Boston and New York, 1922), pp. 62–63; (Commission) Wilkerson, *Public Opinion*, pp. 110–11.

44. (Correspondents) Joseph J. Matthews, *Reporting the Wars* (Minneapolis, 1957), p. 148; (boats) Mott, *American Journalism*, p. 537; (Post) Post, *Little War of Private Post*, p. 162; (prisoners) *Journal*, July 6, 1898.

45. Quoted in Swanberg, *Hearst*, p. 168.

46. Quoted in Oliver Carlson, *Brisbane: A Candid Biography* (New York, 1937), p. 97.

47. Creelman, *On the Great Highway*, p. 176.

48. Abbot, *Watching the World Go By*, p. 150.

49. Ambrose Bierce, "A Thumb-Nail Sketch," in *Collected Works,* XII, 307.

50. Alleyne Ireland, *Joseph Pulitzer: Reminiscences of a Secretary* (New York, 1914), p. 109; Godkin, "Public Opinion," p. 7.

51. Mott, *American Journalism,* pp. 488–89.

52. Creelman, *On the Great Highway,* pp. 187–88.

53. Shafter to Alger, July 24, 1898, "Correspondence Relating to Cuba," War Department Historical.

54. Fish, *Path of Empire,* p. 144. Kennan, *Campaigning in Cuba,* p. 43, claims that in the first two months of the war, correspondents "lost almost as many men from death and casualty [proportionate to their numbers] as did the Army and Navy . . ."

55. Creelman, *On the Great Highway,* p. 205. In similar fashion, Richard Harding Davis joined charges; he was cited by Roosevelt for his participation in the skirmish at Las Guasimas. Langford, *Richard Harding Davis Years,* pp. 201–2; Roosevelt, *Rough Riders,* pp. 96–97. Frank Norris captured two Spanish soldiers at El Caney and Stephen Crane delighted in accepting the surrender of a Puerto Rican town. Franklin Walker, *Frank Norris, A Biography* (New York, 1932), p. 189; Davis, "Our War Correspondents," p. 943.

56. Creelman, *On the Great Highway,* pp. 211–12.

57. Creelman, "Joseph Pulitzer," pp. 242–43. Creelman credited to Pulitzer the "revolutionary plan of government by newspaper—the detection and conviction of criminals, the distribution of coal and food to the poor, the investigation of prisons and asylums, the suppression of brothels, the passage of laws, and every kind of scheme that could advance the public interest and sell the *World.*" Here Creelman, at the time of writing a friend of Hearst's political enemies, ignored Hearst's more ambitious program and attributed to Pulitzer sentiments that were in 1898 more properly those of Hearst and himself.

58. O'Connor, *Bierce,* p. 256. Governor-elect of Kentucky William Goebel was shot and killed in an election dispute.

59. Melville E. Stone, "Stone's Analysis of World's Value," *Editor and Publisher,* Nov. 30, 1912, in the Papers of Joseph Pulitzer, Library of Congress; Seitz, *Pulitzer,* pp. 213–14.

60. Swanberg, *Pulitzer,* p. 252.

61. Pulitzer to Bradford Merrill, Aug. 29, 1898; Pulitzer to Don C. Seitz, Sept. 10, 1898; Memorandum of *World* news staff meeting, Nov. 28, 1898, in Pulitzer Papers.

62. Ireland, *Reminiscences,* pp. 144, 146.
63. James W. Barrett, *The World, The Flesh and Messrs. Pulitzer* (New York, 1931), p. 34.
64. Ireland, *Reminiscences,* pp. 68–69.
65. Swanberg, *Hearst,* p. 61.
66. Rammelkamp, *Post-Dispatch,* p. 114.
67. Tebbel, *Hearst,* p. 151.
68. Ibid., pp. 99–100.
69. Joseph Pulitzer, "Has Congress Abdicated?" *North American Review,* CLXIX (Dec. 1899), 889.

Index